Reformation Europe 1517–1559

Blackwell Classic Histories of Europe

This series comprises new editions of seminal histories of Europe. Written by the leading scholars of their generation, the books represent both major works of historical analysis and interpretation and clear, authoritative overviews of the major periods of European history. All the volumes have been revised for inclusion in the series and include updated material to aid further study. *Blackwell Classic Histories of Europe* provides a forum in which these key works can continue to be enjoyed by scholars, students and general readers alike.

Published

Europe Transformed: 1878–1919
Second Edition
Norman Stone

Reformation Europe: 1517–1559
Second Edition
G. R. Elton

Forthcoming

Europe: Hierarchy and Revolt: 1320–1480
Second Edition
George Holmes

Renaissance Europe: 1480–1520
Second Edition
John Hale

Europe: Privilege and Protest: 1730–1798
Second Edition
Olwen Hufton

REFORMATION EUROPE
1517–1559

Second Edition

G. R. Elton

with an Afterword
by
Andrew Pettegree

BLACKWELL
Publishers

First published 1963

Re-issued in 1985

Second edition published by Blackwell Publishers Ltd 1999

2 4 6 8 10 9 7 5 3 1

Blackwell Publishers Ltd
108 Cowley Road
Oxford OX4 1JF
UK

Blackwell Publishers Inc.
350 Main Street
Malden, Massachusetts 02148
USA

British Library Cataloguing in Publication Data

A CIP catalogue record for this book is available from the British Library.

Library of Congress Cataloging-in-Publication Data

Elton, G. R. (Geoffrey Rudolph)
      Reformation Europe, 1517–1559 / G.R. Elton,—2nd ed.
          p.   cm. — (Blackwell classic histories of Europe)
      Includes bibliographical references (p.) and index.
      ISBN 0–631–21508–5 (alk. paper).—ISBN 0–631–21384–8 (pbk. :
alk.paper)
      1. Reformation. 2. Europe—History—1517–1648. I. Title.
II. Series.
      D228.E4   1999
      940.2'3—dc21   99–26416
                                                                          CIP

Typeset in 10.5 on 12pt, Sabon

by Kolam Information Services Pvt. Ltd, Pondicherry, India

This book is printed on acid-free paper

MAIORIBUS

Contents

EUROPE IN 1550

☐ Habsburg Possessions (Empire of Charles V)	■ Lands of Bourbon–Navarre
■ Lands of the Constable Bourbon (to France, 1529)	☐ Detailed map of this area below
•••••• Holy Roman Empire	

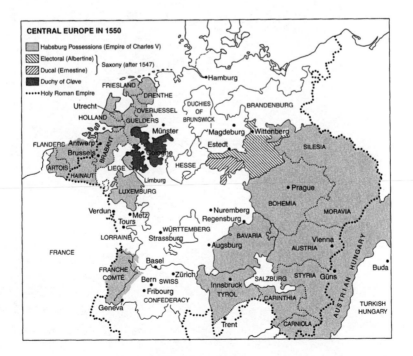

CENTRAL EUROPE IN 1550

☐ Habsburg Possessions (Empire of Charles V)
▨ Electoral (Albertine) ⎫ Saxony (after 1547)
▩ Ducal (Ernestine) ⎭
■ Duchy of Cleve
•••••• Holy Roman Empire

Preface to the First Edition

Europe in the early sixteenth century remains a magnet to student and reader alike. The continued flood of studies is one justification for this attempt to tell the story once more; the continued and lively interest in it of so many people is another. However, it is idle to hope that in a relatively short compass one could adequately deal with all aspects of the age, and I have thought best to centre the narrative on the religious upheaval. The Reformation as a movement in religion and theology, placed within its setting of politics, economics and society, is the theme of this book. This has involved me in passing judgement on some very controversial people and issues, and I must fear that I shall not always seem to have observed the impartiality which it has been my ambition to attain. However, if I cannot hope to have pleased all sides, I can at least suppose that I have in different places displeased them all equally.

My sincere thanks go to those whose counsel and encouragement have helped in the writing of this book: a pleasure in itself, rendered more pleasing by the interest of others. In particular, Dr. J. H. Elliott has generously saved me from error, and Professor G. R. Potter, in addition to performing the same service in other parts of the book, has added enormously to the pleasant burden of obligation by reading the proofs. My overriding debt is recorded in the dedication.

Cambridge
December 1962   G. R. ELTON

Chapter 1

Luther

I The Attack on Rome

On 31 October 1517, Dr. Martin Luther, professor of theology in the recently founded Saxon University of Wittenberg, nailed a paper of Ninety-Five Theses to the door of the Castle Church in that town. There was nothing unusual about this. Any scholar who wished to defend any propositions of law or doctrine could invite learned debate by putting forth such theses, and church doors were the customary place for medieval publicity. Luther's Ninety-Five attacked the practice of selling indulgences—documents offering commutation of penance for money payments. Certainly Luther had no thought of starting a schism in the Church. These were not the first theses he had offered for public disputation, nor did they embody necessarily revolutionary doctrines. Nevertheless, the day continues to be celebrated in Lutheran countries as the anniversary of the Reformation, and justly so. The controversy over indulgences brought together the man and the occasion: it signalled the end of the medieval Church.

Martin Luther (1483–1546) was the son of a miner of Eisleben in Saxony. Since he early showed intellectual promise, his father intended him for the canon law, a profession of honour and profit; he was extremely angry when the boy instead found that his studies at the University of Erfurt inclined him to theology and contemplation. In 1505, Luther entered the order of the Austin Friars at Erfurt; in 1508, he was appointed a professor at Wittenberg. For nearly ten years he read and thought, wrestling with his humanity in his desperate search for salvation. This young friar and academic, obscure enough in all conscience, hid behind the heavy peasant's face a mind exceptional in its passion, intensity, stubbornness and subtlety, a mind which could not rest at ease with the prospect of pastoral and professional success for which in other ways he seemed so well fitted.

He was a solid scholar, trained and for a time sunk in the late-medieval scholasticism of Occamist nominalism, as transmitted by the pietist Gabriel Biel who taught that despite the Fall man had power to seek salvation of his own free will. These teachings soon ceased to satisfy Luther who was to revolutionise theology because in fact he found himself in a state of despair before God. He wanted the assurance of being acceptable to God, but could discover in himself only the certainty of sin and in God only an inexorable justice which condemned to futility all his efforts at repentance and his search for the divine mercy. In vain he tried to solve his difficulties by all the mortifications and other means advised by his Church and Order. When he found the answer, it grew directly out of his total sense of helplessness in the face of God (*coram Deo*), and out of his reading of St. Paul with the assistance of St. Augustine. He went back to the Fathers and finally to the Gospel, till he understood that "the righteousness of God" (*iustitia Dei*) meant not God's anger at sin but His willingness to make the sinner just (free of sin) by the power of His love bestowed freely on the true believer. Luther held that man was justified (saved) by faith alone: the words *sola fide* came to be the watchword and touchstone of the Reformation. Man could do nothing by his own works—whether works of edification like prayer, fasting, mortification, or works of charity—to compel justification. But if he believed, God of His grace would give him the gifts of the Holy Spirit—salvation and eternal life. The means of grace were in Jesus Christ; faith was created by abandoning oneself to the message of the gospel, to what Luther called the Word.

Of course, this doctrine was not new; it hardly could be in a religion which for 1500 years had explored every possibility within itself. Luther did not think it new: to him it was the truth of the gospel. The study of his lectures in the years before he became a public figure has shown the development of his theology and illuminated its close links with late-medieval teaching and mysticism, with views, that is, on the relationship of God and man which laid the stress not on institutional and sacramental expedients but on the search of the individual soul. Nevertheless, Luther's views proved revolutionary because they concentrated with such incisive single-mindedness on the total inability of man to help himself to his own salvation. He took seriously the accepted doctrine of God's omnipotence and therefore (as it were) sole monopoly of free will. In consequence, as the event was to show, Luther had rendered superfluous the whole apparatus of the Church, designed to mediate between man and God. If man's justification depended solely on God's infusion of grace into the believing soul, there was no need for a priesthood alone capable of performing the sacramental acts through which (as the Church taught) the way was opened for grace to enter man. Beside the doctrine of justification by faith alone there soon stood its companion, that of the priesthood of all believers. At first, Luther had no quarrel with the pope, the hierarchy or the Church, and he never lost his conservative sense of an order embodied in institutions. He proved in many ways a most reluctant revolutionary who never wished to abandon tradition, unless his reading of scripture compelled him to it. Thus, when a more radical disciple protested against the elevation of the host in the mass, asking, "Where does Christ command it?" Luther replied: "Where does He forbid it?" But he shared the widespread dissatisfaction with the standards of the clergy and in particular had been shocked by what he saw of the papal Curia when he visited Rome in 1510. He had his share of German nationalism and bigotry, with their violent dislike of all those subtle Italian devices which, prejudice alleged, were milking honest Germans and sending them to perdition. His own experiences had turned him against the futility of monkish asceticism as well as the indecency of its hypocrisy. Thus he was ready enough to give voice to the prevalent anticlericalism of the day.

Throughout, however, there was more than politics, prejudice or envy in the attack on the traditional Church which Luther developed under pressure of controversy, until he left little of it standing. If all men were "priests", able to seek salvation without intercession, the priesthood were not only unnecessary but a hindrance, blurring or destroying the truth behind a magic mumbo-jumbo of ritual in order to preserve a privileged position. Luther therefore denounced the whole concept of a special priesthood, blamed it for keeping God's message from the Christian people, and assigned to the clergy only the function of informing man of his way to God by preaching the Word. As it turned out, the spirit had visited a man unusually capable of making himself heard, so much so that the sceptic may wonder whether the word that broke the old Church was God's or Luther's. For thirty years the powerful mind and large heart of Martin Luther poured forth in an unbelievable output of books, pamphlets, sermons and letters; it has been calculated that he published at the rate of a piece a fortnight. And if the vigour was often coarse, the undeniable humour foulmouthed, the controversial method ruthless and the strong conviction at times only pernicious prejudice, this, needless to say, did not lessen the impact or repel the many who were willing to hear. The Reformation was no more the work of one man than any such upheaval can ever be; but without Luther there would still have been no Reformation.

Nothing of all this could be suspected when Luther attacked indulgences. But it is important to realise that even at that early date the essentials of Luther's theology were worked out. To a man so overwhelmingly aware of the problem of salvation, indulgences touched the essence of things. Indulgences were remissions of the penance imposed on confessed and absolved sinners. The danger of leaving such power in lesser hands had led earlier popes to reserve the granting of them to themselves; the fiscal possibilities were soon seen; and by the later middle ages a reasonable practice had grown into an abuse. Though official doctrine was always careful to stress the need for genuine penitence and the impossibility of obtaining valid remission of sins by merely buying an indulgence, the manner in which the business was represented to, and taken by, the simple people was much cruder. In practice it came to be thought that by the act of buying a papal indulgence men could at least shorten their own time in purgatory, and by the fifteenth century it was commonly held that the souls of the dead in purgatory could also be helped by indulgences bought on their behalf. Though indulgences were always proclaimed for an ostensibly religious purpose—a crusade, or the building of a cathedral—they came in fact to be no more than an important source of papal revenue. In 1517 Pope Leo X permitted the new archbishop of Mainz, Albert of Hohenzollern, to recoup by their sale the heavy outlay incurred on entering his dignity. This sale was very efficiently advertised; despite perfunctory safeguards, the stress lay on the chance offered to people to buy themselves and their relatives out of so much time in the fires of purgatory by a money payment which would enable them to participate in the merits of the saints without going through the tiresome process of contrition, absolution and penance. Moreover, the business was put in the hands of crude salesmen like the Dominican John Tetzel who operated near Wittenberg. Electoral Saxony, where Luther lived, was closed to Tetzel because the Elector Frederick the Wise wanted all money available for pious uses to be spent on his own unique collection of supposed holy relics. But Luther's souls were crossing the river and bringing back bits of paper to prove their freedom from sin. They found their pastor mountingly indignant and distressed.

Thus Luther attacked indulgences, not as just another abuse but as something close to the central truth of religion. Even so, his theses need not have led to more than an obscure academic dispute. They did question certain papal powers, but in a moderate manner and by way of opening up debate. Luther had published them in Latin, but they were at once translated into German and spread abroad by the printing press. Interest in them was general, sudden and unexpected. Unfortunately for itself, the Church tried to silence the critic. Indulgences were too precious to be given up; Tetzel's Order jumped to his defence against a mere Augustinian; John Eck, professor at Ingolstadt in Bavaria and a professional disputant, decided to take a hand by publicly accusing Luther of heresy. The case was referred to Rome: a fateful step. Attacked by Eck, Luther demonstrated his readiness with the pen, and his views grew less circumspect. Called by his own Order to answer for himself at a provincial chapter at Heidelberg in April 1518, he only made converts. While Germany began to stir in support of this monk who dared call abuses by their name, Rome was reluctantly drawn into drastic action, both by the influence there exercised by Luther's enemies and by his own developing language. In August 1518, Luther, summoned to Rome, appealed for protection to his elector. Frederick secured him a hearing at Augsburg before Cardinal Cajetan, general of the Dominican Order and an outstanding theologian of his day. Cajetan seems to have had a better understanding of Luther's essential lack of revolutionary fervour than did his foes who persuaded the papacy to treat him, before trial, as a notorious heretic. The talks with the cardinal—Luther expected death at the stake—were quite peaceable but fruitless; Luther proved stubborn in his convictions and went so far as to assert that a pope could err. Greatly relieved, he got back safely to Wittenberg; the controversy continued.

By now he was famous, and many looked to him for leadership. In June-July 1519 he engaged in public disputation with Eck at Leipzig. He had not originally been concerned in this affair: Eck had called out Andrew Carlstadt, a colleague of Luther's at Wittenberg and a passionate if woolly follower of the new teaching. But Luther thought himself attacked and decided to face Eck in person. The more experienced conservative soon drove him out of equivocation into the uncompromising assertion that not only popes but even General Councils of the Church could err. Scripture was the only authority. He had now taken his stand on doctrines condemned as heretical a hundred years earlier, in the trial of the Bohemian John Hus; Duke George of Saxony, a sound conservative, who attended the disputation, threw up his hands at this point and exclaimed at the heretic. Indeed, Luther, who had before this rejected Hus, as any orthodoxly trained theologian and patriotic German was bound to do, had by this time come to think that there was point in those earlier onslaughts on the papal rule in the Church. Leipzig proved how far he had gone from his purely theological beginnings: too far to retreat.

The battle continued, in the study and in the press; the Church was in turmoil. In 1520 Luther decisively burned his boats in the three great treatises which remained the foundation of his beliefs, his teaching, and his historic importance. In the *Address to the Christian Nobility of the German Nation* he analysed and destroyed the "paper walls" put up by the "Romanists" in defence of their usurped powers, and called upon the Germans to reform the Church by summoning a General Council. *The Babylonish Captivity of the Church* is a theological treatise in which he attacked the papacy for depriving

Christendom of the true religion, described the basis of the new theology, and declared that only three sacraments (baptism, penance and the eucharist) were scriptural. This removed the other four recognised by the Church (confirmation, extreme unction, orders and marriage) and altered the whole concept of a sacrament from a means to salvation created by the officiating priest to the occasion on which the believer can receive grace. In due course the reformers were to dispense with penance, too. Lastly, *The Liberty of a Christian Man*, in a last attempt to establish contact with the adversary, rehearsed in conciliatory terms the doctrines of justification by faith and the priesthood of all believers. However, in general these works, selling in great numbers and to a wide public (only the *Babylonish Captivity*, addressed to scholars, was written in Latin), served to define Luther's now schismatic position and to rally support. Leo X, taking fright rather too late and now rather too drastically, excommunicated Luther in the Bull *Exsurge Domine* (June 1520), made operative in January 1521 by another, *Decet.*[1]

Luther's reaction was both characteristic and symbolic. The three years' struggle had greatly increased his self-confidence: a self-confidence of humility, for he saw in the support given to him the working of God's will and assurance of his rightness. They had also persuaded his eschatological mind that the pope was the Antichrist of the Apocalypse; both his own pronouncements on the point and the busy propaganda literature of the day, with its proliferation of telling, if often crude, woodcuts, grew more recklessly violent and abusive. In 1519 Luther had genuinely believed that the pope was misinformed and needed only enlightenment; in 1520 he knew that this great beast must be destroyed. The chasm was unbridgeable. Now he took his spade and dug it deeper still. In December 1520, he publicly and ceremoniously burned *Exsurge Domine* at Wittenberg, together with a number of his opponents' books and the volumes of the "popish" canon law. For him, and for his followers, the cause of Luther was the cause of the gospel, and the cause of the gospel involved cleansing the Church of all the means of power and government which the papacy had created in the previous 500 years.

Within three years of coming obscurely into the open with his attack on Tetzel, Luther had thus become the spiritual—and to many the political—leader of a movement convulsing most of Germany, drawing large numbers of the influential into his following, and attracting both notoriety and some support well beyond the borders of his own country. It is no wonder that to Luther this marvellous growth was a sign of God's approval; the historian, however, may ask whether there were not conditions present which enabled this one friar's protest to swell so rapidly into a movement threatening the unity of the Church and the supremacy of the pope.

II   The State of Germany

In the early sixteenth century, the complex of principalities and territories known as Germany was at a height of prosperity and population. In particular, there had been a growth of towns, of trade and crafts. The collapse of the thirteenth-century agrarian boom in the population crisis produced by plague after about 1350 had only promoted the wealth of the trading towns—in the north, where the Hanseatic League dominated the Baltic and the North Sea, and in the south where the Danube and Rhine towns controlled the profitable trade routes over the Alps into Italy and from France and Burgundy in the west to flourishing industries and markets in the east. Germany was at this time the centre of the European economic system, left in possession after the decline of France in the wars of the previous two centuries and of Italy in the Franco-Spanish wars of the previous thirty years. Wealth and population growth resulted in the growth of industries organised in craft gilds, while the country-side also profited from the increasing market; by 1500 the old "kernel" lands of the south and south-west harboured a reasonably well-to-do peasant agriculture, while east of the Elbe beginnings were made to open up the great plains for the commercial production of grain. Natural resources were exploited as never before: Germany was the centre of mining and therefore of metal and armament manufactures. Commerce and wealth produced a vigorous money market and such finance houses as the Fuggers who, secured on the Tyrol mines leased from the Habsburg dukes of Austria, were able as capitalists to rival the age-old monopoly of Italian firms in international finance. The Fuggers, and their rivals the Welsers, both of Augsburg, had interests extending from the edge of Hungary to the Spanish colonies in America; they and their like had contact with every government of the day. Wealth was also reflected in the proliferation of civic culture. This was not only the age of the Fuggers but also of Lucas Cranach and Albrecht Dürer, artists fit to stand by the side of the great Italians; of such printers as Froben at Basel, Erasmus' publisher; of the rapid spread of lay education in the towns, the founding of universities, the rise of men trained in the linguistic disciplines of humanism and the practical arts of the Roman law. Luther's Germany was in many ways the most alive, the most flourishing part of Europe.

However, this prosperity and vigour could not hide some serious problems and strains. Above all, Germany was not a political unit; it would not be excessive to call it a political mess. Nominally identical with the Holy Roman Empire, it really lacked all central authority. Not only had outlying parts of the Empire (the Swiss Confederacy,

most of the Netherlands, Bohemia, Milan) severed all significant
connection with it; in Germany itself the authority of the emperor
had nearly ceased to have any meaning. The imperial crown, in
theory elective, had come to be almost hereditary in the House of
Habsburg which possessed extensive lands round the upper Rhine
and in the Austrian provinces. The Emperor Maximilian I (1493–
1519) greatly enlarged Habsburg power when he married the heiress
to the Burgundian domains, built up in the fifteenth century till they
included not only the Free County of Burgundy round Besançon (the
duchy proper had been surrendered to France in 1477) but the great
commercial and manufacturing centres of the Netherlands (Brabant,
Flanders, Artois, Luxemburg, etc.). The increase in his family's power
could not, however, be turned to profit in the organisation of Germany; attempts around 1500 to create central institutions—a
national government, national law courts, national taxation—
languished almost as soon as they were made. Maximilian, a charming, reckless, irresponsible and unreliable adventurer (and very popular with it), pursued no policy except dynastic aggrandisement with
sufficient consistency to promote success.

In the absence of imperial authority, and in turn assuring its
continued weakness, the splintering of Germany devolved the task
of government and the possibilities of ambition upon the rulers of the
separate territories. In particular, the princes showed signs of being
able to read the times aright. From the greatest—the seven electors
who composed the college qualified to choose the emperor[2]—to the
last count or lord with territorial claims, they were in the fifteenth
and sixteenth centuries engaged upon the twofold task of consolidating their power internally and protecting it against encroachment
from outside; though in many lands active representative bodies
existed, these in general assisted princely leadership against even
further fragmentation. For the time, at least, the so-called imperial
cities, who recognised no authority except the emperor's, were able to
hold their own; some eighty-five in number, they jealously guarded
their independence and maintained their defences, some—like Nuremberg—acquiring in the process quite extensive landed possessions,
but most of them relying on their privileges, wealth and town walls.
Inside the towns oligarchic pressure was steadily increasing, but
except in Nuremberg, which was firmly in the hands of the patricians, the lesser citizens and craftsmen still commanded considerable
power in their gilds and therefore in town government.

Ground between the millstones of princes and cities, especially in
the south-west where the Swabian League of cities and territories
imposed some order by force of arms, were a great body of the lesser
nobility, the imperial knights (*Reichsritter*). These men, claiming to
be tenants-in-chief of the imperial crown, had been the most notable

victims of the fourteenth-century agrarian crisis, nor had they ever recovered. Ruling tiny possessions dominated by their ancestral (and usually very uncomfortable) castles, and burdened with a great deal of ancestral pride, they could make ends meet only by surrendering their independence and taking service with the princes, or by preying on the countryside. Trained to arms and leading bands of often professional soldiers, they could not be ignored; yet they formed a sterile and declining class, capable of dangerous nihilism and generally feared. Possibly it is unfair to generalise about them; not all were robber barons and hedge-knights. A man like Franz von Sickingen, proud condottiere and military adventurer and (for money) the backbone of the Swabian League, no doubt answers the description; as does in a lesser way Götz von Berlichingen who was to play a dubious part in the Peasants' War as the allegedly conscript leader and certainly rapid deserter of one band of peasants. But what is one to make of the many who became princely or imperial counsellors, the few who threw in their lot with the towns, or Ulrich von Hutten who combined the anarchic instincts of an imperial knight with the training of a humanist, the pen of a poet, and the dreams of a utopian reformer?

The other body of men who in the early sixteenth century were beginning to feel the pinch were the peasants—or rather, to translate *Bauer* by its sixteenth-century English equivalent, the commons of the countryside. For the peasantry of the German south, including Switzerland and Austria, were men of some substance and more rights, rarely totally unfree, burdened with few compulsory services, possessed of arms, often small proprietors protected in the law. But the economic and political situation, which had on the whole favoured them in the fifteenth century, was turning against them in the sixteenth. Growing numbers were pressing on the available land; growing prices—an inflation in great part initiated by the yield of German silver mines and the vigour of German trade—were forcing landed lords to increase their income from their properties. This was a problem not peculiar to Germany; all over Western Europe, a prosperous peasantry found themselves under attack. In Germany, however, the absence of any national authority capable of offering some protection, the abundance of greater and lesser lords, and the intermingling of territories with different customs and policies, combined to aggravate the lot of the small man. Ecclesiastical lords, especially monasteries, were particularly prominent in their attempts to re-impose old burdens, enlarge seigneurial rights, enforce new claims. The peasants reacted predictably: the fifty years before 1520 were full of sporadic risings around Lake Constance, in the Black Forest, in Württemberg, in Styria and Carinthia. In these parts the demand was for the "old law", a return to customarily fixed rights and duties; the peasants were in effect protesting against innovating lords who employed Roman law precepts and experts to alter the traditional relationships in the body politic. But around the upper Rhine and in Alsace a more ominous movement still made itself felt, the movement which adopted the *Bundschuh* (the peasant's laced boot) as its symbol: here demands were heard for the "law of God" in which truly radical and revolutionary tenets, often reminiscent of the many millenarian and anarchic outbursts of the later middle ages, threatened all authority in the name of natural equality and the triumph of the poor. The discontented peasantry found allies among the urban artisans and lesser craftsmen, especially in the small towns which, often barely distinguishable from villages, dotted that countryside. If lay lords were resented, the more pressing ecclesiastical lords were hated; and with it all went a general animus against Jewish moneylenders and shaven priestlings which several times burst out in violence.

Indeed, these social strains reflected in great part on the standing of the Church. Its reputation for corruption, envy of its wealth, hatred of its spiritual claims so little accompanied by a spiritual life—none of this was peculiar to Germany. Notoriously, the whole Western Church, from the pope downwards, stood involved in a crisis of confidence. Both as a means of salvation and as a temporal institution, the Church was suspect; from the fourteenth century onwards, the lay people at all levels had been freeing themselves from need of it, while the clergy, and especially the religious orders, had become steadily more worldly and uninspiring. But again, the problem was particularly developed in Germany where the Church stood in an even worse case and had earned more deserved resentment than in other countries. Its high places were monopolised by the aristocracy, with the usual abuses of simony and nepotism rampant. While French and English bishops and monasteries occupied much land wanted by an expanding lay population and lived off lavish rents, their German counterparts were in addition often territorial rulers with powers of life and death. Perhaps a fifth of Germany was in the hands of the great prince-bishops (Münster, Würzburg, Magdeburg, Mainz, Salzburg, and so forth), with possessions as large as any duke's. The lower clergy were poor and grasping, and often ignorant, everywhere; in Germany they were also quite exceptionally numerous. As for the papacy, that had been tamed in France, subdued in Spain, acclimatised (for the moment) in England; in Germany, its international pretensions, its financial demands, and its interference with appointments met only sporadic resistance because the empire had lost all meaning.

It is true that long before the Reformation many German princes, and quite a number of the self-governing towns, had begun to interfere in the running of Church affairs. This was, as is well known, true of the western monarchies where the secular ruler exercised a great deal of control over the supposedly independent order of the clergy, but even in Germany many lay authorities supervised monastic discipline, kept out—or at least kept down—the influence of pope or bishop, taxed their clergy. Of so minor a prince as the duke of Cleves the proverb ran that he was pope in his lands; so good a Catholic as Duke George of Saxony allowed no practical limitations to his control of his Church; the bishops of Geneva were nominated by the dukes of Savoy. But while these rulers might to some extent subject the Church to their wills, they had less concern with their people's experience of the Church; and in a region in which so many ecclesiastics held independent sway, the temporal power of the Church survived more formidably than elsewhere.

In any case, quite apart from the secular hatreds and grievances, the signs were clear that Western Europe in general, and once again Germany in particular, was in the throes of something that can only be called a spiritual crisis. The Church's ultimate failure did not lie in its wealth, its frequent worldliness, its somewhat exaggerated immorality, its obedience to a foreign pope who was no more than an Italian princeling: it lay in its total inability to bring peace and solace to troubled generations in an era of dissolving certainties. Plague, war, economic decline, all marked the later middle ages with an unmistakable spiritual malaise. Medieval society, and with it the medieval Church, had suffered a really bad shock in the disasters of the fourteenth century, and the fifteenth bore all the signs of the aftermath. So far from being shelved in the allegedly increasing materialism of the age, the problem of salvation announced its presence in striking and often bizarre forms. The consolations of the Church failed to satisfy. For the first time since St. Bernard revived monasticism in the twelfth century, retreat into the cloister had ceased to attract; though in other parts the number of religious kept some sort of pace with increasing populations, in Germany the fifteenth century witnessed numerous escapes from vows taken without vocation. The best spirits sought the answer in mysticism, in the search for a direct union between the soul and God, which not only bypassed the Church as an institution but also undermined its claim to have united reason and revelation in a workable whole. The powerful German mystic tradition, deriving from Master Eckhard (1260–1327) and John Tauler (d. 1361) had its parallels in England and Italy; Tauler certainly influenced Luther whose theology of grace in a way represents a universalisation of the individual case-history of the great mystics. It must, however, be stressed that in doctrine and obedience these medieval mystics remained entirely orthodox. The same was true of the cognate but less exalted devotional beliefs

of the Brethren of the Common Life in the Netherlands; Thomas à
Kempis (1380–1471), whose *Imitation of Christ* was a best-seller,
accepted all the teaching of the Church but laid the stress on man's
inner life and the individual's emulation of Christ's example. The
regions affected by this *devotio moderna*—the source from which
Erasmus' Christianity sprang—were to prove fertile ground for the
new reformed ideas.

Among the less pure souls and the socially disaffected, dissatisfaction with the Church took more disquieting forms. No doubt a good
many people resorted to a mixture of formal observance, practical
scepticism, and monumental indifference; but this was by no means
true of all. There ran through medieval religion a strong strain of
apocalyptic revivalism, sometimes rising to the madness of self-
appointed messiahs and commonly associated with radical notions
on the rights of the poor and dispossessed. Again it was in the
Netherlands, especially among the industrial classes of Flanders,
that these outbreaks occurred most frequently, culminating perhaps
in the Free Brethren of the fifteenth century who, holding themselves
to be God's elect and free of the Law, believed not so much in
community of goods and sexual freedom as that all things and
women belonged to them, to be taken by violence, if need was. But
Germany, too, had known the phenomenon, most memorably perhaps in that prophet of radical revolution, the Drummer of Niklas-
hausen (1476), who proclaimed the millennium to thousands of eager
pilgrims and excited wild expectations before the authorities burned
him for a heretic. His ideas, however, survived him among the South
German peasants and played their part in stirring up the repeated
Bundschuh risings. The frequency of such extravagancies and the
ease with which they inflamed the common people demonstrate the
instability of the situation.

Mysticism and millenarianism threatened the rule of the Church
over men's souls; among the educated, humanism undermined respect
for its authority and learning. Again this was particularly true of
Germany. Italian humanism, from Petrarch's rediscovery of the
ancients to the Platonic reinterpretation of Christianity by Marsilio
Ficino and Pico della Mirandola in the Florentine Academy of the
1480s, had indeed often attacked the Church, the papacy and scholastic theology; but the Italians managed on the whole to live in both
worlds, especially as the Renaissance popes from Pius II to Leo X as a
rule patronised humanism. On points of doctrine these writers were
either orthodox or silent, the very few conscientious pagans excepted.
Nor were the humanists of the north particularly heterodox. Their
great leader, Desiderius Erasmus (1466–1536) remained faithful to
his upbringing in the *devotio moderna*; despite all his criticism of
abuses and his inmost conviction that the end of religion was a life

lived in imitation of the founder, not the rescue of fallen man by miraculous means, he saw no reason why the central doctrines and ceremonies of the Church should not be preserved for the generality of men. However, his preoccupation with the inner life encouraged his many followers and disciples, as hostile as Erasmus to formal observation and priestly pretensions but less cautious, to think at first that in Luther they had found another of their kind; Erasmian humanists in the beginning smiled (not without patronage) upon the surprising figure of a monk espousing such sensibly personal doctrines.

Humanist learning assailed the intellectual foundations of the Church by studying the bible and the Fathers in new and better editions. In particular Erasmus' Greek *New Testament* (1516), with its pointed glosses against the traditional interpretation of such key-words as *ecclesia* or *presbyter*, did much to draw attention to the gulf between the contemporary and the original Church. Humanist contempt for traditional philosophies and lack of learning, justified in its academic setting, added yet another element to the general anti-clericalism of the day. It came out most powerfully in the controversy over John Reuchlin (1455–1522), the leading Hebraist of his time, who from 1509 courageously stood forth as the champion of Jewish books against the attempts of an apostate Jew, John Pfefferkorn, to get them destroyed by imperial edict. There ensued the usual battle of abusive pamphlets, complicated by the fact that the Dominicans, representing conservative scholastic philosophy, espoused Pfefferkorn's obscurantist case and tried to get Reuchlin indicted of heresy. Reuchlin advertised his strength by publishing the letters of support he had received, under the title *Letters of Famous Men* (1514). This suggested to the more spirited among his champions the production of one of the most successful satirical *coups* of history: the *Letters of Obscure Men* (1515 and 1517) in which the "monkish" defenders of tired traditions were exposed, in all their ignorance, stupidity, vanity and selfseeking, in letters allegedly written, in excruciating Latin, by Reuchlin's opponents. The gale of laughter which swept those two volumes through Germany both testified to common opinion of the old learning and added to it.

One of the authors of the *Obscure Men* was Ulrich von Hutten (1488–1523), in some ways the epitome of German humanism. A scholar and poet, a journalist of genius, a violent hater of popes and monks and priests, he used his talents to support the interests of his nation and his knightly order against foreign usurpation and bondage. Liberty and the free intellect were his watchwords; extravagant and dangerous as he was, he deserves respect for his unhesitating attack on obscurantism and exploitation wherever he saw them. Hutten was one of the first to welcome Luther's appearance; in him

he saw the saviour of Germany for whom he had been waiting. But
Hutten was by no means alone. The humanists were all inveterate
theorists of education, such outstanding writers on the subject as
Erasmus and the Spaniard Juan Luis Vives (1492–1540) excelling
the multitude only in penetration, not in interest. Quite a few, though
not Erasmus, also practised as teachers. In Italy and France, and
ultimately also in England, they concentrated on the education of
the aristocracy and the production of the civilised gentleman; hence
such influential books as Baldassare Castiglione's *Courtier* (1528) or
Sir Thomas Elyot's *The Boke of the Governour* (1531). In Germany,
they established a really firm hold on the schools and universities.
Nowhere else did men trained by humanist teachers occupy so many
important posts in administration, especially as town clerks and the
counsellors of princes. And at first, at any rate, the men of the new
learning thought of Luther as one of themselves. George Spalatin, for
instance, secretary to the Elector Frederick, saved the reformer at the
first crisis of his protest in 1518, by persuading the elector to oppose
the summons to Rome which, if obeyed, would almost certainly have
been the end of Luther. At the same time, while Hutten and Spalatin
stood by Luther to the end, most other humanists soon found that his
attack on traditional theology and the power of the Church went well
beyond their desires. Indeed, despite the old saying that Erasmus laid
the egg which Luther hatched, there was little in common between
the humanist trust in man's potentialities and the Lutheran conviction
of his helplessness, between Erasmus' cool reason and Luther's passion. Nevertheless, while the alliance lasted it assisted the spread and
penetration of Luther's message.

It is, therefore, obvious that the state of Germany helped Luther; it
helps to explain the extraordinary speed with which his ideas—
assisted by the new weapon of the printing press—seized upon the
imagination of a whole people. Not that these conditions—anticlericalism, nationalism, hatred of a foreign pope, social discontents,
political ambitions, intellectual and spiritual turmoil—in any way
form the "causes" of either Luther or the Reformation. The situation
was thoroughly disturbed, but the disturbance could have developed
into anything. As it happened, the particular line taken by the
Reformation was in some ways predictable and in others nothing of
the sort. That it should have assisted the further growth of regional
Churches under lay control is no doubt in line with previous developments. The decline of the knights could be foreseen, but hardly
that of the peasantry and the towns, in a measure a direct outcome of
the Reformation. Nor was it at all to be expected that the spiritual
upheaval should have been accompanied by so little social revolution
as in fact happened: the signs were all the other way. The Reformation's revival of theology as the foremost intellectual concern of

men—scholars and others—was quite out of step with the growingly informal and merely ethical Christianity which had come in the wake of the Renaissance, as it was a break with the multifarious secular interests of the humanists. The new theology and new Church did not bring in liberty of opinion; on the contrary, its uncompromising certainty put a term to the free speculation characteristic of the age of Ficino, Machiavelli, Erasmus, the young Thomas More. We are not dealing in causes and consequences, but with the development of human fortunes within the conditions of the time and under the impact of particular personalities.

If the German situation helped Luther, he derived much benefit also from the failure of the two alleged leaders of Christendom to stop him breaking up the supposed unity of the Church, never an entirely real thing even in the middle ages. The pope, Leo X (1513–21), a soft and kindly man, did not wake up in time. In the Reformation, the papacy in a sense reaped the nemesis not only of its notorious Renaissance decline but also of its frequent earlier victories. An institution which had survived exile to Avignon in the fourteenth century, the long schism of 1378 to 1417, and the attempt to replace monarchy in the Church by the constitutional government of recurrent General Councils; an institution which had so successfully disposed of Wycliffe's and Hus's heresies, and which had so neatly absorbed the sceptical attacks of both Occamism and humanism on the orthodoxy set out by St. Thomas Aquinas in the thirteenth century; such an institution could hardly take seriously the vapourings of an obscure German professor. Experience had shown how to deal with such aberrations. Unfortunately for the Church, the drastic action sanctioned by tradition and demanded by Luther's enemies only made matters worse; confronted by Luther's obstinacy and a constellation of circumstances interposing a wall between him and that stake which had been the fate of Hus, the formidable weight of ecclesiastical censure only created a more formidable reaction. As for the emperor, it was only late in 1520 that the new holder of that crown reached Germany and faced the problem of Luther. In the critical years from 1518 to 1520 there had been a virtual interregnum. All had waited upon the resumption of rule; all, that is, except Luther.

Chapter 2

Charles V

In the affairs of this world, the Reformation lay under the often brooding presence of Charles V. Born in 1500, this residuary legatee of Habsburg marriage alliances and the accidents of death ruled by 1519 an empire which covered much of western and central Europe and was beginning to include the best part of the recently discovered New World. From his father Philip's death in 1506, Charles was titular ruler of Burgundy—Franche Comté, Luxemburg, the Netherlands—and in 1515, declared of age, he became its real duke. In 1516, his grandfather Ferdinand of Aragon bequeathed to him the crown of Aragon, with Sicily and Naples, as well as the regency (soon turned into a kingship) of Castile with its American conquests; regency, because his insane mother Juana remained his nominal co-ruler throughout his life. The personal union of Ferdinand and Isabella, the Catholic kings, which had created something like a Spanish realm, was thus embodied in one man, and from this time one may, with reservations, speak of a king of Spain.[1] Then, in January 1519, his other grandfather, the Emperor Maximilian, also died, leaving Charles heir to the Austrian lands (Austria, Tyrol, Styria, Carinthia, Carniola) and the original Habsburg family lands round the upper Rhine, between Switzerland and Burgundy.

The event also vacated the crown of the Holy Roman Empire. Even here, though the dignity was elective, heredity played its part. The negotiations and intrigues preceding the election arose from the fact that Charles was not the only candidate; his rivals included for a short time Henry VIII of England, and more especially Francis I of France who had ascended his throne in 1515. The seven electors were much torn between their dislike of Habsburg power and their fear of the notoriously heavy rule of the kings of France; for a while they thought of electing one of themselves, Frederick of Saxony, but found that simple and stalwart worthy unwilling. They extracted money and constitutional concessions as best they could; the Fuggers produced 543,000 florins of the 850,000 which helped to turn the tables against France. But in the end it was not only his superior resources which secured Charles's unanimous election (28 June 1519), but even more the fact that he was a Habsburg, member of an imperial family and—as all Germany falsely thought—a German himself. The election gave him some further access of power; above all, it made him, in his own mind, the secular head of Christendom.

The young man who by these rapid stages gathered in the fruits of a hundred years of policy was a slight, rather ugly, man with a reserved manner. His mind was slow but, though unoriginal, far from negligible. He suffered from a high sense of duty and a powerful conviction of God's demands upon him. Brought up entirely in the traditions and atmosphere of the Burgundian court, he liked display and loved the ideals of its somewhat hot-house-grown chivalry; his physique notwithstanding, he found his favourite recreations in hunting and the tournament; later he prided himself on personal prowess in war. Certainly, his courage never failed; and even though the years, assisted not only by his labours but also by a gout which his vast eating and drinking did little to cure, aged him more rapidly than was usual even for the sixteenth century, there is justice in the well known equestrian portrait by Titian which as late as 1547 showed him as the armoured and conquering knight. By then he could barely sit his horse any longer. As he grew older, the force of experience, readily assimilated in a retentive memory, increased his stature until he appeared as a truly formidable ruler and the outstanding monarch of his day. In an age of brilliant princes and courts, Charles V proved that an unprepossessing exterior and the absence of a great intellect were no bar to eminence if a reasonable intelligence was allied with a sense of purpose and a dedication to work.

What maintained Charles through his trials and disappointments was his own notion of empire. This, which in part he learned from his brilliant chancellor Mercurino de Gattinara (d. 1530), involved much more than mere territorial power. Charles quite consciously thought of himself as the heir of Charlemagne, the secular head of a united Christendom, God's vicar side by side with the pope whose spiritual rule it was his duty to defend. If (as he was to find) the pope himself failed to share this conviction, being rather inclined to dread the power of his coadjutor and to work against it with all the weapons of secular diplomacy, this did not alter Charles's purpose; if the pope would not do his duty, the emperor must constrain him to it. Charles V was assuredly the last of the medieval emperors, born well out of his time and enabled to play the part at all only by the physical power of his dynastic empire. Ever aware of his God-given mission, he could not face the Lutheran revolt with anything but unrelenting hostility. From first to last he was determined to end the

schism, one way or another. In the struggle, his empire lost its
original bias towards Germany and the Holy Roman Empire, as
well as its original Netherlandish foundations. As time went on,
Spain, its resources, troops and ideas, more and more dominated
the territorial complex of Charles's dominions. Though Charles himself never became a real Spaniard (the truly Spanish empire awaited
his son Philip II) there was symbolic justice in the fact that the man
who in 1516 had come upon the scene as a valiant knight of Burgundy should in 1556 have retired, defeated and worn out, to the
neighbourhood of a Spanish monastery.

Even without the Reformation, the problems of Charles's empire
were enormous, possibly quite beyond solution. His very power and
greatness would have been enough to draw upon him the hostility of
others, especially of France, the one consolidated and independent
kingdom strong enough to act as a brake on his activities; but in any
case he inherited with his lands several long-standing disputes with
that monarchy. The ruler of Burgundy and the Netherlands had a
claim to the duchy of Burgundy, lost to France in 1477. The counties
of Flanders and Artois were in Habsburg hands but owed feudal
allegiance to France. Both these contrasting claims were not given
up until 1529. The king of Castile was at odds with France over the
Pyrenean kingdom of Navarre. The king of Aragon inherited the
ancient Aragonese-Angevin dispute over Sicily and Naples, as well
as the struggle for Milan dating from Charles VIII's invasion of Italy
in 1494; these elements composed the background to the prolonged
Italian wars which again were to endure until 1529. When Charles V
came to the throne, his hold over southern Italy was secure; but in the
north, the French had established their ascendancy by the decisive
victory of Marignano (1515). Milan was technically a fief of the Holy
Roman Empire; so was the Alpine duchy of Savoy which played
French and Habsburgs off against each other to preserve a precarious
independence, also threatened by the aggressive policy of the Swiss
Confederacy. In Alsace and Lorraine, imperial and French interests
had clashed for centuries, a situation only aggravated by the Burgundian attempt to recreate the ancient Middle Kingdom and by the
Habsburg succession to that ambition. In all this, there was plenty of
material for war, as there was plenty of cause for Francis I to feel
encircled and frustrated in his search for military glory. Personal
rivalry made certain of the conflict: Francis, a flashy and superficial
and often ill-advised exponent of Renaissance passions, could not
bear the greatness of his opponent, while Charles was at first jealous
of the other and later came to hate his unreliability and treachery.
Thus the forty years after 1519 were dominated by the Habsburg-
Valois struggle, an era of intermittent war only ended by the peace of
Cateau-Cambrésis in 1559.

As though this were not enough, Charles found himself challenged also by the formidable power of the Turks. Indeed, he had three reasons for fighting them. Aragon and Italy made him a Mediterranean prince, heir to the Catalan and Genoese commercial empires; throughout his life he depended heavily on Genoa for ships and money, did his best to keep the great admiral Andrea Doria sweet, and late in life warned his son never to break with that necessary city. After the conquest of Rhodes in 1522, the Ottoman empire thrust forward also by the sea routes; in alliance with the Muslim pirates of the Barbary coast from Tangier to Tunis, it soon disputed the control of the Mediterranean with Spain. A second point of contact lay in the east. After the collapse of the Jagiellon power in Hungary and Bohemia in 1526, the Habsburgs, in the person of Charles's brother Ferdinand, inherited claims to those lands for which they had to struggle with the sultan's victorious advance upon Christian Europe up the Danube. And thirdly, Charles's chosen position as head of Christendom would in any case have forced the problem of the mighty infidel upon his attention, the more especially as his reign coincided with the expansion associated with the rule of Sulaiman the Great (1520–66). Throughout his life, he never lost sight of that mission and that danger, dreaming of crusades and more practically trying to repel the sultan's progress.[2]

War was therefore the keynote of Charles V's reign, war and the expenditure it demanded. Of course, his resources in men and money looked to be very large, too, but even if he had ruled a united and consolidated empire he would have had great difficulty in meeting his needs. As it was, he ruled nothing of the sort. His empire had come to him by dynastic accident, and dynastic unity was the only unity it knew. His own power alone held it together, and he was for ever on the move in order to show his face in his various dominions. His absence always threatened discontent. True to the dynastic principle, he governed as far as possible through members of his family. Ferdinand looked after Germany for him. In the Netherlands, an aunt, Margaret of Austria (1519–30), and a sister, Mary of Hungary (1531–5), successively acted as highly competent regents. His wife headed the government of the Spanish kingdoms. But in the last resort he alone mattered. Though he showed himself able to delegate authority and allow action by deputies, he always reserved the last word and demanded constant reference to himself. He kept to himself also as much as possible of the one great weapon of unity: his rights of patronage. Patronage in the bestowing of lands, offices, ecclesiastical appointments and direct "rewards" (money gifts) was the main social and administrative cement of all western Europe in this age;[3] but no ruler commanded so much of it or had to use it so purposefully as Charles V. In the result he bound increasing numbers especially of the nobility to his faithful service; the Burgundians had been there from the first, but Spaniards, Italians and even Germans found first a substitute for loyalty, and ultimately the thing itself, in their feelings for this fountain of honour and profit.

This did not make his rule any less personal, but it enabled him to translate personal rule into practical terms, to direct the affairs of his scattered realms with some success, and even to wage victorious war by deputy and at a distance. For Charles never attempted to develop a single administrative organisation for all his territories. Gattinara, his chief minister after the death, in 1521, of his tutor, Guillaume de Chièvres, who had brought him safely through his Burgundian youth and set him on his Spanish thrones, had such a plan: he tried to extend his powers as chancellor of Burgundy to all the empire and make Charles monarch of an integrated state. But it never proved possible, and after Gattinara's death in 1530 Charles abandoned such unworkable and very expensive schemes. He ruled in person, and though his two secretaries—Francisco de los Cobos for Spain and Italy; Nicolas Perrenot, lord of Granvelle, for Burgundy and Germany—provided a little co-ordination at the centre, every part of his dominions continued essentially to live by its own system of government, customs and laws. As Charles moved about Europe he changed character from king of this to duke of that or count of the other; if only the Spaniards demanded that in Spain he should call himself their king and not use the imperial title, the rest of his subjects behaved very much in accordance with the same notion.

His old homeland, the Burgundian inheritance, was as complex as any; but it remained essential for him to command its allegiance. Franche Comté supplied a disproportionate number of his civil servants from among its many highly trained Roman lawyers. (Granvelle was one of them; so were others, legists and secretaries of courts and councils all over Europe). Even more urgently, the industrialised lands of Hainault, Flanders and Brabant supplied much needed wealth. Flanders, the medieval Lancashire, was by this time in decline. The rising English cloth industry and the heavy taxation of the Burgundian dukes had undermined its prosperity; out of this had come a chronic state of disorder, expressing itself in frequent risings of the urban democracy against both the *haute bourgeoisie* and the count. Bruges and Ghent revolted against Maximilian; and Ghent tried the old game once more in 1539–40 when for the last time a popular government was set up by the unemployed craftsmen and proletariate. It took a major military operation, conducted by Charles V in person, to overthrow this and destroy the power of the gilds.

The decline of Flanders proved the making of Brabant, and especially of the great Scheldt port of Antwerp. From 1504, when the Portuguese transferred the spice staple there from Lisbon, to the

Habsburg bankruptcy of 1557, Antwerp was the commercial and
financial centre of Europe, supplemented rather than rivalled by
Lyons, Augsburg and Genoa. Its ascendancy rested in part on its
own flourishing industries—cloth-finishing and metal trades in particular—and in part on its convenient and exceptionally free markets
which turned it into the great entrepôt of European trade. More
particularly, it imported the unfinished cloth which was the staple
produce of England and, after working it up, conveyed it further to
the markets of central Europe; but it also exploited a north-south
route of trade, from the Baltic and down the Rhine, and had contacts
with every significant centre of primary production and manufacture.
The pressure of business attracted merchants from all parts who
either resided or kept factors there; it also rapidly developed the
machinery of international finance and made Antwerp the main
money-market of Europe. The creation of Charles V's empire gave
the city natural advantages inside his extensive political system and
made it the obvious place for feeding the precious metals of the
Americas into the European trade stream. Its wharves, workshops
and bourse were as much the economic centre of Charles's empire as
his court was its administrative centre; more even than the prosperity
of the Netherlands, its highly developed machinery for liquidising
resources and raising loans was essential to the conduct of policy and
especially of war.

Yet the Netherlands remained a political problem, for two main
reasons. On the one hand, only the duke's person held them together.
It is true that Charles's regents used central councils to give some
cohesion to the régime; but every province had its own governor and
more particularly its own estates whose consent had to be obtained,
often with great difficulty, for every grant of taxes. Though the States
General met at Brussels occasionally, anything they agreed had to be
ratified by the provincial estates. Secondly, the collection of provinces
was not complete when Charles came to the throne. By escheat and
conquest he added Tournai (1521), Friesland (1523), Overijssel and
Utrecht (1528), and Groningen (1536). Another territory caused him
more trouble. With the duchy of Burgundy he also inherited the old
enmity of the Egmont counts of Guelders, repeatedly stimulated by
France, which expressed itself in constant raids and much destruction
in the northern parts. In the end, even Holland and Zeeland, despite
ingrained suspicions of the Walloon south, grew tired of Guelders,
and in 1543 Charles V was able to end both the threat and the
independence of that county.[4] This made possible a measure of
unification for all the provinces, even including the prince-bishoprics
of Liège and Utrecht, though to the last the emperor remained very
cautious in these matters and respected separatist traditions. The
problem was further complicated by the Reformation which after

1530 began to make progress in the Netherlands. Among the lower orders, especially, it met and reinvigorated ancient sectarian traditions of both the quietist and the apocalyptic kinds; Anabaptism, as we shall see, had much success in this region. On the other hand, its spread gave Charles the opportunity of using a violently repressive policy against heretics in the interests of centralised authority, and to do this with the approval of the nobility and the town oligarchies who would have jealously watched any such endeavours if they had not been directed against hated dissentients.

If the problems of Burgundy and the Netherlands, aggravated by taxation and heresy, tended to get rather worse during the reign, those of Spain moved the other way. True, in Castile, temporary prosperity disguised some disquieting weaknesses. War and American silver caused a rapid inflation which, though it ultimately affected all Europe, hit Spain first; Charles continued the disastrous policy of his predecessors against the industrious classes who were mostly crypto-Muslims and crypto-Jews; the burden of taxation was gradually allowed to fall more and more on the poorer sort. Thus despite its flourishing wool-production, cloth-exports to the Americas, and the constant influx of bullion from the colonies, Spain grew no richer, to the amazement of contemporaries who could not understand the situation at all. Although this generation witnessed some active commercial enterprise in the towns, the social structure of Castile, dominated by a greater and lesser nobility contemptuous of all trade except that of arms, did not permit Spain to benefit permanently from the rain of silver which, by stimulating prices and profits, promoted marked economic advances elsewhere—in Germany, Antwerp and England in particular. Exclusion from the American trade, Charles's dependence on Genoese bankers, and bigoted Christianity operated against the revival of the much more commercial traditions of Aragon; trade in the western Mediterranean, for which Barcelona had fought so long, now fell largely into Italian hands, and the gardens of Valencia followed those of Granada into decay. In the end only Andalusia and the port of Seville, the entrepôt for the Atlantic trade with the new colonies, showed much life; and here it is notable that despite the supposed national monopoly in these matters many of the merchants resident there and regularly engaged in the Caribbean trade were foreigners—Germans, English, Italians.

However, Spain's decline was more insidious than rapid; Charles just about quadrupled the yield of taxes from Castile (as against a doubling of price levels); and if the American silver ultimately ruined the country, it could for the time be used to pay troops, repay loans, maintain the running of the empire. To all appearance, this was a great age for Spain. Dragged into a European—even world-wide—complex, it came to dominate it. In his early years, Charles encoun-

tered the greatest difficulties in getting himself accepted by his penin-
sular subjects. His Burgundian entourage, his lavish court, his foreignness, not to mention the tactlessness and folly which left behind
in his absence a Dutch bishop (his old tutor, Adrian of Utrecht) to
rule the pride of Castile—all this set up serious strains. The *Cortes*
(parliament) of both Castile and Aragon reluctantly recognised his
kingship and even more reluctantly voted him money; as soon as he
left the country again, to receive the imperial crown which the
Castilian *Cortes* had already told him was worthless, trouble broke
out. In 1519, the towns of Valencia formed a *Germanía*, or armed
revolutionary government, nominally in support of their king against
the nobles but in fact against all authority; this lasted precariously
until 1523 when it was finally destroyed by the grandees. A more
serious rebellion broke out in northern Castile in 1520, when the
towns there refused to pay taxes, drove out the royal officials, and
formed the league of the *Comuneros* which for a time threatened all
royal rule. But as the movement, under extremist leaders, grew more
radical and anarchic, it lost its moderate followers; in 1521 the
Castilian nobility defeated the *Comuneros* in battle at Villalar and
handed the kingdom back to their absent king.

Surprisingly enough, after such stormy beginnings, the Spanish
kingdoms remained henceforward unswervingly loyal to a sovereign
whose frequent absences they nevertheless continued to resent. The
truth is that the monarchy had in effect formed an alliance with the
Church and with the nobility who in Castile even ceased to pay taxes
after 1538. The glory of Charles V's monarchy captured the imagination of these soldiers born and bred who served him in Italy, Germany and across the oceans with devotion and high skill. Spanish
troops even more than the German professional foot-soldiers—the
renowned *Landsknechte*—formed the backbone of all Charles's
armies. The alliance between the warrior king and the warrior nobility—grandees and hidalgos—of Castile certainly brought splendour
to Spain for the moment; the future was another matter. No more
than in the Netherlands did Charles try in Spain to destroy ancient
privileges and constitutional customs, except that the towns were
reduced to subservience after the defeats of *Germanía* and *Comuneros*; the *Cortes* of both kingdoms continued to meet, those of the
Crown of Aragon (theoretically very powerful) continued to limit
their financial contributions; even the office of *justicia*—protector of
Aragonese liberties against the king—continued to exist. There was
much growth of organisation at the centre, especially a hierarchy of
councils served by professional secretaries which administered the
Spanish kingdoms; Aragon's council was reorganised on the Castilian
model in 1522, but it was the latter (which went back to Isabella)
that provided unified government for Spain. In this task it had the

valuable help of the Inquisition, in Spain a royal instrument with powers that cut across the regional divisions and the customary rights of the lay people. This mixture of old and new, of entrenched privileges and modernised administration, was in general characteristic at this time of Europe and of Charles V's empire in particular. It was all a trifle haphazard, but the establishment of bureaucratic practices and traditions, and the growing dependence on a personal monarch were beginning to create in Spain conditions favourable to a true royal absolutism. However, in the age of Charles V any such tendencies were still markedly modified by the customary law, by the power of the *Cortes*, and by the continued semi-independence of the nobility. On the other hand, it is probably true that the real bulwark against royal despotism disappeared with the destruction of urban liberties.

In 1524, another council was set up, for the Indies. Whether Charles V ever fully appreciated what was happening in America is by no means clear; certainly all his preoccupations were with European problems. The age in general, however, saw the point all right; few things so disturbed settled notions and comfortable convictions as this discovery and opening up of a vast and populous continent totally unknown even to the apparently omniscient ancients. The first shock of discovery had been absorbed before the reign of Charles V began, but it was in his time that the wonders of the New World really came to light. In 1519, Hernán Cortéz landed at Vera Cruz; by 1521 he had conquered Mexico, destroyed the Aztec empire, and added a new realm to the Spanish crowns. After tentative exploration southwards in the next few years, the conquest of the Inca kingdom in Peru by Francisco Pizarro and his four brothers—a bunch of illiterate thugs and conquerors of genius—was even quicker. It took only a few days in 1530 to break the power of the military empire which the Spaniards came to replace. Though several years were needed to exploit the victory, it is a significant fact that by 1537 the triumphant Spaniards were able to indulge in the luxury of civil wars.

These conquests and the news of these marvellous lands made the world gape, but they raised fundamental difficulties for the king of Castile and his advisers. Though the *conquistadores* usually professed complete loyalty to the crown, it was a far from easy task to govern territories 3000 miles away and men of such marked individuality; quite apart from securing the king's lawful share of the profits, especially the fifth, or *quinto*, of all silver and gold mined. In addition, the native Indians, horribly maltreated and exploited by their first conquerors, were yet thought of as full subjects of the crown and soon demanded attention. It is much to the credit of the Spanish clergy that they took the lead in protecting these victims. From the first the missionaries, intent on baptising the heathen, resisted the Spanish habit of treating the Indians as animals; and the missionaries—especially the Dominican Bartolomeo de las Casas who devoted his life to the rescue of the Indians—soon had the ear of the government. In the 1530s, Francisco de Victoria, professor of law at Salamanca, asserted that the American heathens had their rights and that war against them, unless specifically provoked, was unjust: a formidable indictment of the whole crusading principle which had played such a part in Spanish expansion overseas.

If the government were to protect their Indian subjects, they would first of all have to break the power of their Spanish henchmen, and this difficult task was energetically undertaken. The conquest of Mexico had led to the granting of *encomiendas*—great landed estates with rights to Indian labour—to the first settlers; since these could easily develop into near-independent principalities, they were thereafter consistently broken up. An organised system of royal courts (*asdiencias*) and officials, headed by a viceroy, took hold of the country. The same methods were applied to Peru and the other conquests. In the process, some injustice was done to such as Cortéz. That relatively civilised man, in whom ruthless selfishness did not overbalance intelligent statesmanship, tired in the end of the petty persecution to which the government subjected him, returned to Spain, and died disillusioned in 1547. Charles never used his great talents in his European wars. Pizarro escaped a similar fate by being murdered (1541); his brothers, and other equally brutal and successful men among that extraordinary generation, died violent deaths at the hands of each other or of Spanish governors. By the 1540s the situation was ripe for settlement, and in 1542 the "New Laws of the Indies" ended the *encomienda* system and replaced it by a general structure of royal rule at a distance in central and southern America. The wonder is that these endeavours had as much success as they did. New Spain and New Granada settled down to become true provinces of the Spanish crown, exploiting cattleranching, mining (in 1545 the inexhaustible silver mines of Potosí were opened, to swell the flood of bullion into Europe), and trade with the Old World—legitimate trade with Seville and illegal trade with French, Portuguese and English interlopers. The rapidity and extent of the conquest are perhaps no more remarkable than the speed with which it was at once settled in depth or the enlightened attention given to the problem of colonial government. Spain, thinly peopled and absorbed in European and Mediterranean concerns, yet found the energy and men to colonise in two or three generations an area much greater than Europe.

For Charles V, however, these problems, though not ignored, remained somewhat marginal. He faced struggles in Italy and

Germany before he could turn to the Americas. These he was bound
to regard as a source of money rather than a manifest destiny. In Italy,
he was at least lucky to find both Sicily and Naples permanently loyal
in the hands of their nobility; the problems of Milan and the pope,
complicated by the strength of Venice in the north and the feebleness
of Florence in Tuscany, recurred throughout his wars and must be
noted there. In sum, he effectively established Spanish ascendancy
over the whole peninsula, turned the pope into something very like an
imperial chaplain, and in the end settled Milan (long administered by
Spanish viceroys) by conferring the dukedom upon his son Philip
(1546).

Germany was another matter. We have already had occasion to
stress the weakness of imperial authority there, though generalised
sentiments of loyalty to the emperor—or at least unwillingness to
take action against him—continued to exercise quite considerable
influence even on most princes. Such feelings were really powerful
among the cities and the middle sort of men. As long as Germany
thought of Charles V as a German, all parties, very much aware of
the concept of a "German nation"—a community of traditions and
interests which they wished to see expressed not in the creation of a
national state but more vaguely in co-operation and peace among the
splintered entities—put their hope in them. The imperial Diet (*Reich-
stag*), with its separate "estates" of electors, princes and towns, still
offered a genuine arena for a nationwide discussion of policy and
affairs; for all anyone could tell in 1520, it might even have become
the sort of instrument for true unity which national parliaments had
been in other countries throughout the later middle ages. Add to that
the sheer physical power of the new emperor, so much greater than
anything known for centuries, and it is plain that it would be historically wrong to regard as in some way inevitable Charles V's ultimate
failure to exterminate Protestantism and bring centralised unity to
Germany—though, of course, the range of difficulties and rival preoccupations outlined here always made his chances somewhat pro-
blematical.

In fact, Charles did not find it possible to govern Germany in
person; here, too, he needed a deputy. In 1521–2 he surrendered the
eastern Habsburg lands to his brother Ferdinand, thereby in effect
founding the later Austrian empire; there is some irony in the fact
that of the two brothers Ferdinand was markedly the more Spanish.
Thereafter he usually left German affairs to the younger man—or
rather, left him to have recourse in all that mattered to his absent
majesty. In 1531 he secured Ferdinand's election as king of the
Romans or, under the constitution, heir-apparent to the imperial
title. In his last years, as we shall see,[5] he tried in vain to reverse
this policy which split the Habsburg possession into a Spanish and an

Austrian part. Ferdinand's government of Germany was always under the emperor's cold eye, and events frequently compelled Charles V to spend much longer than he wished in central Europe; but he never could find time or inclination to grapple decisively with the particularism, the lack of central authority, or the patchwork intermingling of territorial claims which characterised the country. Yet when in 1520 he crossed the sea to Antwerp and travelled from there towards Aachen and the imperial crown,[6] he summoned the Diet to meet him at Worms in January 1521. He meant to look at the situation and act. There he would sit in state in the assembly of the empire; there he would meet yet another set of subjects. It soon became apparent that he would also be facing Luther there.

At this point it is not easy to see where exactly Luther stood. The years of controversy, culminating in the papal excommunication and his own reaction to it, had made him a public figure. The obscure theologian had grown into something of a prophetic leader, thanks to his own literary genius and the invention of printing. But while his message had found an overwhelming response among all sorts of men, from princes to peasants, there was as yet no Lutheran Reformation, Lutheran Church, or even Lutheran party. The pope might treat him as an heretic and schismatic; Luther was still far from accepting the split. The emperor's arrival seemed at last to offer the chance of setting things in motion. In effect, Luther hoped to appeal from a deluded pope to a reforming emperor; but to do so he would need a hearing. The electors—especially Frederick the Wise whose attitude to Luther (they never met) was a mixture of awe and patronage—asked that he should be called before the Diet to explain himself; the papal nuncio, Jerome Aleander, an ex-humanist frightened by discord into being more papal than the pope, vigorously opposed the suggestion. He dreaded the effect of a public demonstration, and he was right.

Luther's appearance at Worms proved to be the true beginning of the Reformation, a blow to the many hopes placed in the emperor but also the certainty that the new theology had come to stay. Charles V agreed to the elector's request, sent Luther a safe-conduct, and made his way from Aachen up-Rhine to Worms. At the same time, Luther, with the warnings of apprehensive friends ringing in his ears, travelled there from Wittenberg; by coach now, whereas he had walked to Augsburg to meet Cajetan. On April 16 he arrived; next day, he faced the assembly for the first time. As he waited to go in, old George Frundsberg clanked by in his armour and, seeing the tense and at this time palely slender figure, was moved to a rough affection. "Little monk," he said, "thou'rt on a heavy errand." Luther knew it, and he nearly muffed it. On the 17th he was suddenly asked to do no more than acknowledge his works and recant—no chance of

an address or an argument, Aleander triumphant. This was certainly
not the hearing he had expected, but he just managed in a whisper to
ask for time to consider. Despite the nuncio, Charles gave him
twenty-four hours—twenty-four hours which, it is not extravagant
to say, were to cost him thirty-four years of trouble. For on the 18th,
all was different. Luther calmly acknowledged his writings, apolo-
gised for offensive remarks, admitted the existence of debatable
points, but firmly maintained his fundamental doctrines. He had
made his speech and was very much in command of the scene,
presided over by the sombre and silent figure of the young emperor:
in all their joint lives, it was their only confrontation. At last, as
exasperated opponents pressed for a straight answer rather than an
argument, he spoke his defiance. The record does not preserve the
famous words, but what it does give is not far from the challenge of
tradition. Let tradition have its say: "Here I stand; I can do no other;
God help me; amen."

In the German world his appeal succeeded; at Worms, nuncio and
emperor had their way. The Diet's final edict denounced the Lutheran
heresy, demanded that all members should destroy it, and placed
Luther himself in the imperial ban. He was now outlawed by both
the swords, the spiritual and the temporal. With memories of Hus
vividly before them, his friends got him to leave before Charles was
persuaded to break his word. They misjudged the emperor: his
knight's honour would force him to observe the safe-conduct. But
only while it lasted; Luther was wise to get out. Along the road back
to Saxony he disappeared. An armed band of kidnappers carried him
off to the castle of the Wartburg. They were friends, acting by
arrangement with his territorial prince who thought it best to remove
the outlaw from the reach of the authorities. In one way the move
was a mistake because it left Germany Lutherless, bewildered and
torn by rumour, a prey to agitators more violent than Dr. Martin. Yet
it had its uses. Secluded in the Wartburg, disguised in secular clothing
and passing by the name of Sir George, Luther needed work. The
sudden leisure after such crowded years was bad for a temperament
always given to brooding; for him temptation (Luther's word for it
was *Anfechtung*, the devil's attacks) took the form of spiritual lan-
guor and physical discontent. Small wonder he saw the devil and
threw his inkpot at him in the little room above the trees. The work
he found could not have been better chosen for his purpose: he set
himself to translate scripture into German. As he had always said, the
Word would do it all; now the Word was to be made available to all.
If there is a single thread running through the whole story of the
Reformation, it is the explosive and renovating and often disintegrat-
ing effect of the bible, put into the hands of the commonalty and
interpreted no longer by the well-conditioned learned, but by the

faith and delusion, the common sense and uncommon nonsense, of all sorts of men. One country after another was to receive its vernacular bible in this century, and with it a new standard of its language; in 1521–2 Luther, who had for so many people already done so much to bring the gospel to life after its long sleep in the scholastic nightcap began the work for his Germans.[7]

Chapter 3

Years of Triumph

In the eight years from the Diet of Worms to the 1529 Diet of Speyer, Lutheranism grew from a theological and spiritual protest into organised Churches, but in the process lost much of its general support; there appeared new centres to rival Wittenberg's leadership; these advances were made possible by the weakness of the central government and the emperor's absorption in war and diplomacy. Though it is worth remembering that all these things happened at the same time, they will, for clarity's sake, be described in turn.

I The Progress of Lutheranism

Luther's friends soon heard from him after his disappearance to the Wartburg; indeed, his sojourn there began that flood of letters, instructions, advice and exhortation which, flowing from him for twenty-five years, was his chief instrument in spreading the new teaching and in holding the new Churches together. Nevertheless, his absence from the scene posed immediate problems. Wild rumours circulated about his fate, and the orphaned multitude looked to new leaders. Especially was this true in Wittenberg itself. Without his restraining influence, it was not the scholarly and cautious Philip Melanchthon (1497–1560), the systematic thinker of early Lutheranism, but the enthusiastic and unstable Andrew Carlstadt (1480–1541) who took charge. Carlstadt determined to follow direct inspiration and carry out radical reform at one blow. He preached against the mass and clerical celibacy, followed his precept by taking a wife, encouraged violence of expression and action till Wittenberg was riven by conflict and overrun by image-breakers. The extremists enthusiastically welcomed the arrival of the socalled Zwickau prophets, religious maniacs of a familiar messianic pattern: men of the people who had seen visions and made a deep impression both by their patriarchal appearance and by their exaltation. The moderates turned to Luther: he must come back and restore order; in the end, despite the elector's fear for his safety, he complied. The lost reformer reappeared like a portent and a judgement. Eight sermons did the trick: the Wittenberg laity shamefacedly abandoned Carlstadt, and the moderate progress of the Reformation, by persuasion and consent rather than violence and puritan excesses, was assured. Exiled by the elector, Carlstadt turned up at intervals and various places, his unhappy wife in tow, inciting to radical action, stirring up strife, and complaining of his misfortunes. His is a well known type of academic enthusiast, and he was as ineffective as one might suppose.

Luther now faced a great decision. Hitherto he had been a preacher and teacher. But now that he had broken with Rome and removed one accepted order of things, he had to become an organiser and an actor in the world. As he had seen, if he did not accept the task, there were others only too willing to do it for him. It would be wrong to suppose that he now recognised the permanency of the split; he and his followers continued to think in terms of reforming the one and universal Church. But they were now forced to supply their own machinery, and Saxony came to be the proving ground of what, after all, turned out to be a new Church. The Lutheran doctrines of grace and justification and the nature of the priesthood, the demand for vernacular services and lay communion in both kinds, enforced far-reaching changes in ceremonial and worship, even though Luther insisted on progressing by degrees. The mass, later the chief target of reformed hostility, was for the moment altered rather than abolished, until by 1526 it emerged in Luther's *Deutsche Messe* as a new liturgy. The sermon gradually replaced the miracle of the eucharist as the centre of the service. By trial and error, by exchange of views with associates soon spread over most of Germany, the evangelical Churches acquired their characteristic form. Melanchthon supplied the systematic theology of which Luther's wayward genius was not capable. This infant prodigy—at twenty-one a professor of Greek at Wittenberg, a learned Hebraist, the most distinctively humanist influence on Lutheranism—aptly complemented his master's gifts with his own; his *Loci Communes* ("Commonplaces"), first published in 1521 and frequently reprinted with alterations, provided definitions of doctrine highly necessary in the uncertain situation created by Luther's explosion. John Bugenhagen (1485–1558) supplied the organising and constitution-making talent needed by the new Churches. Thus Wittenberg became a busy centre of missionary activity. Luther practically never left it, but the press and his immense output in effect made him present everywhere, while disciples gathered to be instructed and go forth. From 1525, when Luther broke his vows to marry the escaped nun

Catherine von Bora and live quite happily ever after, his household provided both an advertisement for clerical marriage and a somewhat rumbustious centre for the growing community of evangelical pastors. He continued to be the main inspiration of the movement, not least because he discovered in himself an unexpected talent for the writing of hymns, the battlecries of the Reformation (Luther's are often superb, the general output is another matter). But many other men increasingly contributed to its success.

More difficult than doctrinal change and liturgical reform was the problem of organisation. Although Luther's theology of justification contained hidden within it a notion of God's Church as confined to those upon whom God had bestowed His grace—a Church of true believers only—the reformer himself accepted that while the Invisible Church of the saints in heaven was assuredly of that kind, the Visible Church on earth must necessarily comprehend all who call themselves Christians, even though in fact they may be sinners. Since only God knew for certain who was saved, men must not exclude any souls from communion with the Church, except by way of punishment for an open sinful act. (Excommunication, the great ecclesiastical weapon, never became much of an issue in Lutheranism.) Luther's teaching therefore preserved the medieval principle of the universal *res publica Christiana*, even if organised in separate entities; he had no time for sectarian notions which confined the true Church to the self-known chosen of God. In addition, the question of public order was always very much in Luther's mind, as it was in that of the civil authorities with whom he had to deal.

All this demanded uniformity—the existence of one organisation and general conformity to it. But in trying to secure this Luther was thrown back upon the territorial ruler who alone could support ecclesiastical discipline with physical power. When Frederick the Wise, never a Lutheran, was succeeded by the Elector John (1525–32), Luther had to hand a prince willing to follow his lead. The result was a disciplinary organisation called the Visitation, a committee of two electoral councillors and two theologians, who took over the government of the Church from the bishops. They enforced devotional uniformity, reformed the morals and manners of the clergy, and supervised the moral and spiritual welfare of the laity. Bishops, now called superintendents, continued to be appointed, subject to the Visitation's authority; that authority itself, however, really emanated from the secular arm. Luther ascribed to the Christian magistrate a duty and a right to see to the well-ordering of God's Church, and the Visitation, embodying his political doctrine, in effect turned the Lutheran Church of Saxony into a state-Church. The system was copied, with modifications, wherever the Lutheran Reformation established itself. The princes in their territories, the councils in the cities, in alliance with evangelical clergy, took effective charge of the new Churches emerging in the process. Their willingness to do so was greatly encouraged by the invariable disappearance of regular orders and the confiscation of their property; throughout the 1520's the secularisation of Church lands and their resumption by territorial rulers added a very powerful element of self interest to the genuine religious feelings which assisted the spread of Luther's reform.

This organisational growth, territorially fragmented if denominationally uniform, reflected the great crisis of support which struck the Reformation in the years 1524–5. A nationwide popular movement collapsed in those years, authority triumphed, the failure of the reform to conquer all Germany (let alone all Christendom) became predictable. Luther had from the first refused to carry out his Reformation by the sword, but his refusal had not stopped others from trying to do so. The first to go were the imperial knights. Though the grievances and ambitions of that decaying order of society were really, as we have seen,[1] social and political—a desire to recover the influence in affairs to which they reckoned their birth entitled them, but which economic decline and the powers of princes had partially destroyed—their leaders, Sickingen and Hutten, tried to appeal to the Lutheran reform as a national movement. Hutten, a true idealist, was serious about this; Sickingen, the mercenary captain and devious politician, hoped simply to attract wide support for self-aggrandisement. In 1522 he pursued a personal vendetta by attacking the archbishop of Trier, but the prelate proved a trifle too warlike and his spiritual position too little resented to explode Sickingen's revolutionary mine with any success. The condottiere retired in discomfiture and in 1523 was defeated at Landstuhl by an alliance of princes. He died soon after of his wounds; Hutten fled to Switzerland, to die of syphilis, exhaustion and despair at the age of thirty-five. The collapse of the knights removed a standing threat to peace and order, but also an obstacle to princely despotism; it did not harm the Reformation which had not really become involved in the affair.

More serious in every respect was the general uprising known as the Peasants' War which started in the Black Forest in June 1524, spread rapidly through southern Germany, and in the months of March to May 1525 had not only the south but the centre and parts of the north in uproar. The conventional name is liable to mislead: leadership came from the yeomanry and the smaller craftsmen of the towns, while the following consisted largely of the more solid and propertied lower orders. The roots of the rising went a long way back;[2] the immediate causes were those which had provoked rebellion before this—economic pressure and an extension of legal demands upon those who thought themselves protected by ancient custom; the extensive spread reflected in part a general malaise and in part the failure of the authorities to act in time. The interesting fact that Bavaria remained untroubled despite the violence of rebellion all round it, demonstrates the essential grievance: here alone the duke had enforced discipline on lesser lords and prevented their aggressive exploitation of claims against their tenantry. But the Reformation played its part in the story: the recent growth of demands for rights granted by the law of God readily coalesced with the belief that Luther, unbridled in his attacks on fat priests and monks, had called to action—that the restoration of the gospel included restoring the rights of the commons. Since Luther had assaulted one aspect of the existing order, it is no wonder that men with grievances interpreted his message as encouraging attacks on other parts of the system.

More directly influential were the radical reformers some of whom preached the promise of salvation for the poor if they would only rise up against their oppressors and do God's work by destroying the devil in rivers of blood. Thomas Müntzer,[3] the demonic genius of the early Reformation, took his share in whipping up rebellion and died for it after fleeing from the final battle. Not that the peasants' demands were in general extreme. The Twelve Articles of Memmingen, accepted as a programme by most of the individual bands, combined traditional and legitimate grievances concerning rights of pasture, fishing and hunting, labour services and excessive rents, with evangelical desires for pastors elected by the congregation and a general willingness to have everything judged by scripture and the law of God. As the revolt spread, some men got out of hand and excesses occurred; monasteries were regularly sacked, and there was some killing. On the whole, the peasantry at least of Baden and Swabia, the original areas of trouble, behaved with extraordinary restraint, though in Salzburg and the Tyrol they showed up worse. Rumour exaggerated the violence. The governing classes were shaken to the core, and after much delay their reaction was a good deal more savage than the threat they were fighting. The peasants proved to have no leaders of either military or political capacity; worse, they rarely showed either valour or vigour in action. An air of bewilderment hangs about most of their efforts. When the armies of the Swabian League, professionals commanded by that competent general, George Truchsess, got going in the south and east, and when Hesse, Brunswick and Saxony joined forces against Müntzer's pathetic theocracy in Thuringia, the end came very quickly. Thousands—some estimates reckon 100,000—of peasants were killed, mostly in the aftermaths of so-called battles that were only routs, the princes' men-at-arms having great sport in running down the fugitives. But after the hot blood had cooled, revenge was much modified; the lords could not afford to destroy the tillers of the soil on which their own wealth depended; there were few hangings.

Instead the peasants lost their weapons and were heavily fined; it says something for their previous and not altogether terminated prosperity that they could and did pay up. Nevertheless, the war had a profound social consequence: an essential characteristic of late-medieval Germany disappeared overnight when the rural commons and urban poor suddenly ceased to have any further power to influence events.

Luther had watched the war with horror. At first he told the lords the truth: they had only themselves to thank for the rebellion. But as the reports of violence came in, and of appeals to his teaching, he took fright and grew angry. He had never meant to start a revolution, least of all a social upheaval destructive of the inherited order of society. His deeply conservative instincts reinforced his growing fears that his real message—salvation in another world dependent on faith in God's love and mercy—would be swamped by the radicals' perversion of it to temporal ends, and his fatal gift of violent language provoked him into hot denunciation. His notorious tract, *Against the murdering, thieving hordes of the peasants*, was written when the rebellion seemed to carry all before it and in the circumstances was even an act of courage; the rapid collapse of the war made it come out after the event, so that it read like a brutal call to stamp on the defeated. But while Luther was unfortunate in his timing, and while his resentment of revolutionaries taking his name in vain can be understood, he had, as so often, been carried away by his temper and his vocabulary. The tract remains a sad example of the crudity to which he could sink.

In southern Germany, at least, the authorities were now firmly in the saddle; the Reformation had thrown in its lot with the princes. On the other hand, it has recently been shown that the traditional view, which regards 1525 as the year at which the Reformation ceased altogether to be a popular movement, overstates the case. Luther's general appeal declined but did not disappear; in the northern cities, especially, reformed after the crisis, the initiative came from below.[4] It must also be said that the consensus of opinion which deplores the failure of the "popular" Reformation would seem to misread the situation. As the Peasants' War itself demonstrated, the secular backing which the Reformation was bound to need if it was to survive the enmity of pope and emperor could be supplied only by the princes. Furthermore, among the generality the spiritual upheaval of the new doctrines deteriorated rapidly into the sort of millenarian visions and messianic dreams which, as events had shown before this, could only end in anarchy, lawlessness and bloodshed.[5] It is not only the case that the reformed princes preserved the Reformation, but also that without them it could almost certainly not have been preserved.

By a curious coincidence, 1525 also marked Luther's break with the main humanist reform movement from which he had at one time drawn much support. As the revolutionary impact of his teaching become more and more apparent, Erasmus and his followers grew increasingly doubtful. Attacks on bad popes, worldly clergy, rapacious and ignorant monks were all very well; but this man was throwing out the good with the bad, destroying instead of reforming. The distance widened between the world of academic ideas and the reality of things; many who had enjoyed criticising the seemingly invincible drew back in fear when they saw where their own propaganda was leading. The entrenched forces of the old order turned savagely upon the humanist reformers and accused them of having brought all this about: Erasmus was under violent attack from the *viri obscuri*. Moreover, Luther turned out to be too fully convinced of man's total corruption to suit the scholar's vision of a rational Christianity evolving from man's fundamental goodness. So Erasmus tried his hand at theological controversy. In 1524 he produced his *Discourse on Free Will* in which he attacked Luther's concepts of grace and justification, only to be flattened by Luther's reply, *The Will in Bondage (De Servo Arbitrio)*, published the year after. Although Erasmus lived till 1536 and still had much honour, his day was really over. Some of his closest friends deserted the bright promise of the humanist dawn; Thomas More dropped criticism and free argument in order to battle against heresy by pen and stake; the cardinals of Medicean Rome rallied behind the papacy. Though ideas of moderate reform within the old framework lingered on,[6] humanism as a general reforming ideology had shot its bolt.

Again, however, one must object to some of the inferences drawn from the split between Luther and Erasmus. Many of the older generation of humanists did turn away from the Reformation, but some did not; nor was Protestantism to be independent of the humanist tradition. A humanist training continued to predispose many towards acceptance of one or the other Protestant Church. The real contribution of humanism to the future history of all the denominations lay above all in the break with scholastic traditions of education and the incorporation of a rediscovered antiquity in the mainstream of European culture. These achievements endured; they supplied the intellectual backbone of reformed Churches everywhere (even, up to a point, of the reformed Church of Rome) and survived the struggle of the religions to become the basis of school and university curricula all over Europe until the later nineteenth century. Certainly, Luther and the Reformation could not work hand in hand with a humanism which reduced religion to ethics and respected the unassisted competence of man to lead the good life; as certainly, however, the continued support of men trained as humanists saved the Reforma-

tion from that total denial of the intellect and that total contempt for
man to which much of Luther's teaching tended.

In politics, however, 1525 did mark the triumph of the state in the
affairs of the new Churches. That this was not contrary to Luther's
opinion on civil government has already been shown. Man's fallen
nature demanded government, and God's order for the natural creation—including the institution of civil magistracy—demanded obedience. As Melanchthon put it in words which were in general
characteristic of the major reformers: "The magistrate's administration of the sword [that is the maintenance of secular order] is con-
sonant with piety...If princes command anything contrary to God,
this is not to be obeyed...If they command anything arising out of
the public interest this must be obeyed...If any of their commands
are tyrannical, here too the magistrate is to be suffered for charity's
sake in all cases where change is impossible without public commo-
tion and sedition." Such relatively cool acceptance of civil authority
(written in 1521) changed readily into a precept of general obedience
to God's deputy as the problem of order came to the fore; there was
but a short step from seeking the lay ruler's help in setting up a
reformed Church to ascribing to him a divinely instituted authority
to rule the Church. The duty of obedience came to be qualified only
by the reservation that things contrary to true religion must not be
done. But even then—and Calvin, for one, agreed with this—while
obedience, being an offence to the higher authority of God, is wrong,
resistance is equally so: God will punish the wicked magistrate, men
must suffer him. In varying degree, this doctrine of obedience characterises all political thought of the period, Catholic as well as
reformed, with the exception of the radicals to be described in the
next chapter. It reflected the actual power of secular princes and
national rulers; but it was also, of course, a convenient thing for
them to use.

At any rate, in 1525 Albrecht of Hohenzollern, grand master of the
Teutonic Knights, a military order which ruled a remnant of territorial power in East Prussia, shocked the world by beginning the trek
into the Lutheran camp. He dissolved the Order, secularised its lands,
and, as a vassal of the king of Poland, became the first German duke
of Prussia. In Germany itself, several territories soon officially
adopted the Reformation: Hesse, under its young and unpredictable
landgrave Philip, by 1526; in 1528, the margrave of Brandenburg-
Ansbach, the dukes of Schleswig and Brunswick, the count of Mansfeld. In these regions, the ruler imposed the new order from above,
and the model of organisation was that developed in Saxony. Later
events made these princely conversions seem more important than
any other, but in the 1520's the Reformation seemed more likely to
succeed in and by means of the towns. Nuremberg, the most

powerful of them, admitted the evangelicals before 1524; Strassburg, Ulm, Augsburg and many lesser southern cities soon followed suit; between 1528 and 1531, the leading northern cities—especially the episcopal see of Magdeburg—did likewise. In the upshot some two thirds of the imperial cities accepted the Reformation in one form or another; of the major cities only Regensburg, overawed by the loyally Catholic Wittelsbach dukes of Bavaria, and Cologne, held together by its archbishop, adhered consistently to Rome. In the cities, the reform was usually promoted from below, not by the town government but by the craft gilds; it was as a rule a selfconscious triumph of the laity who secularised lands, reformed worship and introduced evangelical pastors in despite of the cautious fears of conservative oligarchies. Only in proudly patrician Nuremberg did the authorities welcome and install the Lutherans without hesitation, and Nuremberg remained always the most definitely Lutheran of the Protestant cities.

This spread of reformed Churches was a different matter altogether from the wide and unorganised support which Luther had enjoyed from the first. It took place in the teeth of the Edict of Worms, feebly maintained by the regency council (*reichsregiment*) which Charles V had left behind in 1521. Attempts to govern through the princes or the Diet were no more successful in maintaining unity and peace. Under the rules laid down for the regency, three Diets met at Nuremberg between 1522 and 1524; at each of them the jealous policy of the princes prevented any effective assertion of imperial authority; at the last, the useless regency council was dissolved. The assemblies invariably shelved the question of the Church with vague and pious talk about the need for a General Council of the Church to settle the dispute. In the absence of central control, self-help became the order of the day, and in 1524 the formation of the Catholic League of Regensburg—an alliance of Ferdinand of Austria, Bavaria and the south German bishops, blessed by the pope—initiated the fatal policy which was to produce armed camps in Germany and end in religious war. The Regensburg leaguers enforced the Edict of Worms where they could; the Lutheran League of Torgau (1525) tried to prevent its enforcement.

In 1526 the Diet assembled at Speyer. Charles V, recently victorious in Italy,[7] hoped to be there and bring matters to a conclusion; instead he was prevented by other concerns from attending at all, and in his absence the estates could agree only on a famous recess (decree) of toleration. Each ruler and city were recommended so to order themselves as they would trust "to answer it to God and his imperial majesty". The Worms Edict appeared forgotten. With the Turkish danger growing and France once more a problem, Charles could not afford to dictate, but he was from the first determined to get the 1526 recess rescinded and never forgot his resolution to end the schism. The Lutheran estates were divided; most of them, especially Saxony and Nuremberg, followed Luther's own lead in regarding armed resistance to the emperor as inadmissible. The result was that at the second Diet of Speyer (1529) the new cause suffered a bad defeat: the 1526 recess was repealed and the enforcement of the 1521 edict once more made compulsory; no more Church lands were to be secularised. In reply, the six Lutheran princes, supported by only fourteen of the reformed cities, signed a Protestation in which they affirmed their right to answer to God alone for what concerned "God's honour and the salvation... of the souls of each one of us". The document gave to the reformed party the name of Protestants, which has stuck ever since. It is worthy of notice that the protest came from the heart. These princes were, no doubt, eager to augment their power, consolidate their authority in their lands, acquire Church property; they were also persuaded of the need to serve and save the gospel. It is presumably an improper reflection that they would very likely have caused less trouble if they had stuck to selfishness alone.

Yet perhaps the most significant aspect of the Protestation was the abstention of some of the reformed cities. The parties of 1529 were no longer simply old and new; the danger, always stressed by conservatives, that tampering with tradition could end only in a general dissolution of all unity, had indeed become real; Lutheranism was no longer the sole inspiration on the side of reform. Zwingli had set up the Swiss city of Zürich as a rival pole.

II Zwingli

Although Huldrych Zwingli (1484–1531) was less than a year younger than Luther—was in fact thirty-seven when he first made his mark as a man of new ideas—he always carried an air of relative youth, even adolescence. Born at Wildhaus, in the mountainous region of Toggenburg, he followed the conventional career of the intelligent child of poor parents by going to university. He attended both Vienna and Basel, came under the oddly assorted influences of humanism and that Scotist philosophy modifying Aquinas (*via antiqua*) which Luther's nominalist teachers had rejected, and got his first cure of souls in 1506. On two occasions he acted as chaplain to Swiss Armies in Italy. Meanwhile he studied, became an Erasmian, read the New Testament with new eyes. He himself liked to assert that he had arrived at his theology independently of Luther, but modern scholars think him a little deceived in this; certainly, his reforming activities followed in the wake of Luther's impact on the Swiss cities.

In 1518 Zwingli was appointed common preacher[8] in Zürich cathedral. It was from this minor office that he initiated the Swiss Reformation. In his sermons, a continuous and consistent exposition of scripture, he not only attacked the common abuses but soon cut very deep indeed, proclaiming a radical theology to the destruction of the existing order. Like Luther, he laid the stress on the direct relation between man and God, denied the validity of good works, and demanded a purification of ceremonies and observance. Unlike Luther, he wanted a complete break with the recent past, encouraged image breaking, and denounced the mass from the first. Zwingli's theology was more uncompromisingly "spiritual"; that is to say, to him salvation was more definitely a purely inner experience in which sacraments and ceremonies played no part at all. His preaching caused a good deal of unrest, until in January 1523 the city council decided to put the matter to the test of a public disputation. The presence of evangelical pastors of Zwingli's acquaintance turned this into a demonstration and triumph for the reformers. In the years 1523 to 1525 he gradually reformed the whole Church at Zürich, abolishing the mass, introducing vernacular services, embodying his interpretation of scripture in new orders of baptism and communion service, and using his influence with the council to enforce uniformity. Despite the radicalism of his ideas, Zwingli always proceeded with caution. Though he married in 1522, he did not publish the fact until 1524; though he attended at the curious occasion in 1522 when some friends of his demonstrated for the Reformation by eating sausage in Lent, he himself did not join in the meal. What made him a radical was his conviction that salvation depends on faith alone and is confined to those whom God has chosen; his idea of the Church was more exclusive than Luther's and anticipated the narrow and disciplined body of Calvin's Church. His caution saved him from following his tenets to their logical conclusion, a conclusion which rapidly led to the growth of Anabaptist sects.[9]

The character and effect of the Zürich Reformation can be understood only within the setting of sixteenth-century Switzerland. The Confederacy, which in the fourteenth and fifteenth centuries had won its independence in struggles with Habsburg overlords and Valois dukes of Burgundy, was no more than a loose association of mostly self-governing states. The forest cantons of Uri, Unterwalden, Schwyz with Zug, Glarus and Lucerne were poor peasant republics, suspicious of the rich and powerful city states of Zürich, Bern and Basel. Bern's expansionist ambition westward threatened the cities of Fribourg and Solothurn which therefore inclined to ally with the rural districts. In the north and north-east, Schaffhausen and Appenzell formed independent partners; the abbey of St. Gall stood in a client relation to Zürich; small units like Mülhausen, Rothweil, Biel,

Toggenburg and the town of St. Gall tried to preserve their identity against that city's dominance. Across the Alps to the south, the districts of Valais and Grisons, though nominally affiliated members only, were treated in most respects as full cantons. Such central organisation as there was consisted of a diet of delegates which usually referred action to one of the great cities. Despite the existence of a few small provinces administered nominally by the Confederacy as a whole (Aargau, Thurgau, etc.), there was no central government. The Swiss economy was thoroughly unsound: the country had to import corn and salt, and the money was supplied by the pensions and wages earned by Switzerland's chief export—soldiers. The peasantry suffered much the same troubles as afflicted their fellows north of the Rhine; but while in Swabia and the Black Forest the agents of oppression were feudal lords, in Switzerland their place was taken by centralising city oligarchies. The unsettled and resentful state of the peasants expressed itself frequently enough in risings, and the 1525 Peasants' War found its echo in the Confederacy, especially round Lake Constance. In the towns themselves, prosperity was in decline, except that Basel harboured a flourishing paper and printing industry and St. Gall made linens. Except in Bern, whose command of several trade routes had concentrated power in the hands of wealthy patrician merchants, the smaller craftsmen, organised in powerful gilds, were usually at this time increasing their influence on city government.

Switzerland mattered in the world because it supplied some of the finest troops available to the greater powers. Until 1515, the Swiss infantry, inheriting the traditions of the wars of independence and reckoned to be invincible in its tight, pike-bristling formations, had been hired to the highest bidder; in that year, its defeat by the French at Marignano ended the legend and forced the Swiss into dependency on the victor. In 1516 the Confederacy agreed that in future its people would serve only in the armies of Francis I. When the treaty came up for renewal in 1521, Zwingli persuaded Zürich to abstain from it. He bitterly resented the wastage of Swiss men and blood in those mercenary wars; his protests from the pulpit first brought him popularity and renown. Himself given to military dreams and amateur strategy, he did not object to war as such, but only to war without a cause and to the destruction of Swiss manhood for mere money. Yet while Switzerland remained an importing country, prevented by geography from finding work and food at home for its expanding population, the export of soldiers was a simple economic necessity. Nor did it end, though after Bicocca (1522) the dominance of the Swiss regiments in the Italian wars was definitely over. Both France and the papacy, however, continued to employ regiments of Swiss guards.

Despite its famous liberty, its prowess and its ancient towns, the Switzerland of the 1520s was not, therefore, a happy, contented or well administered country. The situation offered ready openings for one form or another of revolutionary action. But as in the case of Luther it became apparent that conditions might assist but could not produce reform, so in Zürich the fact of religious and spiritual aspiration, centring upon Zwingli and his associates, must not be overlooked in any concentration on the political problems or social unrest of the day. On the other hand, the political situation was decisive both for the form which Zwingli's Church took and for the manner in which the Reformation spread. Zwingli held much the same views as Luther on the civil magistrate's duty to supervise the proper rule of the Church; but in Zürich this naturally meant control by the city council, not by a single prince. In addition, Zwingli ascribed an important place to the minister's supervision of the laity's ordinary lives. The effect was drastic for the individual. Private morals and behaviour were subjected to a court containing both councillors and pastors; the council became responsible for introducing reforms and for excommunication from the Church; faced with Anabaptist sectarianism, Zwingli eagerly embraced the assistance of the "godly magistrate" and encouraged the creation of a true state-Church. The same principle was applied by the other cities which adopted the Zwinglian reform, especially Bern in 1528 and Basel the year after. The characteristic process of evangelical preaching, popular demand, public disputation, acceptance and enforcement of the reform, operated here and elsewhere. The reformer of Basel was John Oecolampadius (1482–1531), a solid scholar and a gentle soul who wished to reserve more autonomy for the Church than had become customary, but though he influenced Bucer at Strassburg[10] he had to allow the Swiss cities to accept the practical triumph of the laity and the lay magistrate.

By about 1528 Zwingli confronted a double problem. Certain cantons, especially the forest ones, remained firmly attached to Rome; and the question of his relations with Luther grew pressing. Zürich had come to fear an alliance between the Habsburgs to the north and the Catholic cantons to the south, a danger which drove Zwingli to preach war. He laboured to construct a league of evangelical cities and also stretched out his hand to the German reformers. The link was provided by the spread of the Reformation in the south German cities. Strassburg in particular became a centre of the new order under the guidance of Wolfgang Capito (1478–1541) and Martin Bucer (1491–1551). Both these men, and Bucer more especially, were remarkable for a desire for peace, even at the cost of absolute rigour; Bucer came to see the necessity for distinguishing between essential and inessential (*adiaphora*) points of the faith, and to seek collaboration by agreement to differ on the second. Unlike Zürich, the city of Strassburg lay right across one of the imperial highways—out in the open and potentially liable to attack. From 1523 it became a refuge for evangelical preachers and therefore a hotbed of reform, and from the year after the city was, to all purposes, reformed. But here the council held more aloof than in other cities—it was not until 1538 that a complete reconstruction took place—so that the Strassburg Reformation remained more flexible. The example of Zürich and Strassburg exercised its influence on other towns which had previously accepted the Lutheran reform. By about 1528 it was clear that the southern German cities—those of Upper Germany, as they are called—differed quite noticeably from those of Franconia and the north where Lutheranism was triumphant. The difference lay in the greater degree of lay participation, of democracy in government, and of diversity of opinion which the Zwingli-Bucer line encouraged. Unlike Luther, these two reformers thought in terms of towns, and their ideas proved more congenial to people cherishing traditions of urban communalism and independence.[11] Zwinglians were strong among the gilds: in Augsburg, for instance, the Reformation was forced on the greater burghers, tied to the Habsburgs by their financial interests, by the lower orders who ruled the city in these organisations.

These differences between Lutheran and Upper German regions became so important because the two Reformations discovered a fundamental point of conflict to quarrel over, and because in the later 1520s the "cause of the gospel" had to begin thinking about defence against imperial and conservative reaction. The issue over which the reformers were divided touched the central mystery of Christian worship, the Lord's Supper. All the evangelicals were agreed in rejecting the Roman Catholic concept of the sacrifice of the mass, according to which each celebration is a re-enactment of Christ's sacrifice; they stressed the unique, once-and-for-all sacrifice of the Cross. Equally they denied the doctrine of transubstantiation, that is to say that after consecration by the priest the elements of bread and wine are transformed into the elements of Christ's body and wine. Luther and Zwingli both regarded transubstantiation as an unscriptural piece of priestly magic, but their own views of the eucharist differed widely. Luther, laying the stress on Christ's words, "This is my body", felt compelled to believe in a real presence, though this could not, of course, be produced by any human action. He held that for the believer the sacrament contains the substance of Christ's body and blood co-terminous with the substance of bread and wine, the former being imparted to the latter by the action of saving grace responding to faith, a doctrine which he rested on a difficult notion of the ubiquity of Christ's body throughout creation. Many of his later disciples have been unable to follow him in this and speak, perhaps oddly, of the regrettable survival of "medievalism" in his thinking. The difficulties of the doctrine and his more spiritual inclinations led Zwingli to deny a physical real presence altogether; he saw nothing but symbols in the bread and wine. Salvation came by faith; in the sacrament, grace entered the believing soul through the spirit, with no physical means at all. Although it would seem that this involved, for him, a spiritual "real presence", it is no wonder that he was generally thought to have reduced the communion to a service of commemoration for Christ's sacrifice. To Luther's scriptural citation he riposted by treating "is" as "signifies" (there was scholastic authority for such interpretations) and laid the emphasis on another passage, "It is the spirit that quickeneth, the flesh profiteth nothing." Real enough as these controversies were to the participants—eucharistic troubles ran right through the Reformation—one must also recognise that we have here an early example of that *odium theologicum* which was to destroy so much and kill so many people in the next 150 years.

The debate convulsed the reformers from 1524. Behind it there lay a temperamental difference which perpetuated the split. Zwinglianism disliked the flesh and thought the spirit more refined; the purity of a religion apprehended by the soul should be free of all traces of primitive physical stand-bys. The humanist, Erasmian tradition played its part here, as did late-medieval mysticism, with its doctrine of the inner spirit and its contempt for outward forms; but so, it seems to me, did a kind of "modern" squeamishness. Luther, on the other hand, was a man who needed solid and palpable things to hold on to; he had a sufficient understanding of the spirit, but—as the concrete, not to say carnal, imagery and style of his writings show— he visualised spiritual matters in earth-bound form. If he lacked the intellectual elegance of the Zwinglians, he also lacked their puritanism. Certainly, he represented in all this the common feeling of his day better than the south Germans; "sacramentarians" as Zwingli's followers on this issue came somewhat incongruously to be called (since to them alone the sacraments themselves possessed no grace-giving quality) were disliked and persecuted even in countries like England which were beginning to tolerate Lutheran infiltration.

By 1528, the profound division among the reformers alarmed their political leaders. It was becoming apparent that Charles V would shortly be able to turn once more to the suppression of the new religion, and the prospect found the evangelicals very much at odds. Luther at this time still held firmly to the view that nothing could justify armed resistance to the Holy Roman emperor, and Nuremberg especially backed him up on this. That city had risen to eminence by supporting emperors against particularist princes; its prosperity depended on a wide-ranging trade and therefore on general peace; of all the segments of Germany, it clung most tenaciously to the idea of imperial unity. On the other hand, the impetuous Philip of Hesse feared Charles's power and listened to lying stories of plots; he foresaw disaster unless the reformed communities prepared at least for the possibility of war. He found ready allies among the Swiss cities which had only traditions of enmity to the Habsburgs to look back on, and also in Strassburg, a town long used to participation in military alliances. While before 1529 no one had yet given up all hope that the emperor might still prove helpful, Hesse, Strassburg (under the leadership of the energetic Jacob Sturm) and the south-German reformers (especially Bucer) wished to close the ranks, even at the risk of being charged with separatism and disloyalty to their distant liege lord.

In his endeavour to promote the alliance, Philip, in October 1529, brought Luther and Zwingli together in the colloquy of Marburg, in Hesse, to see if they could not end their differences. The meeting was a disaster. Ever returning to the words "This is my body"—indeed, keeping his finger pointing at where he had written them on the table before him—Luther ridiculed Zwingli's symbolical interpretation: if any term could signify anything one wished it to say, one might as well translate the opening words of Genesis ("God created earth and heaven") as "The cuckoo ate the hedgesparrow". Zwingli remained equally obdurate, and both great men displayed signs of pettish anger. However, Zwingli, as he knew, was the real loser. The failure of a general evangelical alliance coincided with his failure to carry all Switzerland with him. His violent propaganda for action against the Catholic cantons resulted at length in war, and at Kappel in 1531 the forest cantons destroyed the forces of Zürich. Zwingli, who had gone to battle armed and ready, a soldier, as he thought, for Christ, was himself killed. Though his death, followed rapidly by that of Oecolampadius, might have been expected to endanger the continuance of the Swiss Reformation, other men in fact took up the torch, especially Henry Bullinger (1504–75) at Zürich whose vast correspondence and pacific temper gave him a position of great authority in the second generation of the Reformation. Although in due course Zwinglianism was to retreat from south Germany, it found a more unexpected area of influence in the England of Edward VI which also received Bucer and with him the eirenic doctrine of *adiaphora*. In Switzerland itself, the failure of the Reformation by conquest compelled the provinces to accept co-existence, as indeed Zürich had for some time been willing to admit, even though Zwingli had pressed for war. The peace of Kappel (1531) left the Confederacy divided into reformed and Catholic parts. In 1536, the First Helvetic Confession provided a common, Zwinglian basis for the Swiss

Protestants. After the rise of Calvin this was superseded by the 1549 Agreement of Zürich and Bullinger's Second Helvetic Confession (1566) which set up the characteristic Swiss Reformed Church of modern times. Zwinglianism as such disappeared; however, not only had Zwingli's Zürich been a forerunner of Calvin's Geneva, but the more gently human and humanistic traditions of Zwingli's teaching also modified the fundamental rigour of that Church's Calvinist basis.

III   The Wars of Charles V

We must now go back to the early 1520's and see how the problems of politics and war so absorbed Charles V that he had to give the Reformation a clear run in this decade. When Charles, in 1520, travelled back from Spain, he had two matters mainly in mind. He would have to settle Luther, but that was the lesser thing. Foremost in his calculations stood the power and attitude of France. No one really supposed that the two monarchs would keep the peace; to the old causes of conflict—Italy, Burgundy—were added personal rivalry and the recent struggle for the imperial crown. From the first, both Charles and Francis manœuvred with war in the offing; in particular they sought the alliance or neutrality of England. In the summer of 1520, Henry VIII and Francis I demonstrated their unshakable amity in the junketings of the Field of the Cloth of Gold near Calais; but even before this, Charles had come to an understanding with Henry's minister Wolsey at Gravelines. Late in 1521 Wolsey negotiated the treaty of Windsor, an alliance with the Habsburgs. Ancient hostility to France, the economic ties of the cloth trade, and the lead given by papal policy (at this time directed against French predominance in Italy), all ensured the alignment. The war in Italy had indeed broken out before this; with brief respites, it was to last until 1529.

At about this time, the art and science of war entered a new phase which was in part responsible for the fact that campaigns rarely brought solutions and conflict continued. The forces opposed to each other, though hardly in balance, matched sufficiently to ensure attritive warfare; if Charles disposed of high-quality Spanish and German infantry, Francis commanded the finest cavalry of the age and after 1521 almost monopolised the supply of Swiss mercenaries. Artillery by now formed an indispensable part of any army, but infantry still dominated battles, as it had done since the eclipse of the heavily armoured knight at the hands of English archers and Swiss pikemen in the fourteenth century. On the other hand, infantry tactics themselves were changing: the day of the solid phalanx of pikemen, charging at a trot, which had made the Swiss specialists so formidable, was just about over, as the use of firearms—wheel-lock arquebus and horse-pistol—was coming to be universal. Normal practice now carefully intermingled pike and shot, the former to protect the arquebusiers from a charge, especially when engaged in the painfully slow process of reloading, the latter breaking up enemy attacks before they could get near enough to cut gaps in the forest of pikes. This sort of formation, and the drill connected with it, required a high standard of professional skill. In consequence, though every prince tried to develop native man-power resources, only veteran standing armies could really do useful service, and among these mercenaries continued to play a leading role. This was particularly true of the German *Landsknecht*, a self-conscious professional whose loyalties were first to his trade, second to his captain, and last to his employer (if he got paid). *Landsknechte*[12] found their way into every army, but Charles could rely on the bulk of them, especially as long as the great captain George Frundsberg lived who had a paternal hold over the affections of these extremely obstreperous men. As time went on, Spanish volunteers, professionalised by experience, and French native troops, several times reorganised to increase mobility and efficiency, came to dominate the battlefields.

The decline of the Swiss and German mercenaries was assisted by the decline of the war of manœuvre which had characterised the thirty years of Italian conflict down to 1525. The battle of Pavia in that year was the last of the great set pieces—if the name is appropriate for what seems to have been the usual scene of confusion. The ascendancy of shot, both artillery and small arms, compelled commanders to be more chary of full-scale engagements: at Bicocca (1522) and Pavia it destroyed respectively some of the finest infantry and cavalry of the day, and what is more, thanks to the growth of skirmishing tactics it prevented the main body of armies ever coming effectively to grips—to push of pike. At the same time the art of fortification developed very rapidly; many towns rebuilt their old walls and designed new ones; theoretical discussion reached an impressive height in the work of Niccolò Tartaglia (1546); modern forts, with low silhouettes, round towers to deflect shot, and designed to cover every inch of wall by enfilading fire from bastions, protected even the English south coast. Siege warfare became the order of the day, with mining and sapping often more effective than cannonades, and disease and hunger invariably most effective of all. War slowed down, so that it became longer and even more expensive. As it was, the new weapons, the new size of armies, the problems of supply were all driving up the cost of war to a point where the lesser practitioners had to drop out, while even wealthy princes ought to have recognised that they could quite simply not afford it. France was best placed because her monarch had extensive rights to tax his people without consent, but this impoverished the nation; England, in the 1540s, joined in only at the expense of wrecking her coinage and endangering her economy; Spain, with all the wealth of the Indies at her disposal, had to default on her debts in 1557.

Even though war was so ruinous and achieved so little—points often enough made by writers of the time for whom the miseries of war supplied, as usual, a familiar stylistic exercise—it goes without saying that governments did not contemplate abandoning the use of war as a means to glory, aggrandisement, or the advancing of some more rational concern. The moving factor was rarely "national interest", a principle the age had not yet invented; instead, the dynastic ambitions of princes or their private feelings were the usual makers of war, and nations thought these quite as compelling as did monarchs. The prince's honour was something that his loyal subject held himself bound to defend. Some wars, of course, especially against the Turk, were thought to be entirely just, and all wars were "just"—that is, acceptable to God and forced upon the combatant by the wickedness of others—in the propaganda of the participants. But if the apparent futility of war did not lead anyone (except some Anabaptists and the occasional professor) to question the whole idea, it did lead governments to develop that other means of policy, international diplomacy. Though the older practices of formal challenges by heralds, moves in accord with the book of chivalry, and the sending of occasional special embassies continued to be used, and to have some real meaning in them, they were increasingly replaced by the maintenance of regular ambassadors, trained and experienced professionals, often legists and sometimes of pretty lowly origins, rather than showy noblemen of ancient lineage and sufficient wealth to pay for all the glitter themselves.

The Italians had led the way; Venice, in particular, covered Europe with a network of "orators" who protected the interests of the republic and supplied it with the detailed and usually accurate information on which it based its policy. In the reign of Charles V, most of the powers followed suit; resident ambassadors, diplomatic negotiations, ramifying intelligence services all began to assume a recognisably modern form. As yet, rules of conduct were uncertain; such principles of international law as existed still rested, somewhat uselessly, on an assumption of common interests and standards among Christians on the one hand and belted knights on the other. An ambassador's life could be difficult: if he was not murdered by an exasperated foreign government, his servants might very likely suffer that fate, and his correspondence was regularly violated. Still, practice in due course developed principle; the beginnings of a *corps diplomatique* are visible not only among the Giustinianis and Michiels of Venice, but especially among the Burgundian legists—

men like Eustace Chapuys and Simon Renard—who served Charles V, or the French professionals (a Castillon or Marillac) who were superseding bishops and noblemen in the service of the Valois. England continued for a while to rely quite a lot on ecclesiastics, but that was because these were less clerics than professional civil servants; lay professionals were just about taking over towards the end of our period.

Nevertheless, in spite of these developments the most obvious feature of the age was the near-absence of any coherent set of principles against which policy could be measured. We stand between the *res publica Christiana* and the concert of the powers. This is not to suppose that the earlier or later conventions ensured either peace or honesty; it is only to suggest that the era of Charles V had difficulty even in finding words for its hypocrisies. This troubled the emperor least: he had his own vision of his place and purpose. But it makes the proceedings of Francis I and Henry VIII, not to mention those of Leo X and Clement VII, appear peculiarly pointless and selfish. Perhaps they were.

In 1520 Francis tried to sidetrack Charles by suborning raids upon the Netherlands, but the conflict soon migrated to Italy again. In the summer of 1521, imperial and papal forces began a systematic campaign which really destroyed the French hold over the northern parts of the peninsula. Parma and Piacenza were brought within the papal grasp; Milan reverted to the Sforza family (under Spanish control); Genoa, previously French but henceforward usually Spain's ally, was captured and sacked. When the French suffered a disastrous defeat at Bicocca early the following year—the battle, among other things, deprived them for the moment of their Swiss mercenaries who decided they had had enough—Charles's triumph seemed complete. He had also tried to transform the papacy from a doubtful ally into an attached friend. Leo X, last of the true Renaissance popes, died in December 1521. Though Wolsey had his hopes, Charles secured the election of his old tutor Adrian of Utrecht, now a bishop in Spain. Rather to Charles's disgust, Adrian VI determined to pursue an independent and peaceful policy which in the circumstances of Spanish success tended to benefit France; he also annoyed the Curia by being both genuinely incorruptible and somewhat ostentatiously austere. Before this disconcerting pope could completely bewilder the experts who had learned their business by studying Alexander VI and Julius II, he died in 1523; with a sigh of relief, the cardinals, electing Clement VII, reverted to type and the Medici. The new pope had been an admirable secretary of state, and no one has ever seriously impugned his private morals. Intending to preserve the independence of the papacy, reform the Curia, and not to overdo the Medici family interest, he was a better man and potentially a better pope than Leo

X could ever have been. It will therefore surprise no one versed in the ways of history that the pontificate of Clement VII put the pope into hispano-imperial bondage, made certain of the Protestant schism, and lost England to Rome. With all his good qualities, Clement was weak, hesitant and always a little late; and he tried to play the old Italian political game in circumstances which no longer permitted it.

After Bicocca, things for a time continued to go well for Charles V. Though the French retained some garrisons in the Milanese, Spain controlled Italy. In 1523, the defection of the Constable Bourbon, who had a private quarrel over some lands with his sovereign king, Francis I, opened the way into France itself. But though the French king was very hard pressed—moneyless, his army in ruins, invaded in the north (a futile English demonstration) and south (Bourbon and the Spanish)—he rallied well; Bourbon was beaten back from Marseilles, to prove that you could beat France in Italy but not at home; and the emperor's triumph produced the usual alliance against him. Clement VII, following old papal precepts, thought he could redress the balance of power so essential to the independence of the see of Rome by bringing Venice and Florence into accord with France. At first it seemed to work: the Spaniards were once more driven from Milan, and French forces even reached the borders of Naples. It looked as though things would again go as they had always done since 1494—by see-saw. But one battle altered everything. The French army laid siege to the main imperial remnant shut up in Pavia; the defence was unexpectedly determined; a relieving army led by Bourbon and Frundsberg rushed incontinently to the attack when by the rules of experience it should have held off; the French made several bad mistakes; and in the general mêlée which ensued the power of the Valois was decisively broken (24 February 1525). The better part of the French chivalry lay dead (a French habit this, reflecting unthinking bravery: Crécy and Agincourt had had the same result); the king himself was a prisoner, speedily removed to Madrid.

Well might Charles offer pious thanks. He was master not only of Italy and the pope, but to all seeming also of Europe. The only power that could have rivalled his was destroyed. By the treaty of Madrid (January 1526) Francis renounced his claims to Milan and Naples, surrendered the Burgundian territories either claimed or held by him, and engaged himself to marry his conqueror's sister. But, as so often, Charles was to find that victory evaporated in his hand simply because there was no way of really following it up. Francis I as a prisoner was something of an embarrassment, and the treaty could not be put into effect until he was back in France. So he left Madrid, assuring Charles of his good faith by solemn oaths and by leaving his two sons as hostages. Charles, who had his doubts, felt compelled to trust him; in any case, there was no other way out. No sooner, however, was Francis once more in his realm than, revoking all agreements and concessions, he prepared to recover his fortunes again. Barely more than a year after Pavia, Charles faced the League of Cognac (1526) of France, Venice and the pope, with Florence and Sforza (driven out of Milan by the Spaniards) joining, and England— Wolsey was being pressed by the pope—looking kindly upon it. Pavia seemed to have been an emptier victory than Marignano which, after all, had secured French primacy in Italy for nearly ten years.

One other event of 1526 tilted the balance once again against the emperor. In April, the armies of Sulaiman the Magnificent, advancing from Belgrade, destroyed the Hungarian forces on the plain of Mohács. The young king Lewis, last of the Jagiellon kings of Bohemia and Hungary, died in the battle; the victorious Turks occupied all Hungary and steadied themselves for the next move into central Europe. The danger was very pressing, even if for the moment Sulaiman had to draw back into the Balkans. His usual problems—overextended lines of communication and trouble at the other end of his empire, in Asia Minor and on the Persian border—compelled him for the present to postpone the end of Christendom. Nevertheless, Charles now found the east another call on his time and resources. There was the general threat, for which he tried in vain to mobilise men and money at the first Diet of Speyer; there was also the problem of the succession to Lewis. Once again, marriage connections opened wonderful prospects to the Habsburgs, and Charles's brother Ferdinand claimed both Bohemia and Hungary as brother-in-law to the childless Lewis. The Bohemian nobility accepted him; but in Hungary, the native aristocracy preferred one of their own kind. In this they had the support of the sultan who for the moment was content to rule Hungary through a puppet king. At any rate, he did not propose to let the powerful Habsburgs establish themselves right across his line of advance. Thus the next few years saw Ferdinand involved in a struggle with John Zapolyai, *voivode* (duke) of Transylvania and the Hungarian choice for the vacant throne; and even when in 1527 he succeeded in expelling his rival from the country, he only drove him into Turkish arms. These eastern preoccupations prevented Ferdinand from attending to the growing power of Lutheranism and soon provoked the Turkish danger once more, in worse form. For he overreached himself when he arrogantly demanded the return of some Turkish conquests on the borders of Hungary, and in 1529 Sulaiman went on the war-path again. This time he overran Hungary quickly enough, restored Zapolyai to his dubious throne, and appeared before the gates of Vienna.

After Mohács, Charles would have been glad to rally Europe against the Ottoman threat; instead, he had to deal with the League of Cognac. Throughout 1527 the French more than held their own in

Italy; Charles's only success, if it deserves the name, sent a wave of horror through Latin Christendom. In the spring the imperial troops mutinied; as usual, they had not been paid for a long time. Frundsberg suffered a stroke when his efforts failed to restore order among his "lambs"; Bourbon thought to do better by putting himself at the mutineers' head. They marched on Rome, home of that pope who had betrayed their prince and in addition was Antichrist to the many Lutherans amongst them. Rome, it is to the point, was also quite correctly reported to be fabulously rich. On 6 May, Bourbon dying in the first assault, the veterans stormed the city and sacked it amid such scenes of violence, murder, rape, looting and destruction that the *Sacco di Roma* has remained in the European memory even after many still more frightful events. The pope fled to the castle of San Angelo and later to Orvieto; though both he and his successors were at intervals to attempt strokes of independent policy, the papacy was really from that moment the emperor's reluctant client. As for the city, the sack was rightly seen at the time as the end of a great age. The Rome of the Renaissance was no more. Though palaces might rise from the ruins, and though no doubt the city lived again, it was no longer the home of art, beauty and free speculation. The sack prepared for the emergence of that more sombre and much less attractive Rome which was to be a fitting setting for the Counter-Reformation.

Charles disclaimed all responsibility and was sincerely shocked, but he still could not help feeling that God had emptied the vials of His wrath over that unfaithful steward, the pope. Though attempts were made throughout 1528 to countervail the Spanish power in Italy, events moved somewhat inexorably towards a predictable end. In September 1528 Genoa deserted its temporary alliance with France and rejoined the emperor. Shortly before this, Francis's one competent general, the marquis de Lautrec, had died in an over-ambitious attempt to attack the Spaniards in Naples. Wolsey intelligently chose this moment to enter the war on the side of France and pope, only to find his country entirely unwilling to support him. Then, in June 1529, Charles won his last victory in Italy, at Landriano. Francis I and Clement VII recognised the end, and Charles on this occasion proved less demanding than in 1526. The Ladies' Peace of Cambrai (negotiated by Francis's mother and Margaret of Austria) in August 1529 terminated not only the struggle that had been going on since 1521 but also a whole phase in the history of Italy and Europe. Spain now ruled the peninsula, and the emperor ruled the pope. Except for the mad efforts of Paul IV,[13] there were to be no more anti-imperial alliances and machinations at Rome; the papacy had learned its lesson. France kept the duchy of Burgundy and the lands of Bourbon; Sforza was restored at Milan, but now as a Spanish client. Above all, though the struggle between Habsburg and Valois was not over, it was in future to be less continuous and less vigorous. Francis I, growing older, seems to have worked some of his restless "chivalry" out of his system, and Charles was content with the result. Italy ceased to be Europe's battlefield.

In the summer of 1529, one thing only stood between the emperor and the problem of the schism in the Church: the Turks were advancing up the Danube and in September invested Vienna. At last even the German estates recognised the danger, and the 1529 Diet of Speyer found them uncharacteristically willing to vote men and supplies for defence, though Philip of Hesse, true to the narrower view, wished to refuse these to an emperor who was likely to attack the gospel and princely independence. In fact, the gallant defence of the city owed something to the quality of its garrison, rather more to the weather and disease which weakened the Turkish army, and nothing to German generosity. After three weeks, Sulaiman decided to call off the enterprise; mid-October was no time to sit among the snows and gales which added to the pleasures of Danube floods. The situation in Hungary returned to normal: a struggle between the Habsburgs and Zapolyai, the latter allied with the sultan, for the whole vast realm. It also returned to normal in Germany where princes and cities recovered from their access of near-unanimity. Late in 1529 it suddenly became plain that Charles V, victor over France, ruler of Italy and the pope, and for the moment free of worry over the Turks, would come to his realm of Germany to deal with disaffection in religion and politics. But the eight years during which Germany had not seen the emperor had left their mark. Not only had they permitted the steady and spectacular advance of the schismatic Church; they had witnessed the growth of even more disruptive radical movements and the spread of the German Reformation to all parts of Europe.

Chapter 4

The Radicals

While the Church might stand horrified at the radicalism of Luther's or Zwingli's break with tradition and authority, the truth soon became plain that these leading reformers were in most things quite as conservative as they claimed to be. For in the wake of the early Reformation, a genuine radicalism soon made its appearance. Luther's attack, though never designed to overthrow the existing secular order and only partially critical even of the ecclesiastical order, encouraged more violent ambitions among the masses and among certain over-enthusiastic religious leaders. Radical movements will never lack material, since men's condition will never be perfect. As we have already seen, in the early sixteenth century it was definitely growing worse for some men, the middling peasantry and the independent craftsmen being the chief victims of economic pressure produced by a rise in population and prices. Significantly enough, it was they who provided the main support for radical religious movements. The prophets and leaders of sects were usually parish priests, or laymen of some education and standing; their followers did not noticeably include the outcasts of society, the poor and destitute, but rather the yeomanry and solid peasantry of the countryside, town artisans like weavers and fullers, and especially the miners of Saxony and the Tyrol who regarded themselves as a labouring aristocracy.

The social and economic conditions which assisted radicalism were, of course, serious enough; hardship and misery were endemic in a society constantly plagued by disease and harvest failure, to mention only the causes ascribable to Providence rather than man; but the situation grew critical not because a lot of people had always been badly off (as they had) but because a lot of people believed that things were getting worse for them. Helpless and uncomprehending, they naturally charged this up against their social superiors, many of whom were also in great difficulties. It will not do to treat the radical reformers as though only their theology mattered; neither the spread of their ideas nor the reaction of others can possibly be understood unless the secular discontent to which they gave a tongue is kept in mind. In even the most pacific and world-withdrawn sectarian movement, opposition to the existing distribution of power was implicit and usually freely expressed. History does not often record the feelings and aspirations of those without privilege; but the cauldron is always there, even if the lid is only occasionally taken off so that we may observe the broth bubbling in it. One cannot do justice to Luther's (and also Calvin's) teaching about the magistrate's right to exact obedience unless one comprehends their awareness of the abyss opened by the denial of all authority. The liberal mind must always regret that Luther so firmly took his stand with princes and Calvin so sombrely erected authority on a basis of moral censorship. No doubt it is always a tragedy that in the struggle distinctions between legitimate grievances and excesses tend to disappear. But what enabled Luther to maintain himself where earlier reformers had failed was in great part his recognition that religious reform need not mean social revolution. Where Wycliffe and Hus had become identified with the protests of the underdog and his desire to overthrow the existing order, the Protestant leaders secured the reform of the Church by remaining careful of the support of governments. Naturally, they did not, in the process, produce quite the Church which they and others had dreamed of. The trouble with the Word is that it differs by more than one letter from the world.

In the sixteenth century, movements of protest were bound to take a religious form and draw their strength also from spiritual dissatisfaction. Here the radicals extended Luther's teaching, amalgamated it with inherited traditions both mystical and millenarian, and refined it further by independent bible study and inspiration. In their interpretation of the Christian religion, they went to extremes of enthusiasm—that religious enthusiasm (*Schwärmerei*) which, according to one's view of it, abandons or transcends reason and is so rightly distrusted by all organised religions. Denying all earthly authority, they would as a rule not even accept scripture as binding; to Luther's emphasis on the Word they opposed their emphasis on the inner spirit. By this they meant that revelation came not from the bible as such but from the illumination given to each man by God direct, speaking to him personally and interiorly. Of course, this was not particularly new. A recent summary has identified six medieval sources for this theology: the sectarianism of the Netherlands Free Brethren, the mass movements of the Waldensians and Hussites, an anti-Augustinian tradition of free will which regarded man as capable of working actively for his salvation, the German mystics, the *devotio moderna*, and the subtleties of such fifteenth-century spiritualists as Nicholas of Cusa.[1]

Not that the radical reformers deliberately borrowed these ideas; it was rather that they were profoundly and half-consciously influenced by spiritual traditions which had for long existed by the side of the official sacramentarian doctrines and institutions of the Church. In any case, they exceeded tradition by making the inner spirit their sole guiding light. In this attitude lay manifest danger. Anarchy was almost inevitable if nothing mattered but each man's conviction that he was chosen by God. So also was a strong strand of antinomianism, the belief that the law, whether of God or man, had no force or meaning for those whom God had saved by infusing His spirit into them. Plenty of precedent existed to demonstrate how easily such notions could boil over into an orgiastic display of unbridled service of self. The radical movements of the sixteenth century were not immune to the danger, even though their enemies, suspecting the worst, usually wildly exaggerated their charges of communism and sexual licence. Still, consciousness of election, of being the righteous few among the mass of deluded sinners, is a dangerously exhilarating experience; time and again, genuine spirituality and often humble piety degenerated into wild ravings and vicious action.

The enthusiasts were in great part saved from the logic of their beliefs by the need to hold the sects together—so that discipline came to play its part even among these believers in the inner spirit—and by their marked puritanism. Moralistic and ethical attitudes played a major role in the growth of radicalism. Since dislike of the Church, contempt for its behaviour, and a general desire for the purification of life had so much to do with preparing the ground for the Reformation, the failure of Lutheran and Zwinglian reform altogether to overthrow the old institutions and really to produce an outburst of holy living disappointed the more earnest. Protests against the laity's morals ran right through the history of the sects. Apart from the occasional wild outburst, the radicals therefore insisted on high standards of conventional behaviour and exercised a strict control over the ordinary lives of their followers. Where the major Churches of all denominations, regarding it as impossible to set up the true Church anywhere but in heaven, accepted the fact that the Church on earth must include sinners, the sects wished to establish the kingdom of Christ on earth and to confine His Church to the minority of true believers (themselves). This sectarian puritanism could again lead either to millenarian dreams of creating the heavenly kingdom in the here and now by violence—by washing the sins of men away in blood—or to a near-pietistic withdrawal from the contamination of the sinful world. It is not, therefore, surprising that in the long run the proper place for these sectarian ideas came to be the empty continent of North America—rendered empty if found occupied—where not only the English puritans but later also Moravian, Dutch and Swiss brethren found not so much a refuge as a Canaan.

All these tendencies appeared in the radical Reformation before Luther's movement was more than a decade old. Only a few men stuck rigorously to the full spiritualist ideal, becoming in consequence isolated from the rest; but these included two of the more attractive personalities of the age, Caspar von Schwenckfeld (1489–1561) and Sebastian Franck (1499–1542). Schwenckfeld formed altogether an exception in his time. Of aristocratic birth, and a privy councillor to the duke of Liegnitz in Silesia, he was the only enthusiast who came from the upper ranks of society. His piety was both deep and personal, and his temper was uncharacteristically gentle. He came early under Luther's influence and in the 1520's assisted the reform in Silesia; but by 1525 the two men quarrelled over Schwenckfeld's spiritual interpretation of the sacraments, and in 1529 he arrived, like so many of the heterodox, in Strassburg. Here he lived until driven forth in 1534; the rest of his life was spent in wanderings, interrupted by persecution. To Schwenckfeld, a true mystic who had experienced personal conversion, the spirit was so much the only valid thing in religion that he denied the need for any Church; he fell out even with the Anabaptists when it became plain that they were seeking to add organisation to the workings of the inner spirit. Despite his many writings, his wide friendships and his exemplary temper, he consequently exercised little influence on contemporaries, though he had some disciples; but to posterity he has become an early apostle of toleration.

This is even truer of Sebastian Franck. A parish priest influenced by Erasmus and converted by Luther before 1525, he was not content to stop at this stage. In 1528–9, resident at Nuremberg, he turned to the spirit and rejected all formed Churches, among which he included the sects. All physical things were of no significance: Christ, he said, was the invisible Word, the inner revelation, and he refused to allow either the historical Saviour or the bible (that "paper-pope", as he termed it) any place in his scheme of things. Unlike Schwenckfeld he could be combative, and since he specialised in the compiling of histories and chronicles designed to show that none of the Churches in existence had the truth, he was naturally in general unpopular. A man who held that the true believers might be found among non-Christians as easily as among Christians was no doubt a praiseworthy preacher of universal tolerance, but somewhat out of turn. So he suffered some persecution, was driven out of Strassburg, earned a pitiful living boiling soap. In the end, Basel received him and permitted him to write his books. Like Schwenckfeld he was essentially a pacific man, and since he too denied the very possibility of organised Churches he could hardly be a dangerous revolutionary. This purely spiritual element had some influence on the proliferation of sectarian ideas and probably played its part in persuading at least a few people that religion was a matter for the individual. But though the second half of the century witnessed some serious propaganda for toleration, the happy day when possession of the truth was no longer regarded as a warrant for the extermination of dissentients was yet a long way off.

In any case, the vast majority of radicals were less pure and simple than these out-of-the-way spirituals. Both the major centres of the early Reformation—Saxony and Switzerland—produced extremist movements which came to have a good deal of influence on each other and finally emerged into the so-called Anabaptist movement, a number of sects holding often differing views but sharing a common belief in the necessity and validity of adult baptism as the instrument of that regeneration in Christ which assured the believer of salvation here and now. Other influences were to play across the main sectarian lines, but for the present it will do to deal with the Saxon and Swiss manifestations. Luther's radical incubus was Thomas Müntzer (1489–1525). A youngish man full of violent hatred for all the things that were other than they should have been, university trained, an idealist of the kind familiar in all revolutions, he held a cure of souls at Zwickau in Saxony when in 1521 he came under the influence of the weaver Nicholas Storch, one of the "prophets".[2] He now broke with Luther whose follower he had been, partly because he disagreed with his doctrine but mainly because in his view Dr. Martin had become Dr. Soft-Life and had sold out to the powers that be. In Müntzer there met three distinct strands. He arrived in due course at the pure form of the inner-spirit doctrine, with its stress on election or regeneration; he added to this a very powerful measure of apocalyptic and millenarian passion, believing that the Second Coming was close at hand when the wheat would be sorted from the chaff, but that the wheat had better begin the sorting and hasten the Coming by burning the chaff; and he had a genuine hatred of oppression, a sincere feeling for the lot of the poor, even if he was often carried away from true sympathy into plain rabble-rousing. His ministry at Zwickau came to a sudden end when the town got tired of his inflammatory preaching. After some wanderings he settled in Allstedt, a small Saxon town which he proceeded to turn into the prototype of his heavenly kingdom on earth.

Müntzer was a genuine revolutionary, willing to follow ideas to their logical conclusion, and a truly dangerous man. He was dangerous because his passion greatly exceeded his understanding, and because he was utterly convinced of his own rightness and righteousness. He preached well and knew how to stir up a congregation;

his social teaching naturally attracted the discontented, especially the strange, closed community of miners on the Mansfeld estates near Allstedt, always ready material for rebellion. There was pleasure in hearing Müntzer call the people of the elect the instrument of God's sovereignty; it was splendid to applaud when one of his followers announced that "princes born will never do good". There was no limit to Müntzer's teaching, and all the commonplaces of medieval apocalyptic violence poured forth once again. Man can seek God and become His elect. He can prove his chosen status only by exterminating the rest. Take the goods of this world from those who wickedly monopolise them (though whether Müntzer was really a communist remains disputed: he may only have been encouraging a rough and ready re-distribution). Blood must flow. And so forth. In this welter, Müntzer's nobler thought—his concern for the poor, his belief in man's capacity to reach God through the spirit—vanished without trace. The Elector Frederick hesitated to act; he was always slow at the best of times, and here he was further hindered by the awe he always felt in the face of anyone who just possibly might be a true prophet. What had saved Luther now benefited Müntzer. Luther was almost absurdly enraged, not so much by Müntzer's foulmouthed attacks on himself, which he knew how to repay, as by the fact that Müntzer was using the protection of the evangelical Reformation to flaunt his fantasies and burrow from within. So the Wittenberg pastors demanded an end to Müntzer's activities, and in June 1524 the elector at long last authorised an investigation: his brother and nephew went to hear Müntzer preach at Allstedt. The "Sermon before the Princes" was Müntzer's masterpiece, both daring and impudent. He chose to preach on that apocalyptic *locus classicus*, the second chapter of Daniel: Nebuchadnezzar's dream of the great statue of gold, silver, bronze, iron and clay, which symbolises the succession of world empires and is destroyed by the mountain grown from a stone, signifying the kingdom of God. Müntzer appealed to the princes to take heed of the fate of secular rule and to lead the revolution which would bring in the rule of Christ. "Be not deceived by your hypocritical parsons, nor held back by a false notion of patience and mercy." He meant Luther and his doctrine of grace which counselled submission in this world.

The princes heard and were astonished; the sermon proves not only Müntzer's ability but also his rather characteristic lack of the barest trace of common sense. Exiled, he drifted into Thuringia where he set up another of his cells at Mühlhausen. Here he was when the Peasants' War broke out. The flood spread to neighbouring Franconia, and Müntzer reckoned his time had come. There appear to have been no serious grievances among the peasants of his region, nor did they ever formulate any demands. But this did not deter

Müntzer who saw visions: the peasants' rising was the beginning of Christ's coming. He called for blood, and at the hands of the princes he got it. His fanaticism could drive the peasants into the field; it could not make them win. He was captured after the rout of Frankenhausen (May 1525), tortured and killed. The war ended his brand of radicalism, as it put a stop to dreams of social justice. The meteor was shattered in its fall, and Luther, breathing more easily, could bring the Saxon Reformation back to an even keel. However much one may admire Müntzer's genuine concern for the poor and his exalted spiritual state—and whether this latter deserves admiration is a matter of opinion—one must recognise him for what he was: not so much a constructive revolutionary as an unrestrained fanatic, and in his preaching of violence a dangerous lunatic.

Meanwhile, Zwingli, too, had found that one cannot make a revolution without calling forth revolutionaries more extreme than oneself. The Anabaptist movement proper started in Zürich, almost as soon as Zwingli initiated the reform there. In 1524 he was arguing about the nature of the Church with certain of his erstwhile followers, especially the patrician Conrad Grebel and the priest George Blaurock. Grebel's doctrine rested on a logical, even fundamentalist, interpretation of the bible and more particularly on a desire to put its ethical precepts into practice. He held that the true Church consists only of those who deliberately enter it as free agents, that baptism is both the symbol and the means of entry, and that the true believer must follow the ten commandments and the Sermon on the Mount without compromise. In consequence, infant baptism was wrong; only the adult, able to make the surrender of his sinful nature and, so to speak, choose Christ, could and should properly be baptised. His type of Church was what the English sectarians later called a "gathered Church": a community of believers, of saints on earth, who elected their own pastor to guide them and would have nothing to do with the institutions of this world. Since they were saved, the law and the magistrate—God's government for sinners—were irrelevant to them; they must have nothing to do with the "sword" (the civil authority), must not bear arms, swear oaths, carry out the duties of citizens or take part in government. They must not obey civil dictates, though, like most Anabaptists, Grebel also held that they must not actively resist but must patiently bear all the tribulations which the sinners put upon them. On the other hand, their freedom of the law will not become licence because, as men saved by God and regenerated in baptism, they will behave well ("imitate Christ") as a matter of course. The Zürich Anabaptists had contacts with the spiritual teaching of people like Müntzer, especially through Carlstadt who had been captivated by the prophet of Allstedt and in his travels had reached southern Germany; but in many of their ideas they were independent, and they certainly did not share Müntzer's violent and apocalyptic dreams. Zwingli quarrelled with Grebel over the theological implications of his doctrine of baptism which leant towards free will; the city authorities were horrified by the denial of obedience; in 1526 there began the persecution which was to be the main history of the Anabaptist sects. Imprisonment, exile and drowning scattered the rapidly increasing numbers of the Swiss Brethren, until Zürich could claim to have stamped out the movement in its first home.

However, the only real consequence of the persecution was to set the Anabaptists on the move. Blaurock went to the Tyrol, to be executed in 1529; he found in Jacob Huter a man to carry on the work. The Tyrolese Brethren thereafter formed something of a recruiting ground for the growth of the movement further north, as well as a link with the restless dissatisfaction of northern Italy. How far they owed their success to the grievances of the lay people against their superiors is not yet clear, but it cannot have been without significance that the Alpine provinces of Austria had for long been seething with peasant discontent. Two of the more remarkable Zürich converts, Balthasar Hubmaier and the ex-monk Michael Sattler, made for the upper Danube region. Sattler, responsible for the Schleitheim Articles (1527) which provided a common basis for the growingly fragmented movement, was in that same year captured and burned in Rothenburg on the Neckar, after a trial which indicates some of the reasons why these peaceful sectaries met so much hatred and violence. He was charged, of course, with a number of heretical beliefs concerning the sacrament of the altar, baptism, and the like; but it was civil disobedience and in particular his refusal to engage in war even against the Turk, "the greatest enemy of our holy faith" as his judges put it, that really roused anger. In reply, Sattler said that "if the Turk comes he shall not be resisted, for it is written, Thou shalt not kill". To this uncompromising statement of a fundamentalist biblicism he added words which were not designed to conciliate: "The Turk is a true Turk and knows nothing of the Christian faith; he is a Turk in the flesh. So you would be Christians and boast of Christ, but persecute Christ's true witnesses and are Turks in the spirit." This mixture of principle, meekness and arrogance is very characteristic of all these puritanical sects, convinced that they had the truth but also constrained by their convictions to avoid violence and to suffer—but not to suffer in silence.

Hubmaier, meanwhile, had gone to Augsburg where he made a convert of John Denck (1495–1527), an interesting exponent of German spiritualism who had also been influenced by a humanist upbringing and by contact with Müntzer's teaching. Denck soon went to such extremes in spiritualising religion—he abandoned as useless all ceremonies, sermons, sacraments and in the end even the bible—that he was clearly well on the road which Sebastian Franck was treading at the same time; but before he could become the major influence for which his personality apparently destined him, he died of plague at Basel. Hubmaier found the Augsburg authorities no more friendly than those of Zürich and trekked on. He discovered his promised land in southern Moravia where he converted some of the territorial nobility and was given the chance of proselytising on the grand scale. In a short time there were dozens of Anabaptist communities and thousands of brethren in the country, and all seemed set fair. It did not last. Hubmaier was soon joined by a much less moderate and peaceful sectary, John Hut, an enthusiast who had been converted by Denck and attracted by Müntzer. He escaped from Frankenhausen when Müntzer was taken, and now this preacher of revivalist fervour irrupted into the peaceful Moravian countryside. A wandering bookbinder and the probable author of a highly mystical tract on baptism, Hut was a formidable man—big, loud, persuasive. He had imbibed a good deal of Müntzer's eschatology and of Denck's spiritualist rejection of all the order of this world. A quarrel broke out between him and Hubmaier over the question of obedience to the "sword"; Hubmaier's moderation was no match for Hut's fanaticism; and in a short while the Moravian Brethren were swept into a general denial of civil authority. They at once lost the support in high places which had protected them and were suspected of revolutionary aims; nor was this entirely unjust. Disobedience to the sword might be a spiritual tenet; but one cannot ignore the fact that the tenet proved attractive because in practice it meant refusal to pay taxes, escape from the jurisdiction of the secular courts, and a bringing into the open of the discontents of the poor.

What was unjust was Hubmaier's fate, burned at Vienna in 1528, his wife being drowned; the unhappy man, a truly pious and gentle preacher of the return to the way of Christ, fell victim to the growing alarms which animated the established order, whether papist or reformed. It was becoming plain that Anabaptism, with its sectarian, social and sometimes millenarian views, was feared and hated by all. Hut again escaped, but soon after died in an Augsburg prison, apparently a natural death or possibly suicide. The Moravian movement was saved by the arrival of reinforcements from the Tyrol, led by Huter who turned out to be a highly competent organiser. Huter and his followers believed in the common ownership of goods and gave to their branch of Anabaptism a tradition of communal farming and community life which was patriarchal, rather touching, and extremely narrow-minded. When he was caught and executed in 1536, the Moravian Brethren, or Hutterites as they later called themselves, had become a well-established collection of groups which could survive the intermittent persecutions they were to suffer in the years to come. Though often driven back and forth between Moravia and Hungary, they were never exterminated.

While Hubmaier carried the message down the Danube, other Swiss Brethren made their way to the Rhine. At first they stopped over in Strassburg which in the late 1520s offered a general meeting place for all branches of evangelical reform. Between 1528 and 1534 the city resounded with the debates and arguments of Anabaptists moderate and immoderate, of Schwenckfeld and Franck, of Carlstadt and Servetus. Despite their basic belief in religious freedom, Capito and Bucer watched all this with some apprehension, especially after they had entirely failed to outargue the extremists. But in 1534 the city acceded to the Lutheranism of the Augsburg Confession,[3] and the Anabaptists found themselves once more on the move. The Rhine seemed to present the obvious highroad. Unfortunately for the good name of the movement, that road led straight to the Netherlands where sectarian traditions of a violent and socially disruptive kind had long maintained themselves; as unfortunately, the way was led not by a pacific moderate like Hubmaier but by the fanatical and extravagant Melchior Hoffmann.

Hoffmann was a furrier's journeyman from Swabia, an untrained dreamer who easily fell under the spell of eschatological fantasies. He troubled Zwingli in 1523, called on Luther, led a wandering life as a preacher in Scandinavia and north Germany. Increasingly he laid the stress on the nearness of the Second Coming: he was one of those who over the centuries have seized on the biblical prophecy concerning the triumph of the 144,000 righteous virgins to inspire his followers. In 1529 he joined the Anabaptists at Strassburg and was soon told to cease troubling the city's air. This drove him to the Low Countries where his exalted visions and passionate preaching found ready echoes among the heirs to the equally extravagant Free Brethren. Melchiorite Anabaptism took hold of the region—of the ordinary people, that is. It differed quite markedly from the Moravian brand by being less concerned with the Christian life on earth and much more concerned with preparing for the day of wrath when all but the righteous shall perish. Hoffmann himself, who believed that the day would come without drastic action by the believers and who claimed to be the prophet Elijah *redivivus*, made the mistake of going back to Strassburg just when opinion there was turning decisively against Anabaptism; he was promptly arrested, spent his last ten years in prison, and died in 1543.

He left a seed behind in the Netherlands which was to produce a monstrous growth. Imprisoning Hoffmann did not stop his dupes from continuing to look for the end of the world, and the vigorous persecution carried out by the authorities (with Charles V urging them on) only inflamed fanaticism. The ancient tradition that the sufferings of the faithful would rise to a climax just before the day of settlement and the triumph of the elect once again paid off; apocalyptic preaching reached the point where only the believer can distinguish it from madness. The new leader was Jan Matthys, a baker from Haarlem who took Hoffmann's ideas a stage further. For Hoffmann the Second Coming was so close that the elect need do no more than await it in confidence. Matthys declared that Christ would not come unless the true believers smoothed his path by disposing of the unrighteous. Revolutionary passions became mixed up with spiritual exaltation. It was all rather like Müntzer's teaching, only cruder; more to the point, it carried on medieval precedents which had played their part in the excesses of Hussite fanaticism. In other words, it was just the sort of thing that the political powers had sufficiently experienced before to fear it the more now. But persecution could not stop the work of Matthys' proselytisers who went about the Low Countries and northern Germany, rebaptising and calling to arms. A very ugly situation hovered uneasily between social revolution and mass slaughter in the cause of Christ. It exploded in the extraordinary episode of Münster, happily unique in the history of Anabaptism but unhappily doomed to rest upon its shoulders for ever after.

Münster, in Westphalia, was the see and seat of one of the powerful prince-bishops who between them ruled most of north-west Germany. The city had the usual history, in such circumstances, of bickering with its ruler; in the process, it had gained a fair measure of independence. The Reformation thus met a ready welcome, and by the early 1530s the Lutherans dominated council and town. Their two leaders were distinctly on the radical side of Lutheranism: Bernhard Rothmann, the minister, shared Müntzer's views about the sufferings of the poor, and Bernhard Knipperdolling, a leading merchant, had been with Hoffmann in Sweden. In January 1534, Anabaptist missionaries appeared in Münster; Rothmann and Knipperdolling went over to them; and the Melchiorites suddenly saw in this strong city, away from Charles V's dominions, a suitable place for the foundation of the new Jerusalem. In February there arrived Matthys' chief disciple, Jan Bockelson of Leyden, a young and handsome ex-tailor so far distinguished solely by his failure to succeed in anything he had tried his hand at. Matthys himself soon followed and took over the control of the city which he proceeded to remodel to his taste. The first task was to cleanse the place of unbelievers; mass baptisings took place, while all stubborn or hesitant Lutherans and Catholics were driven out by armed bands, into the snow or the equally unreceptive arms of the forces which the bishop was bringing up to restore his rule. Under Matthys' violent leadership, the fanatic mob ran riot in the streets. He proclaimed communal ownership of all property; all books except the bible were forbidden and burned, opponents were killed. When the bishop hesitantly invested the city, the sudden involvement in war gave Matthys his chance to complete the dictatorship. Though he himself was soon killed in an idiotic sortie, undertaken in response to a direct command from God and in assurance of invulnerability, the defenders surprised everyone by their fanatic vigour. The siege dragged on.

After Matthys' death, Jan Bockelson took over, and it was his reign as the new messiah which really put Münster on the historical map. The Leyden tailor was both a ruthless, egotistical maniac working out his private fantasies (he had always liked to act in plays) and a skilful exploiter of other people's madness. To communism he added polygamy: because of the presence of many escaped nuns there were far more women than men in Münster, and the women had been from the first the most fanatical adherents of this apocalyptic Anabaptism. Using all the devices of the inspired dervish, Bockelson imposed his absolute rule on a people worked up to believe that they were the only saved congregation on earth and would shortly inherit that planet. A victory over the besieging forces in August set the crown on Bockelson's power—literally so, for he now proclaimed himself king (an Old Testament king-prophet, no less) and created a dramatic setting of splendid robes, attendant court, armed guards and new nobility. Fanaticism not being enough to hold the community together, the usual weapons of a revolutionary terror made their appearance. The whole thing was both a psychological show-case and a logical culmination to centuries of apocalyptic dreams. King Jan managed nevertheless to remember the needs of defence, and his iron discipline backed up a continued trust in God's favour to keep his kingdom going, even though from early in 1535 it was being gradually starved to death by rigorous investment. Anabaptist risings and armed assemblies elsewhere, designed to relieve Münster and its messiah, were scattered by the armed forces of the princes, and in June the town at last fell. Even then it had taken treachery to open the way. The Anabaptist kingdom was destroyed by the significantly odd alliance of the Catholic bishop of Münster and the Lutheran landgrave of Hesse; their troops executed a dreadful reckoning on the sectaries, hunted down to the last man and woman; Knipperdolling and King Jan were tortured to death. Münster reverted to the old religion.

In actual fact, the end of Jan of Leyden's kingdom cleansed Anabaptism of its insanities. There were to be no more apocalyptic, millenarian or messianic enterprises, and after 1536 all the religious life of the age, in whatever denomination, settled down to more sober forms. Politics rapidly took charge of events; neither fanaticism nor social discontent played thereafter anything like the same part in the story. But for the Anabaptists themselves the events at Münster were nearly fatal. The world, and especially all in authority, had been struck with fear and hatred by this apparent dissolution of all moral and legal order. Rumours exaggerated the frightfulness of an outburst the truth about which was quite extravagant enough, and wherever Anabaptist views were thereafter encountered the memories of Münster weighed heavily against them. Persecution now seemed to be the only answer, and it needs no stressing that it was naturally applied with vigour, especially in the Netherlands.

Yet the sects survived. They found new leaders. Pilgrim Marbeck (d. 1556), a highly skilled mining engineer from the Tyrol, from 1544 managed to live at Augsburg as town engineer and to organise from there the south German brethren. In the Low Countries, a middle-aged priest, Menno Simmons (1496–1561), not even converted until 1536, gathered the shattered communities together and by imposing an extremely rigid Church discipline on his followers saved them from extermination. There were other leaders, as for instance the ebullient David Joris, a Flemish disciple of Melchior Hoffmann who clung to his master's teaching on the Second Coming, for a time regarded himself as God's true prophet, but in the end retired to live in disguise at Basel for an untroubled twelve years, respected by all. The town council were horrified when the identity of the notorious heretic was discovered in 1558, two years after his death; they burned his dead body to straighten their account with man and God. The Dutch brethren were cured by Simmons of all forms of violent belief; they became instead quiet gatherings of pious and very exclusive people who perpetuated the gentler traditions of Anabaptism. The movement which had burst forth in Zürich, which had drawn inspiration from Allstedt, which in a bare ten years had covered Germany and parts beyond with sectarian communities, and which had come to grief at Münster, survived now in the meekly suffering rural congregations of Hutterites and Menonites. But it did not lose its assurance of a special revelation and its quietly arrogant rejection of all who did not share this. The Dutch brethren in particular exercised much influence on the growth of sects in Elizabethan and Jacobean England; they helped to develop the puritanical and self-consciously superior attitudes which are characteristic of all these "gathered" Churches. Millenarian doctrines were not, of course, dead, but they did not again trouble the age of the Reformation.

During the heyday of Anabaptism it appeared to contemporaries that there were now three religions to choose from: the popish, the reformed, and the sectarian. It has sometimes been argued that the effective elimination of that third choice wrecked the prospects of early toleration and liberty for the private conscience. This is to mistake the true nature of Anabaptism. Since it always embodied a conviction of sole salvation for the particular group of believers, and often also the chiliastic dreams of salvation realised in the destruction of the wicked with the establishment of Christ's kingdom on earth, it was in its essence markedly more intolerant than the institutional Church. Its victory, where it occurred, led to terror; and that was in the nature of things. No one will deny that the movement also gave prominence to men of true piety, simple belief and gentle manner; but this does not take away from the fact that its enormous appeal rested on the claim to bring power and glory to the poor, the weak and the resentful. It is surely significant that such genuine believers in toleration as Schwenckfeld and Franck fell out with the Anabaptists; as it is significant that neither Schwenckfeld nor Franck could leave a mark on more than the occasional individual. The Anabaptism of the early Reformation—no matter what pious and respectable sects may to-day look back upon it as an ancestor—was a violent phenomenon born out of irrational and psychologically unbalanced dreams, resting on a denial of reason and the elevation of that belief in direct inspiration which enables men to do as they please. Not even the terrible sufferings of its unhappy followers should make one suppose that the salvation of mankind from its own passions could have been found by the path which runs along the clouds.

Chapter 5

Outside Germany

Could the Reformation have spread so far and so fast if it had started anywhere but in Germany? At any rate, the fact that it had its beginnings in the middle of Europe made possible a very rapid radiation in all directions; the whole circle of countries surrounding the Empire came one after the other under its influence.[1] Germany's position as the centre of European trade also helped greatly. German merchants carried not only goods but Lutheran ideas and books to Venice and France; the north German Hanse transported the Reformation to the Scandinavian countries, parcelled up with bales of cloth and cargoes of grain; trading links with Germany did much to encourage the growth of Lutheranism in the eastern lands. Dutchmen trading with London and Hull played a leading part in introducing Lutheran and even Anabaptist ideas into England. Wherever the busy mercantile connections of Germany penetrated, there propaganda, first clandestine and soon open, made its appearance. Pamphlets and books, imported in this way, were soon translated into the local languages.

Not that the Reformation in those countries owed everything to German influence. Luther's revolt met willing sympathisers everywhere. The condition of the Church was much the same throughout most of Europe; corruption, worldliness, spiritual lassitude, immorality and uselessness were not peculiar to the German clergy. In consequence, anticlericalism, too, was to be found pretty well everywhere. So also was the humanist reaction to abuses and unsatisfying doctrine. Before Luther's name was ever heard of, Erasmus' name received honour from Valladolid to Cracow. A network of his devoted followers covered the European universities and schools, promoted his characteristic attacks on ignorant monks and dull scholastics, and absorbed a good deal of his positive teaching on the ethical basis and the spiritual essence of Christianity—the doctrines of Christian humanism. Everywhere there were men, often influential men high up in the Church, who agreed with him that the formal observance and intellectually indefensible routine of the Church did not represent true religion. However far apart Erasmus and Luther really were—and they not only (as we have seen) disagreed but thoroughly disliked each other—it is as true for all Europe as it is for Germany that Erasmian humanists felt an initial sympathy with the Reformation.

Equally, Germany was by no means alone in harbouring a mystical and spiritual tradition which, whether outwardly orthodox or not, sought a return to the simple and personal religion which it was felt the Church had lost. Lollards in England, Hussites in Bohemia, small private groups or individual revivalists in Italy and Spain and France, provided at least a well tilled soil for the seed, even if at times their aspirations were to be no better satisfied by Luther or even Zwingli than had been Müntzer's or Grebel's. The interaction of new and old, of rational humanism and mystic hope, of secular reform and transcendental Reformation, of the personal search for salvation and enthusiasm for the rebel against the Church, is as notable in the non-German countries as it was in the homeland of the Reformation. But even as in Germany the growth of new Churches depended largely on the effects of political alignment and power, so, naturally, it did elsewhere. The working out of Luther's impact on the Christian world varied a good deal from place to place.

I The South

Even in Spain and Italy, the countries traditionally least associated with the Reformation, the victory of the old Church was no foregone conclusion. Here, too, movements of doubtful orthodoxy offered points of entry for the new ideas. Spain had not only its recent converts from Islam and Judaism, not in fact especially inclined to embrace Lutheranism but always suspected of being likely to fall from grace at the first opportunity; there were also the obscure little groups of the Illuminati or *Alumbrados*, gatherings of mystics whose antecedents remain as dark as their tenets, but who at any rate elevated personal union with God above the formalism of the Church. Italy was full of individuals preaching regeneration in one form or another but always to the disregard of the organised ecclesiastical institutions. Fra Girolamo Savonarola (1452–98), with his puritan commonwealth in Florence, had violently cashed in on the unstable situation (aggravated, as usual, by economic decline), though most of these enthusiasts were men who, like the Camaldolese hermit Paolo Giustiniana (1476–1528), preached peaceful reform and a return to pure religion. In both countries, humanist influence was strong. This hardly needs stressing for Italy, the home of humanism, where such native movements as the Florentine Academy with its Platonic Christianity (and the addition of St. Socrates to the list of saints) outweighed Erasmus. Spain, on the other hand, was strongly colonised from Rotterdam, and its intellectuals welcomed Erasmian thought with fervour. Cardinal Ximenez' own foundation, the University of Alcalá—founded to restore learning to the Church, and in the 1520s a flourishing institution—was full of Erasmians, while their presence at the court of Charles V greatly increased their numbers and security. The condition of the Church differed widely in the two countries. In Italy it was as bad as anywhere, with great numbers of often indifferent bishops and always unspiritual popes setting the pace for a general increase in worldliness and corruption among the clergy. The Spanish Church, on the other hand, had been very thoroughly overhauled in the previous fifty years. Even Ximenez had not been able to stamp out corruption and ignorance, but he had greatly reduced these evils and left in Spain alone a Church sufficiently reformed to face the Reformation with confidence.

Above all, the Spanish Church possessed a truly formidable weapon for the destruction of heterodoxy. The Spanish Inquisition was an altogether peculiar institution, created in the struggle to eliminate non-Christian religions from the peninsula. It owed its foundation and power not to Rome but to the Catholic kings, Ferdinand and Isabella. From 1483, Thomas de Torquemada as inquisitor-general commanded in the royal Council of the Supreme and General Inquisition (commonly called the Suprema) an instrument of terror which by its secrecy, its ruthless use of torture and the stake, its freedom from restriction or supervision, and its ability to touch the highest in the land became an irresistible seeker-out and suppressor of the least deviation in the faith. Dominated by the friars, who were unshakably attached to all the teaching of the Church including its most routine practices, it soon went into action against both Illuminati and Erasmians. The former were condemned in 1525; even Ignatius Loyola, later as founder of the Jesuit Order a saint of the Church, fell foul of the Inquisition in 1527 and suffered imprisonment for his contacts with the mystical movement. The humanists were a harder problem, especially as they were well entrenched among the leading bishops and at court. The Inquisition was by no means free of corruption; the secrecy of its proceedings, its refusal to acquaint the accused with the charges and witnesses against him, and the practice of confiscating the property of suspect and family gave openings for abuse and for the persecution of the totally innocent from motives of personal spite or greed. The Cortes repeatedly urged Charles V to take the Holy Office in hand, especially because after the death of Ferdinand of Aragon the crown's control had much relaxed; but by the early 1520's the spread of Lutheranism gave the Inquisition a new lease of life, and the emperor never got beyond good intentions.

Whether, in fact, there were any converts to Lutheranism in Spain is not clear, if only because the Inquisition used the smear-tactics of calling Lutheran all those who did not adhere to its narrow orthodoxy; but Erasmians who ridiculed the friars, denounced the Inquisition, and held the ceremonies of the Church in some contempt there certainly were. A meeting at Valladolid called, in 1527, to investigate their tenets ended in defeat for the friars, but when Charles's Erasmian court departed with him in 1529 the humanists lost the protection they had enjoyed. The Inquisition now had a free hand, even daring to attack men who stood in the emperor's favour, until by 1538 the strong body of Erasmians was destroyed—forced to recant or flee. So eminent a man as the aged Pedro de Lerma (1461–1544), the first chancellor of Alcalá and as peaceful a scholar as one could wish to meet, suffered prison and exile; he ended his days in Paris because, as he rightly said, no one could any longer pursue serious studies in Spain. If the orthodox Sorbonne did not object to his presence, he cannot have been even tainted with Lutheranism: the fact is that the Spanish persecution of heretics had rapidly become nothing but a general and obscurantist attack on any form of intellectual enterprise or independence.

Spain, therefore, produced no movement of Protestant reform but only individuals who dissented from the Church. Francisco de Encinas (d. 1552), who went to Wittenberg, England and Strassburg, seems to have been a fairly straight-forward Lutheran. Michael Servetus (1511–53), on the other hand, was nothing if not devious. An intelligent and thoughtful man brought up to the study of law and medicine, he lacked theological training but not interest. Exercised over the presence in Spain of Jewish and Moorish remnants, he came to the conclusion that only the doctrine of the Trinity stood in the way of their full assimilation, and when he discovered that the doctrine had no explicit scriptural foundation he wrote, at the age of twenty, a book—*De Trinitatis Erroribus* (1531)—which made him the arch-heretic of the day. Ever since it had nearly foundered over the Arian heresy of the fourth and fifth centuries, the Western Church had always been particularly sensitive to antitrinitarian views; all the sixteenth-century Churches inherited the conviction that the denial of Christ's divinity and the personal character of the Holy Spirit constituted the ultimate, the quite unforgivable, heresy. Servetus fled from Spain, to pursue his medical studies in France, engage in controversy with Calvin, and fall victim to the Genevan reformer.[2] His influence on others was negligible. The same cannot be said of Juan de Valdés (1500–41), Spain's chief export to Italy. Valdés was an

ardent humanist, with a like-minded brother Alonso who, as secretary to Charles V, could until his death in 1532 offer some protection
to them both. In 1529 Juan published his *Dialogo de Doctrina
Christiana* in which, following Erasmus, he attacked the outward
and unsatisfactory religion of the Church. Though for a while he
escaped the worst, in the end (and in his absence) he suffered a
process at the hands of the Inquisition, was probably condemned
for heresy (1532), and before the matter ended had decided to
emigrate to Rome in search of safety and employment.

Compared with the Spain of the Inquisition, Italy—even Charles
V's kingdom of Naples—certainly seemed to offer some hope both to
humanists and reformers. The peninsula's division into a multiplicity
of states and small principalities, with the intricate politics characteristic of this European microcosm, prevented anything like a concerted
attempt to suppress heterodoxy. At least until about 1530, many of
the best and most devout of the higher clergy favoured the earnest
concern with reform of manners and substance which in Italy animated both humanists and mystics. Here, too, therefore the teachings of the various reformers at first met no serious opposition,
though attitudes changed as the European struggle developed. In
particular, the Erasmians and moderate reformers among the bishops
and cardinals withdrew into the more easily defended position of
Catholic reform, content to remove abuses without touching funda-
mentals.[3] However, before this happened extremer tendencies had
got quite a foothold in Italy. In this connection, the republic of Venice
was particularly helpful. Its commercial links with Germany facili-
tated the importation of Lutheran ideas; its recently acquired possessions on the mainland, including in particular the famous university
of Padua, offered a sizable area for missionary effort; and its chronic
quarrel with the papacy over lands taken from the old papal states
encouraged a general tolerance. Vicenza, in Venetian territory, was
from 1546 a centre of Anabaptist activity. Small independent states
offered a refuge: thus the court of Ferrara, presided over by its
duchess, Renée of France, was from 1528 almost a reformed cell in
the body politic.

However, the real vigour of the Italian Reformation owed less to
Luther than to Calvin and became really apparent only after about
1535. Before this, it is difficult to distinguish between the general
dissatisfaction with a corrupt Church and a more insidious penetration of truly revolutionary attitudes. It would appear that Lutheran
and Anabaptist influences were widespread, affecting all sorts of men
both lay· and clerical—noblemen, artisans and peasants, as well as
bishops, parish clergy and friars—without ever becoming sufficiently
organised to constitute a threat to the ascendancy of the Church.
When, after 1530, the papacy set itself to deal more effectively with

these sporadic manifestations it found ready support among municipal and other authorities and achieved a rapid success. An exception to this truth was provided only by the group which grew up round Juan de Valdés, from 1533 resident at Naples where he developed his ideas, maintained contact with friends and followers all over Italy, and entertained visitors eager to learn from him. Valdés himself never broke with the Church and died peacefully in its bosom, and his religious beliefs have defied precise definition. Every sort of radical movement, including the Antitrinitarians, has claimed him among its ancestors, but the only certain thing is that he regarded the essence of religion as separate from ecclesiastical institutions. While he shared certain views about the working of the inner spirit and the inessentiality of a formed Church with such as Schwenckfeld, he seems altogether to have lacked the enthusiastic temperament and remained more attached to the traditions of Erasmus and the *devotio moderna*. Certainly he denounced those who thought that true religion lay entirely in observing the Church's rule for outward performance— fasting, confession, invocation of saints or the Virgin Mary: in fact, works, in the Lutheran sense—but so did everybody who thought seriously about religion at all, except perhaps the Dominicans of the Spanish Inquisition who treated criticism of this sort of purely formal Christianity as equal to heresy. Valdés' faith was, in fact, sincere but unspecific, flexible and protean, harmless in any other age, centred upon a personal search for God and that "imitation of Christ" which humanism had reduced to identity with the Stoic virtues.

On the other hand, his influence on a number of *belles âmes* made Valdés something of a minor prophet. Women of the aristocracy, in particular, found him an inspiration, among them the Princess Caterina Cybo and Giulia Gonzaga, the widowed duchess of Faietto, both of whom ended their days in a nunnery. Vittoria Colonna, widow of Charles V's great general, the marquis of Pescara, and centre of the most famous *salon* of the late Renaissance (patron of Michelangelo, friend to such diverse men as the future Cardinal Reginald Pole and the future heretic Bernardino Ochino), also maintained contacts with many of Valdés' disciples. Ochino (1487–1564) was, indeed, probably the most remarkable man to come under Valdés' spell. A preacher of great fervour and power, he sought throughout life for the true Christianity which always seemed to lie over the next hill. Early in life he joined the strict order of the Observant Franciscans, transferred himself to that even stricter Franciscan offspring, the Capuchins, became their vicar-general, began to see inspiration in Luther. By 1539 he was preaching heresy; in 1542, he announced his conversion and fled to Geneva. The rest of a life spent in travels (Strassburg, England, Zürich, Poland) ended in Anabaptism and Moravia. Pietro Carnesecchi, executed for heresy in 1567, was another who had been taken with Valdés. He belonged eminently among those who had believed that a true religion compatible with the continued existence of the Church might emerge from the welter of orthodox, near-heterodox and plainly heretical ideas which filled Italy in the 1520s and 1530s. A nobleman with high connections, he escaped persecution until, in a very different Italy dominated by the Counter-Reformation, he at last fell victim to the reconstituted papal Inquisition. Some of Valdés' friends became Calvinists, others returned to the Church of Rome, others again joined the many small Anabaptist groups which in the 1540s grew up especially in North Italy. Many of these followed Ochino's example, and from about 1545 the emigration of Italian Protestants created quite a *diaspora*, mainly in Switzerland but with offshoots in England and Poland. This included the unquestionably antitrinitarian followers of what came to be known as Socinianism—the teachings of Fausto Sozzini (1539–1604), an active leader of sects in Poland and Transylvania later in the century. In the spread of Anabaptism, as usual the preserve of poor and lowly men, the economic depression which the wars had either brought to Italy or aggravated there played a recognisable part.

II   The West

If the impact of the Reformation on battered and splintered Italy inspired a mass of anticlerical and spiritually dissatisfied men of all classes to seek salvation in one form or another of sectarian belief, it penetrated more narrowly but perhaps more deeply in France. Here, too, similar ideas and protagonists were to be found, but the setting within which they worked provided a different atmosphere and encouraged a less diverse growth than did the political disunity and—for a time—easy tolerance of Renaissance Italy. Humanism had its devotees in France, especially Guillaume Budé (1467–1540), perhaps the leading classical scholar of his day. Budé's interests lay in philology; he edited classical texts and kept away from theological disputes. Erasmus had his followers, but he never exercised so wide an influence as he did, for instance, in Germany or Spain. Above all, his teaching never gained a foothold in the universities. These were dominated by the theological faculty of the University of Paris, the famed Sorbonne, which had for long been the bulwark of orthodoxy and even obscurantism. Budé, who remained outside regular academic employment, laboured instead to have a new humanistic academy founded; in 1530 he persuaded Francis I to grant a charter to what was soon known as the *Collège de France*, a centre of modern studies much resented by the Sorbonne.

The leading Erasmian was Jacques Lefèvre d'Étaples (1455–1536) whose mysticism rested characteristically on biblical and humanistic studies; he, like so many, welcomed Luther's first appearance because it seemed to support his own spiritual theology of grace and faith. Lefèvre became the leader of a small but influential group of moderate reformers. His pupil Guillaume Briçonnet (1470–1533), from 1516 bishop of Meaux, gathered in that diocese a company of like-minded men—Lefèvre himself, Gérard Roussel (1480–1550), Guillaume Farel (1489–1565)—and carried through a local Reformation of his own. He not only energetically improved the standards of the clergy but also encouraged liturgical reforms which came very close to doctrinal heterodoxy. The group at Meaux, a centre of propaganda and an example to others, presented a high-minded and often earnest endeavour to translate the aspirations of moderate humanist reformers into reality. Lefèvre's teaching included some of those anti-institutional and anti-sacramentarian notions so common among the devout followers of Erasmus; Farel, as he later proved in Geneva,[4] was a potential revolutionary; Roussel was a mystic. So was the most interesting of the people only loosely connected with the group at Meaux, Margaret d'Angoulême, sister to Francis I and later queen of Navarre, whose *Mirror of a Sinful Soul* (1531) shows her to have been well in line with the *devotio moderna* and Thomas à Kempis.

Yet these stirrings were not necessarily heretical. The queen of Navarre always thought herself an orthodox daughter of the Church; Briçonnet turned against Luther and Lutheran books as early as 1522; one of his leading disciples, Josse van Clichtove, an ardent humanist, delivered himself of a violent denunciation of Luther two years before that. The group at Meaux included future reformers; itself, it was fundamentally conformist. Both Briçonnet and Lefèvre continued to hope for reform without Reformation, though after 1525 they had to realise that the conservatives of the Sorbonne were making the inaccurate but customary identification of Luther and Erasmus, with consequent danger to themselves. How influential these Meaux reformers were, beyond the restricted circles of a few intellectual and highly placed sympathisers, is not clear. Certainly there was enough discontent in France—social, economic, spiritual—to present an opportunity to evangelical propaganda; Luther's works were soon imported and widely read, and from the early 1520's one hears of people or groups, usually low down in the social scale, who are suspected of heretical leanings. But the essential situation was quite different from Germany. Assuredly, the Church in France was quite as corrupt and often deplorable as any part of the western Church, but it was not in the least independent of the state and much less subjected to Rome than most. The Pragmatic Sanction of Bourges (1438) had created almost a separate Gallican Church by conferring a large measure of self-government on the hierarchy in France. This ecclesiastical liberty was destroyed by the Concordat which Leo X and Francis I concluded in 1516 at Bologna. In that treaty the pope abrogated the Pragmatic Sanction, formally resumed control over the French Church, and in the same breath surrendered the bulk of that control to the king. Ecclesiastical appointments, legislation and discipline were from henceforth very largely in the hands of the crown. Thus the French Church might excite the customary anticlericalism of the laity—best expressed perhaps by that untypical ecclesiastic and downright humanist, François Rabelais (1494–1553)—but it did not rouse nationalist opposition because it was so manifestly French and not Roman.

More important still, the crown did not have to look to the Reformation for a chance to establish monarchical and centralised control over the clergy; it already had the best part of that. Indeed, the fate of the Reformation in France depended to a quite extraordinary degree on the policy and inclinations of the Most Christian King. Francis I acceded to a monarchy which was on the way to absolutism but still had quite a distance to go there. As yet the country was not even properly unified. It was only in 1529 that Habsburg claims to the duchy of Burgundy were abandoned and that the king gained control of the great Bourbon appanage right in the centre of France; only in 1532 was Brittany fully annexed to the crown. The size and geographical variety of France made it at all times difficult to control. Accepted doctrine limited the king's powers by the fundamental laws and customs of his realm; this was the position maintained, for instance, by Claude de Seyssel in his *La Grant Monarchie de France* (1519) which, though recognising the rights and prerogatives of the crown, insisted on such traditional restraints as the need to seek consent from the governed and the inability to alter the laws protecting the subject's basic rights. Even by then, however, that view was ceasing to be altogether realistic; the many contemporary observers from other countries—Venetian, German, English—who felt that, comparatively speaking, the king of France was hard to distinguish from a true despot, had some reason on their side, though they exaggerated.

Ever since the later stages of the Hundred Years' War, kings of France had been able to levy quite sizable taxation without any form of consent, while their edicts carried the force of law. None of the variety of representative assemblies, local or national, took part in lawmaking; though they could and did present grievances, it was entirely up to the king whether he would do anything about them. The limitations of the fundamental law, so stressed by Seyssel, had little meaning when the institutions which could have enforced them failed to do so. Though royal edicts were supposed to need registration by the superior law-courts, the *Parlements* (especially that of Paris) before they were effective, Francis I began the subjection of these once powerful bodies—always potential rivals—to the royal will. Both he and his successor Henry II (1547–59) reduced the *Parlement's* power by the creation of new central courts out of the royal council and weakened its resistance to royal legislation by the frequent holding of *lits de justice*, meetings in the king's presence where criticism and resistance were steamrollered. The principle of consent in popular assemblies might exist, but it had little means of expressing itself. No Estates General met between the two important assemblies of 1484 and 1560, and though Francis I called quite a few more sectional assemblies he progressively confined himself to consulting a devoted nobility or the overawed *Parlement*.

Administrative reforms improved the collection and management of the revenue, multiplied the central law-courts, and reduced the independence of the localities. Francis I continued the policy of transferring local government from local magnates to royal officials; in particular he relied upon a body of trusted servants equipped with general powers, the masters of requests, for the diffusion of central authority among the regions. Admittedly, though the king gained the benefit and for simplicity's sake is credited with these reforms and policies, Francis I deserves much less credit than most kings. His own interests were exclusively courtly—that is to say, war, the tourney, the chase (of deer and women)—and he was most at home with his greater nobles, in his brilliant and superficial court. The patient work of enlarging the royal authority fell to that large and increasing bureaucracy of men mostly trained in the Roman law who both devised the means and earned the rewards of a growing absolutism. Among such legists, at any rate, less conservative doctrines of the monarchy were gaining ground; Charles de Grassaille (*Regalium Franciae*, 1538) and his like, while preserving much of the old framework, exploded it by ascribing to the king the full sovereignty of the Roman *imperator*, and such notions were beginning to influence the monarchy, if not its subjects.

At the same time, it must be said that all this looked rather better on paper than it worked on the ground. The second half of the century—aristocratic faction fighting under the guise of religious wars—was to demonstrate how insecure the monarch's ascendancy could still be in the face of the continued power of the great territorial nobility and the size of the country. Despotism is not, at this date, the right term to apply to the French monarchy. Francis I might not call general assemblies, but especially before 1530 he called many lesser ones (of notables and town deputies) to consider diplomatic or financial business; his earlier treaties were always ratified by some form of consent. The provincial estates, varying in constitution and power, were active enough, and the king's right to tax was limited both by the need to secure the taxpayer's co-operation and by the growing pressure of financial needs which compelled some degree of caution if active resistance was to be avoided. The king favoured the nobility and exploited the bourgeoisie, neither the traditional nor the best policy for the creation of a royal absolutism. By and large, it would seem that the inherited notions of a kingship dependent on the law and compelled to consult the views of the governed still persisted, even though the practice of kings was altering. All this allowed for, it still remains true that under strong kings the French monarchy was the least limited in Europe, and France the most centralised of countries. With its natural wealth (much drained by the royal policy of expensive wars with more expensive aftermaths), its great population, and that attachment to its king which the history of disaster and humiliation had instilled in Frenchmen in the fourteenth and fifteenth centuries, France gave formidable, if sometimes hesitant, support to an aggressive and autocratic ruler who also, as has been seen, could do much as he pleased with the Church.

In itself, the ascendancy of the crown did not necessarily work against the Reformation. Margaret d'Angoulême had much influence on her brother, and there were others at court who agreed with her moderately reformist leanings. Zwingli thought the prospects so good that in 1525 he dedicated the most systematic exposition of his theology, the *Commentary on the True and False Religion*, to the king of France. The stiffest opposition to the new ideas came from the Sorbonne and the *Parlement* of Paris, neither in much favour with a king who prided himself on his appreciation of all that Renaissance and humanism stood for in the arts and learning, and whose only policy towards the *Parlement* involved the reduction of its independence. His Italian policy as a rule made him an enemy of the pope, and always an enemy of the emperor who had declared his view of Luther at Worms. Down to the battle of Pavia, at least, the climate in France was favourable for the spread of the new ideas. However, when the king was a prisoner in Madrid, the regency of his mother, Louise of Savoy, initiated a more repressive policy: the queen-mother was much more orthodox than her son, and for the moment France and Rome sought to ally against Spanish preponderance. The League of Cognac was thus reflected in heresy trials in France. In 1527 the Sorbonne, always single-mindedly hostile to the faintest trace of the Reformation, even extended its disapproval to Erasmus in whose works it condemned a variety of heresies, ancient and modern. The return of Francis I ended this phase; the Meaux group, scattered during the reaction, reassembled; all seemed set fair again. But the king's protection of these moderate reformers implied no inclination to Lutheranism, nor could it survive the pressure of circumstances. Need for money, much aggravated by the ransoms which by the 1529 treaty of Cambrai he had to pay for the sons left behind as hostages in Madrid, forced him to listen to protests from nobles and Church who, as it turned out, had no liking for the Reformation. The 1527 assembly of notables and the 1528 Church councils of Sens and Bourges requested action against heresy as the price of their compliance with financial demands. The Sorbonne gained complete ascendancy in the Church; Lutherans were hunted down and burned; the flow of books from Germany was arrested or even sealed off.

Nearly all the sufferers were of "the people", men and women of no influence. No doubt this represents their greater vulnerability, but it also tells the truth about the early Reformation in France. It did not attract the men of wealth and birth; Louis de Berquin, burned in 1529, remained exceptional as an aristocrat with Lutheran sympathies. The French economy of the sixteenth century was rather backward. The peasants usually farmed plots too small to do more than provide a subsistence yield for the farmer; great lords lived unproductively on the rents paid with great difficulty by peasant tenants; industry and even trade were failing to take part in the general European upswing. The country still bore the marks of over a hundred years of often very destructive war; capital accumulated slowly, and what there was evaporated too readily in the display and wars of extravagant kings. In so far as economic conditions assisted the Reformation in France, it would seem that poverty and distress played a large part, desire for economic freedom and the so-called capitalistic ethos little or none. That is to say, pre-Calvinist Protestantism at least attracted the poor and weak rather than those on the make. Naturally a movement which in the main consisted of the unprivileged was quite remarkably vulnerable, and in the persecution it became clear how little progress the Reformation, or even humanism, had made among the great and powerful. Meaux retired into orthodoxy and decline, and Lutheranism was effectively rooted out.

Though persecution was to be the crown's essential policy from about 1528 onwards, lapses and moments of relief still occurred. Francis I still had not entirely thrown in his lot with the Sorbonne; what is more, he continued to subordinate his religious policy at home to the needs of his foreign policy. From the point of view of his ambitions in the world, any enemy of Charles V was a friend of his. He had demonstrated his freedom from doctrinal bigotry as early as 1525 when he had opened negotiations with the sultan, and his envoys encouraged the Turkish advance which terminated at Vienna in 1529. The beginnings were thus laid for that understanding between the Most Christian King and the Ottoman infidel which at times came near to formal alliance and always ensured some measure of co-operation between these two chief enemies of the Habsburgs.

The understanding scandalised all good Christians and gave Charles V some telling propaganda points, but it also achieved its political ends and proved very useful to Francis I. In the German Lutherans he saw another possible counter-weight to Habsburg power, and from 1530 onwards common interest provided an intermittent bond between France and the Protestant princes. All these foreign involvements were reflected in the ups and downs of the Reformation in France. In 1529–32 Francis tried to attach the Germans to himself: persecution slackened and moderate reformers were encouraged. In 1533 he hoped to win the pope to his side: he agreed to publish a papal Bull against heresy and backed up the Sorbonne. Early in 1534, disappointed in Rome, he switched once more to the Lutherans and allowed some freedom to heterodox propaganda. Unfortunately for the Reformation, this encouraged some hotheads to overstep the mark. One morning in October 1534, Paris, Orléans, Rouen and other cities woke up to find the walls plastered with posters (*placards*) denouncing, in the most violent terms, the orthodox doctrine of the mass and the eucharist. Someone had had the effrontery to post a *placard* on the very chamber at Amboise in which the king had been sleeping. Francis (whose sense of humour was never very prominent) chose to treat this event as a personal insult, and from that moment he stopped playing about with heterodoxy.

The immediate consequence of the *placards* was wide-spread and bloody persecution in which most of the sufferers came, as usual, from the lower orders of society. Though the trials stopped after a few months, the end had nevertheless come. 1534 marked the termination of Lutheran success in France and, despite the later Calvinist explosion, the end of any hope that the Reformation might conquer that country. As long as the crown controlled affairs—that is, to the death of Henry II in 1559—official policy was always strictly orthodox, even if active repression varied in severity. The happy dreams of moderate reform, in the spirit of Meaux or the queen of Navarre, vanished too. Here as elsewhere, the humanist dawn was succeeded by the grim day of Catholic repression and Calvinist subversion. From 1534, French Protestantism drew its inspiration from Geneva rather than Wittenberg.[5] Although it was not until 1540 that the Edict of Fontainebleau put an explicit end to all hope of better times for the Reformation, it was really the radicalism of the *placards* and the growing Calvinistic tinge of French reform which from the mid-thirties dictated the government's attitude. The king discovered that he could enjoy the advantages of a Lutheran alliance without having to tolerate religious dissenters at home; after all, the Lutheran princes on the whole needed him even more than he needed them.

However hostile Francis I and Charles V might be to each other, they thus came to share a common hostility to the Reformation. The emperor, however, could afford to be more singleminded about it from the first, nor did even the considerable number of Erasmians in his entourage and his civil service ever weaken his absolute orthodoxy. The history of the Lutheran movement in his Burgundian dominions was therefore one of instant and consistent persecution. His regents, Margaret and Mary, shared his fundamental opposition to reform; if they did not always agree with his relentless use of inquisitions, book-burnings and executions, that was because they feared unrest; and they could never do anything to ease the repression. By a curious accident, both Charles and the papal nuncio Aleander were at Brussels when the first papal Bull against Luther arrived in 1520; the result was that the Netherlands witnessed the first publication of the Bull and the first counterattack of orthodoxy. The theological faculty of the great University of Louvain, a conservative island in an otherwise humanistically inclined institution,[6] condemned Luther's teaching in 1519; even the Sorbonne did not get round to that until 1521. Thereafter the emperor issued one edict after another, reformed the enforcing agencies by adding general inquisitors to the episcopal instruments of enquiry and repression, and saw to the rooting out, often by the fire of the stake, of all heretics. An ingenious distinction between the crime of heresy (punishable only by the ecclesiastical authorities) and that of disobedience to imperial proclamations enabled him to employ secular judges and to disregard the liberties of people and Church in the self-imposed task of saving the people from perdition and the Church from dissolution.

The persecution achieved its object. Though Lutheranism had found many early followers in the Netherlands—among humanists, among clerics dissatisfied with the Church, among the spirituals left over from late-medieval movements like the *devotio moderna*, and especially in the cosmopolitan city of Antwerp with its large German population—it was by 1530 virtually stamped out. Only the growth of Anabaptism, stronger in the northern provinces than in the better controlled south, kept the authorities on the alert and the executioner's hand in; Anabaptists supplied far more martyrs than did Luther's true followers. One of the difficulties of the situation lies in the inquisitors' propensity to call all aspects of the reform "Lutheran", but it seems clear that in the 1530s the sects had taken over. By 1540 they in their turn had been quite effectively repressed in the south, and for a few years the persecution slackened. It was at this precise moment that Calvin established contact with the Low Countries: like nature, the Reformation, expelled with a pitchfork, promptly came back by another door.

In the south and west, therefore, the Lutheran Reformation never took hold, while its outbreak proved disastrous even to the older

movement for moderate reform which had drawn its inspiration from
Christian humanism and especially Erasmus. It was not particularly
successful even in England, despite Henry VIII's break with Rome in
the years 1532–4, though that event arrested the persecution of
Protestants carried out, under the guidance of the bishops and Sir
Thomas More, in the previous years. In the 1530s Lutheranism and
even more extreme ideas gained some foot-holds in England, occasionally linking up, among the ordinary people, with remnants of
Lollardy; but the leading English Lutheran, William Tyndale,
remained in exile in the Netherlands until in 1536 Charles V's persecution burned him, too, at the stake. Henry VIII's minister, Thomas
Cromwell, had some sympathy for reformed ideas and especially
favoured a political alliance with the Protestant princes; his archbishop, Thomas Cranmer, was on the move towards entirely
reformed views. Though there had been nothing in England remotely
like Meaux or Valdés' congregation, and though such Erasmians as
Thomas More and Bishop John Fisher remained strictly orthodox
(and suffered for it), the younger generation of humanists supported
the king's anti-papal policy and cautiously prepared for doctrinal
advance. However, these trends were arrested in the crisis of 1539–
40 when Cromwell lost his head and the Church of England accepted
the king's order to be entirely conservative in its religion. Some
attempts were made in the reign to reform manners, morals and
shortcomings, but practically none to reform worship or dogma,
beyond the denial of the pope's authority. England remained a country of the mass until Henry died (1547); the reform which came with
a rush thereafter looked to Zürich rather than to Luther.

It is thus very notable that the German Reformation did not
succeed at all in exploiting often favourable conditions in countries
where social discontent and spiritual dissatisfaction were quite as rife
as they had been in Germany, where Erasmus' influence had condi-
tioned the intelligentsia and many in the higher ranks of the Church
to question tradition and open their minds to the possibility of
reform, and where the Church and papacy enjoyed no more respect
or liking than they did in Luther's homeland. It is also clear enough
why this should have been so. Luther's trumpet was heard by all but
listened to most by the poor and powerless—by the craftsmen and
journeymen and peasants of France or Flanders, by the proletariate of
the Italian towns. And not only did this in itself incline their superiors
to disapprove of a reform movement which might involve social
upheaval, but it meant that ideas and ambitions more extreme than
Luther's easily superseded his influence among even those who at first
had seen a prophet in him. Anabaptists and other sectaries soon
predominated among the Italian dissentients; in Spain, the suspicion
was always rife that the new ideas only cloaked the old enemies of

Judaism and Islam; in France, sacramentarian tendencies showed early on, and Calvin's more drastic views quickly replaced a Lutheranism that might have been able to work with the crown. England, with the exception of a few individuals and still fewer small groups, was content to serve its king and wait upon the event. Though Erasmians were put equal to heretics by the stubborn conservatives who ruled the Suprema and the Sorbonne, they themselves not only quite properly denied the charge but tried to blunt it by abandoning reformist propaganda or at least by keeping a safe silence on the subject. Thus, despite initial successes, Lutheranism never achieved in these countries the necessary extent, power and passion to overcome difficulties; it remained the preserve of small and ultimately persecuted minorities. But when all is said and done, it remains surely obvious that the decisive reason for the failures of Lutheranism lay elsewhere. In Italy, Spain, France, the Netherlands, and for the time being in England, the Reformation failed to win the support of princes and magistrates. In part because it had such strong associations with the people and the spectre of revolution, in part because it had little to offer to monarchs already in control of the Church and its wealth, but above all because its teaching practically never attracted anyone in real authority, the Reformation was beaten back in the south and the west. The Word could not after all do it alone; policy and power determined where it should get a hearing.

III The North

In the north, the story was, for this very reason, quite different: here princes found the Reformation a necessary help in their ambitions, and here it therefore established itself. Naturally, Scandinavia, too, had its quota of religious leaders, men trained as a rule at humanist universities, influenced by Erasmus and the new biblical studies, and eager to reform the Church. Paulus Helie (?1485–1534) and Christian Pedersen (1480–1554) in Denmark, for instance, both started from the new learning, though the former, a Carmelite friar, shied away from the Reformation while the latter welcomed it. Sweden and Finland were in less close contact with European intellectual movements, but even here Laurentius Andreae (Lars Andersson, 1482–1552) and Peter Särkilaks represented the characteristic link between Christian humanism and the Reformation. Each country also produced active Lutheran reformers: the Dane Hans Taussen (1494–1561), a missionary preacher, the Swede Olavus Petri (Olaf Petersson, 1493–1552), the master-mind of the Reformation in his country, and the Finn Michael Agricola (1508–57) had all been to Wittenberg. Petri and Agricola reshaped the Churches of their respective countries by an unceasing and most impressive output of writings; Petri, especially, could produce anything from a liturgy to a dictionary or a chronicle. All these men were attacking a Church which suffered from the usual ills of aristocratic dominance and spiritual decay. In addition, it would seem that the Viking north had never become fully assimilated to Mediterranean Christianity, and it is certainly true that the distance from Rome—to the populace little more than fable—eased the break with the papacy and the old religion. Change was further encouraged by close links with Germany, especially through the towns of the Hanse. The Baltic basin represented something of an economic unit dominated by German merchant towns. To Denmark the Reformation spread from the reformed duchy of Schleswig-Holstein, while close relations with the secularised duchy of Prussia opened the way for German missionaries to enter Sweden. It does not look as though the Reformation captivated the peasantry from the start; such opposition as arose came from the remote parts of Scandinavia; the towns, with their advanced preachers and German merchants, provided such spontaneity as there was.

All this allowed for, it still remains true that not only the course but the very fact of the northern Reformation depended on the political situation—on the will of princes. Since the Union of Kalmar (1397) all Scandinavia was technically a single realm under the crown of Denmark. But though the Danish kings had succeeded in maintaining a fair measure of control over Norway and Iceland, they had long had to recognise that Sweden—whose particularist ambitions were supported by the Hanseatic League in its almost unceasing commercial struggle with Denmark—could only be administered through native deputies. This absence of any true territorial unity, together with the enormous size and the inaccessibility of the countries involved, frustrated all royal attempts at establishing an effective monarchy. Instead, Denmark, Norway and Sweden were really aristocratic republics sharing a weak figurehead in a common king, a situation much encouraged, once again, by the Hanse whose prosperity depended on keeping the Sound open. A strong crown straddling the narrows could strangle the Hanse, and throughout the fifteenth century the history of Scandinavia is one of noble faction kept on the boil by intrigues managed from Lübeck, Rostock and Hamburg, with open war (whose fortunes varied) punctuating the story. In the early sixteenth century, the balance of forces began to shift. Though the individual Hanse towns continued to do well, with Hamburg in the west and Danzig in the east rising to peaks of prosperity, the League had for some time been breaking up, a development assisted by the consolidation of territorial states in North Germany and the Netherlands. The very success of the League had led to its decline:

common action seemed less necessary as wealth and power increased, and also less possible as the expansion of the League extended its concerns far beyond the Baltic and introduced conflicting interests into the counsels of these trading cities.

At this juncture, as something of a power vacuum became visible in the Baltic, the throne of Denmark fell to a king eager to follow the example of contemporary monarchs and enlarge his authority. Christian II (1513–23) had some of the qualities necessary. He was a vigorous, ruthless, restless man, aware of the potential strength of the middle sort of men and the towns, and willing to use them and the peasantry in an attempt to break the nobility's power. Moreover, in 1515 he married Charles V's sister and thus gained Habsburg support for his policy, even though he treated his wife abominably. Unfortunately for himself, he combined with these supposed Renaissance virtues the more indisputable Renaissance vices, being thoroughly untrustworthy and treacherous. He allowed himself to be guided not only by a Dutch mistress (murdered in 1517) but, more remarkably, by her formidable mother, at one time keeper of a tavern in Bergen. With this set-up, which recalls bedroom farce rather than the sagas, he struggled to reduce the powers of the nobility and clergy by promoting the interests of burghers and peasants; he attacked noble privilege and vigorously interfered in the liberties of the Church, until he had succeeded in raising the opposition of the strong while earning some favour among the weak. His first check, however, came in Sweden. In 1520 he exploited a struggle in that country between the Danish and the native parties to impose his kingship, but spoiled his success by treacherously executing his defeated opponents. In the following year, the Swedes rose under the leadership of Gustavus Vasa, a leading nobleman and son of one of the victims of 1520. By 1523 the revolt was successful and Sweden had become an independent kingdom.

In the same year, Christian also reaped the reward of his policy in Denmark. An aristocratic rebellion drove him from the country and elected his uncle Frederick, duke of Schleswig-Holstein, to the throne. Exiled in the Netherlands, Christian II remained a disturbing factor in European politics. He tried everything to get back, at one time thinking to benefit from the increasing strength of the Reformation in Denmark by turning Lutheran, at another returning to Catholicism in order to get himself restored by Charles V. In 1531–2 he even managed to mount an unsuccessful invasion; but Lübeck, whose ruling oligarchy supported the Danish nobility, interfered to secure his defeat and imprisonment for the remaining twenty-eight years of his life. Meanwhile, the accession of Frederick I helped the cause of reform. Schleswig was Lutheran, and the pastors began to seize their chance. The king refused to comply with the Church's demands for repression, and by 1530 the Reformation had made such marked progress in the land that two Churches—one official, the other evangelical—virtually co-existed in Denmark. Monasteries were dissolved, lands secularised, Lutheran Church orders and Danish services established, in one province after another. Frederick would not come down firmly on the reformed side, but his insistence on tolerating propaganda and conversion sufficed.

The crisis came at his death in 1533. Though he had secured the acceptance of his son Christian as his successor, the bishops attempted to regain their power by opposing the succession. There ensued nearly three years of civil war, complicated by peasant risings, which reduced the kingdom to bankruptcy and near-collapse. When Christian III finally won in 1536, he therefore faced a ruined inheritance but also a Church widely hated for the part it had played in promoting the troubles. The king soon realised that he could cure the first by destroying the second. In 1536 he abolished episcopacy and confiscated the lands of the Church; in 1537 he called in Bugenhagen from Wittenberg to reorganise the Danish Church; in 1539 he published a Church Order which remained the basis of the Danish constitution. After all the years of piecemeal preparation and progress, the Reformation came in the end at one blow and by dictate from above. The Danish Church was the purest state-Church, its government and rule entirely vested in the crown acting through consistory courts and clerical administrators. In theology the Danish Reformation became increasingly Lutheran. It lost a little of its original simple faith in the bible and the people as such, and learned to accept both the doctrinal complications and the ecclesiastical pretensions of the sophisticated Lutheranism which developed in Germany in the 1530s and 1540s. The monarchy firmly imposed the same system and teaching on its dependent realms of Norway and Iceland, in the face of a mixture of violent opposition and surprised non-comprehension. The victory of the crown, which had broken the Church and tamed the nobility, stands out most clearly; the Danish Reformation redounded to the greater glory of the prince.

Much the same was true of Sweden, though there things happened rather differently, without the sort of drastic break which occurred in Denmark in 1536. Gustavus Vasa found that it was easier to be crowned than to rule. His revolt had been supported by the peasantry who neither would nor could pay any more taxes; the treasury was empty; a strong noble party, looking to the exiled archbishop of Uppsala, Gustavus Trolle, threatened his security. It was clear to the king that only the Church, as wealthy in Sweden as anywhere, could save him, and characteristically he determined to obtain their financial support by force. Secularisation of Church lands became the order of the day. This, as well as papal support for Trolle, involved a quarrel with Rome; and this in its turn suggested the advisability of encouraging the reformers. It must also be added, however, that as far as he had any serious religious opinions Gustavus I favoured the Lutheran Reformation. At any rate, he not only refused to arrest the growing influence of Lutheran teaching but promoted Olavus Petri and his brother Laurentius (Lars, 1499–1573) to places of command; the latter became in 1531 archbishop of Uppsala and with it the administrative guide of the Swedish Reformation, as his brother was its spiritual and devotional inspiration. Matters came to a head at the Diet of Västeras in 1527. Gustavus, a fine play-actor, threatened to resign unless the Church supplied his urgent financial needs, and the threat worked. The Church surrendered all such property as might be thought "superfluous", the definition of superfluity being left to the king; and while the bishops were still reeling, the Diet also enacted ordinances permitting the propagation of reformed teaching.

In effect, the Swedish Reformation dates from this occasion, though its actual consolidation took many years and much trouble, including trouble with the autocratic and unpredictable king. The Reformation was not at first popular; the destruction of monasteries and abolition of the old "superstitions" combined with resentment at heavy royal taxation to provoke frequent risings. Gustavus' temper was never of the easiest, and with age he grew increasingly suspicious. In 1539 even the Petri brothers fell foul of their protector, Olavus because he attacked immorality among the laity and Laurentius because he seemed to be trying to enlarge his episcopal control of the Church. But by then the Reformation was so firmly entrenched that the quarrel led only to a temporary change of agent, not to an ecclesiastical reaction. Disgusted with his archbishop, the king imported an eager German Lutheran, George Norman, and allowed him to batter the Swedish Church with vigorous and tactless visitations and confiscations. This helped to provoke the most serious rebellion of the reign which broke out in the south in 1542; Catholic reaction here exploited grievances caused by Gustavus' burdensome taxation and his interference with local trade. Before the king got the better of it in 1543, the revolt reached extremely dangerous dimensions, but he drew the right conclusions from it when he allowed Norman to disappear into the background and brought back the native Swedes with their more moderate methods of reform. Also, in 1544, he used another Diet at Västeras to complete the work: Sweden was now officially declared to be an evangelical kingdom, its established religion Lutheran. It was fitting and highly descriptive of the true causes of the Swedish Reformation that the same Diet should also have transformed the country's elective monarchy into a hereditary one vested in the house of Vasa. Vasa and Reformation came in together and triumphed together.

If Sweden's Reformation (which also, of course, covered the Swedish province of Finland) owed its origin and spread to the king's policy, it soon penetrated more deeply and so securely fixed itself in popular acceptance that later kings found themselves its prisoners; attempts, for instance, to promote a further Calvinist Reformation failed entirely. When Christian III died in 1559 and Gustavus I in the year after, the north was firmly Lutheran. Its Lutheranism differed in some respects from that of Wittenberg, but there was likeness in all essential matters. Even more than the German state-Churches, those of Denmark and Sweden were the product of monarchic action and encouragement, and in the large kingdoms of Scandinavia the victory of the laity was very markedly the victory of the lay ruler. The generation which witnessed Church reform also witnessed the destruction of noble faction and the creation of strong monarchies.

IV   The East

In the still larger kingdoms of the east, on the other hand, neither Reformation nor monarchy did so well. In the early sixteenth century the vast area between the Oder in the west and the Dnieper in the east, the Baltic in the north and the lower Danube in the south, was nearly filled by the three monarchies of Poland, Bohemia and Hungary. Each of these realms was, in fact, a dynastic union of several parts. The kingdom of Croatia enjoyed a separate existence from the crown of St. Stephen to which it was subject. The Bohemian crown of St. Wenceslas also ruled Moravia, Lusatia and several small Silesian territories. Poland and Lithuania had become linked by personal union, so that the Polish kings governed, as grand-dukes of Lithuania (sometimes the thrones were in different hands), all the Ukraine as well. These three realms represented, in more than geography, the eastern limits and bulwarks of Europe. Though the Ukraine and the Ruthenian parts of Hungary looked in the main to the Greek Orthodox Church—that is, since the fall of Constantinople in 1453, to Moscow—the people of Poland and Hungary proper had for a long time been proud of their loyalty to Rome; and even Bohemia, though largely Hussite, regarded itself as firmly belonging to the universal Church of the west. The Slavs and Magyars of these regions, much intermingled with Germans (traders as well as settlers left behind by the various medieval attempts to "colonise" the east), had every cause to regard themselves as attached to their western rather than their eastern neighbours, outposts of an identifiable European civilization. Poland-Lithuania, in particular, acted as the exponent and protector of Renaissance ideas in their easternmost penetration. The Universities of Cracow and Prague had long enjoyed a European reputation, and the Churches of all three countries had been prominent at the great General Councils of the fifteenth century.

The region was not, therefore, on the fringe though it sat at the edge: it was essentially in Europe. Yet it must be noted that the period with which we are concerned witnessed serious political threats to the traditions and positions of the eastern kingdoms. They were, in fact, being pushed back from further east still. Hungary, for so long no more than a settled kingdom in the middle of a settled area, suddenly found itself turned by Turkish invasions and partial conquest into a characteristically frontier country: the border between Europe and Asia, which had for a century been moving up the Balkans, was in the 1530s and 1540s fixed to run right through the ancient dominions of St. Stephen. The Turks were also pushing back the southern extremities of Lithuania; extending their protection to the Tatars of the Crimea, they had by 1500 laid hold of the southern Ukraine. In addition, Poland-Lithuania experienced the first effects of the newly consolidated threat from the Russian tsars, based on Moscow. Ivan III (1462–1505), who had recreated a Great Russian realm by adding such territories as Novgorod to his possessions and by ending the power of the Kazan Tatars (last echoes of the Golden Horde) on the Volga, also began the attack on the Lithuanian domination of the Ukraine which included the anciently Russian kingdom of Kiev. His successful assault came to a culmination, for the time being, when his successor Vasily III conquered Smolensk.[7] Poland was being squeezed by alliances between Moscow and the Habsburgs, though after 1515 the Emperor Maximilian was forced to abandon such vast dreams; instead he contented himself, in that year, with a treaty which insinuated his dynasty into a new area. He employed the usual Habsburg expedient of marriage alliances: his daughter Mary married Lewis of Hungary and Bohemia whose sister was conveyed to the emperor's younger grandson Ferdinand. Though Poland was still preoccupied with ancient conflicts in the Baltic region, and Hungary still too much concerned with its internal political struggles, the menace from Russia and Turkey was building up. In due course, the success of these essentially extra-European powers was to turn the truly European eastern kingdoms into frontier outposts.

In any case, though Poland, Bohemia and Hungary had such strong ties with the European political system and the civilisation of Europe, they also differed quite markedly from their western neighbours. Power rested in the hands of the great aristocracy and of the large body of lesser nobility or gentry—landowners whose wealth might vary a great deal but who all enjoyed political independence and influence. This ascendancy of the landed nobility arose from the economic facts of the situation. The great eastern plains—

and this goes also for the plains of Bohemia and Moravia, though these were less extensive, hung about and cut through by mountain ranges—were the best arable land in Europe. They offered splendid openings for the commercial production of grain, with cattle and (especially in Hungary) pigs as a side-line, but for little else. The growing populations of the west provided, by the early sixteenth century, an expanded market for eastern corn. However, the plains could be successfully exploited only by large-scale farming, which required an extensive range of possessions and the backing of capital, or failing capital, the equivalent in rights to peasant labour. Thus the only people able to take advantage of the chance were, naturally, the greater landowners. The economic backwardness of the east could be turned to profit only by continuing it—by the creation of vast landed estates given over to agriculture for the market, farmed by the services of what had hitherto been a free peasantry, and for the benefit of the possessing classes.

Throughout the east the nobility were at this time engaged in imposing new burdens on their peasants in order to make the most of their lands. Personal liberty gave way to serfdom; peasant farming to estate farming; and estate farming on that scale created effectively independent domains in the hands of the great owners. A weak monarchy conceded rights of rule. Economic power and aristocratic traditions enabled the nobility to secure not only lordship over serfs but also jurisdictional (that is, political) control in their lands. Only in Bohemia and, up to a point, Transylvania were there any towns with sufficient industry and trade to produce a sector of the population not exclusively concerned with the relationships arising from landownership and tillage; and Transylvania was soon to be lost to the Turks. Indeed, the new dangers from the east helped the nobility; apart from being economically preponderant, they were now also indispensable as the only source of military defence. In Hungary, in particular, the Turkish invasions soon created marcher lordships along the new frontier, with all the usual phenomena of decentralisation, localised government, and private armies.

The political weapon of the nobility was the Diet, the assembly of estates, or rather the great variety of such assemblies which made them instruments of fragmentation rather than unity. The general European development of such deliberative bodies had in the fifteenth century proliferated in the east. The provincial Diets of all three kingdoms gravely weakened the ability of their general Parliaments to make effective provision for the whole realm, and all the estates, provincial or central, were no more than representatives of the landed interest, though disagreement between the greater aristocracy and the middling gentry could provide an occasional touch of conflict. Bohemia alone had an estate of burgesses, reflecting the existence and relative prominence of trading towns in that kingdom, but even here the two estates of the nobility and gentry carried the bulk of influence. This mass of assemblies may be interpreted as a sign of political liberty; their history certainly prevents one from seeing in them a sign of political maturity. The spokesmen of the nobility, admittedly, could regard these constitutions with pride, and a Polish writer in 1549 claimed that in his country alone liberty survived because here alone "popular" assemblies retained free power. It is also, of course, true that the existence and organisation of these Diets very accurately represented the true balance of power in societies so exclusively dominated by a landed aristocracy. Unfortunately it also demonstrated the inability of such societies to adapt themselves to changing circumstances or to resist external danger. If the nobility in their Diets really ruled the country, they did so by keeping monarchy weak and by preventing centralised government from bringing order and efficiency to the system.

Monarchy was weak, above all, because it was elective. The Jagiellons, a Lithuanian dynasty who had ascended the throne of Poland in 1386, and whose cadet branch now ruled Bohemia and Hungary as well, had not proved very effective in resisting the increasing independence of the nobles. Indeed, the native lords who had tried to enlarge monarchic power in the later fifteenth century— George of Poděbrad (1458–71) in Bohemia, Matthias Corvinus (1458–90) in Hungary—had, despite their military prowess, sufficiently annoyed their brethren by their political vigour, so that when the chance offered the Diets preferred to elect a notoriously weak Jagiellon offspring rather than risk any more popular heroes with military reputations. Ladislas I, king of Bohemia from 1471 and of Hungary from 1490, was content to reign without doing any ruling, and before he died in 1516 he had given noble ambition full freedom to do as it pleased. In those decades all the characteristic features of the area reached perfection: the increasing subjection of the peasantry, the economic decline of the towns, the extensive concentration of all power in noble hands.

As things turned out, aristocratic oligarchy—not so much government by Diet as obstruction, through the Diets, of all government— had overreached itself; the threats from abroad frightened even these selfish defenders of "liberty", and Ladislas' successors proved to be of rather sterner metal. Sigismund I (1506–48) showed that even in Poland there was room for a monarchy which took itself seriously, though in the end he failed in his attempts to reduce the nobility to order. All he could secure was that they would agree to accept his son's succession; they did not surrender the essential principle of election, and Poland was to sink deeper into anarchy as time went on. It remained a distracted kingdom, the landed classes becoming only more determined not to allow such another as Sigismund to threaten their constitutional privileges.

In Bohemia and Hungary, developments went the other way, in part because of the Turks, but in great part because here the feeble Jagiellons were succeeded, after Lewis II's death at Mohács in 1526, by a patient, long-headed, determined Habsburg. Ferdinand I could not do very much to reorganise the crown of St. Stephen because he was in the main engaged in clinging to it by his finger-tips. At first disputing the realm with John Zapolyai, and frequently involved in war with the Turks who after 1541 stayed permanently in Hungary, he had in the end (1562) to accept a settlement which divided the country into three: Austrian Hungary in the north and west, Turkish Hungary covering the bulk of the old kingdom, and the Turkish protectorate of Transylvania in the east. He was elected in 1526, by a minority of Hungarian lords, only on condition that he recognised his title to be purely elective and promised to keep all the customs of the realm, that is, to do nothing to promote monarchic control over aristocratic self-interest. As the years passed, as Zapolyai died (1540), and as it became apparent that Hungary would continue to suffer from the Turks, Ferdinand established something more of an ascendancy over his subjects, and before he died (1564) he had extracted the concession from the Diet that the crown should henceforth be vested in his dynasty. Though he saw his son crowned his successor in his lifetime, he had not quite succeeded in eliminating the elective principle.

This he did achieve in Bohemia. There, after a good deal of constitutional conflict with the nobility, he got his chance in 1547 when the Bohemians were so ill-advised as to make common cause with the Protestant princes of Germany. The defeat of the Germans by the emperor[8] left the Bohemians at the mercy of their king. With much skill, Ferdinand attacked only the towns, destroying their independence and privileges; the nobility were pardoned, but only after acknowledging that in future the crown of St. Wenceslas was to be hereditary. In Bohemia, too, Ferdinand used the national assembly to reduce the separatism of the various territories. An attempt to create a general Diet for all his dominions failed, while he made only little progress with the even more significant endeavour to concentrate the government of all the eastern Habsburg lands at Vienna. Centralisation and monarchic absolutism were still a long way off, though the patient work of Ferdinand I prepared the ground for a future in which the crown was to rule with the assistance rather than against the opposition of a subdued nobility, a future marked by German overlordship rather than Slav and Magyar traditions.

In these countries, therefore, the Reformation encountered yet another set of political and economic circumstances. Its impact owed something to both foreign importation and native readiness to receive. Ancient traditions of allegiance to Rome did not prevent both Poland and Hungary from being as dissatisfied with the Church as other countries in the papal obedience. The Hungarian Church, in fact, was effectively dead, controlled and staffed by king and nobles with virtually no spiritual life left in it at all. In Poland-Lithuania, the pressure of a strong body of Greek Orthodox Christians had in a way kept the Church more in being, especially as the attempts to convert Lithuania to Rome had hitherto been unsuccessful; but here, too, aristocratic dominance of the hierarchy was enough to reduce the appeal of the Catholic Church to the people at large. In addition, Cracow provided a centre of Erasmian humanism of the kind familiar enough further west but exceptional in these parts. In Bohemia, on the other hand, all the traditions were against Rome; here the Hussite Church, enjoying the support of nobility and people alike, formed the only area within the res publica Christiana as defined by the pope which had secured separatist independence. It is true that the Hussite extremists had been defeated by more moderate men, and that Prague and Rome had come to an arrangement which preserved the appearance of papal suzerainty behind which the reality of the schism was allowed to persist. The Czechs of 1520 were not the Taborites of 1420. Nevertheless, here if anywhere Lutheran ideas might expect to meet a sympathetic reception from people who already practised and believed some of the heterodoxies promoted by Wittenberg. This was the more likely because by the side of the official and moderate Hussite Church of Bohemia there existed the radical—peacefully radical—group known as the Unitas Fratrum or Bohemian Brethren, a Church resting on democratic and scriptural foundations which had much in common with the sectarianism that spread in the wake of Luther's Reformation.

On the other hand, Bohemia could offer an exceptionally nationalist resistance to the Reformation. Not only could the Czechs claim (as they did) that they who had had Hus needed no Luther; the fact that the Reformation came from Germany and in the mouths of Germans did not help it at all in a country which had been fighting German aggression for a century or more. There were Germans in Bohemia, especially among the townspeople, but they were the only bulwark of full Catholicism in the country and therefore less likely than anyone to welcome Luther (though some of them did). In this respect the other two kingdoms fared very differently; here German influence greatly favoured the Reformation. Its first penetration into Poland came from the Livonian regions where the towns (Riga, Reval, etc.) had been rapidly and violently reformed, with a great deal of image-breaking and destructive attacks on monasteries, in 1523–5. The leader of the Reformation here, Andreas Knopken, was a German from Pomerania, the townspeople who forced the Reformation on reluctant city councils were Germans, and so was Albrecht of Hohenzollern who in 1525 took neighbouring Prussia over to the reformed side.[9] Thus German merchants and preachers brought the Reformation to Poland from the north, and for the time being that was about all there was to it. Lutheranism made very little impression on either the peasantry or the nobility of Poland; it remained the preserve of a few individuals, many of them German immigrants.

In Hungary, the German influence was as notable, especially among the so-called Saxons of Transylvania, descendants of German immigrants who formed a curious enclave in the world of Slavs and Magyars. Zapolyai's Transylvania was predominantly Lutheran. Trading connections helped, but so did the growth of a native Lutheranism. The new religion made remarkable progress among the Magyar magnates and the lesser nobility, especially after Mohács and the destruction, in that battle, of nearly all the Hungarian episcopate; and the magnates protected and encouraged Hungarian preachers—notably Matthew Bíró—who pursued a fruitful ministry in the somewhat apocalyptic atmosphere created by the Turkish triumph. Ferdinand did nothing to arrest the growth of Lutheranism in Hungary; he could not afford to antagonise those of the nobility who were prepared to support him. Nor was he much more active in Bohemia where it became ever more difficult to know whether what was going on was the Lutheranism denounced by the papacy or the Hussite Utraquism with which it had come to terms. As time went on, the Utraquist nobility in particular began to look remarkably like Lutherans, while the popular Brethren became hard to distinguish from Moravian Hutterites. The king urged the Diets to protect uniformity and Catholicism, but without much success.

In short, in its first age the Reformation made some progress in the east but never developed anywhere there into a true movement. It came nearest to it in war-torn Hungary where Lutheran services and practices for a time almost drove out Catholic traditions. In Poland, it did little more than prepare the ground for the more serious impact of Calvinism. And in Bohemia it added to the general air of heterodoxy which had characterised that country since the early fifteenth century. There was little persecution; such as there was resulted from temporary fears that the reformed preachers were advocating social revolution—fears which in the two southern kingdoms naturally did not survive the widespread conversion of the upper classes. Both Sigismund and Ferdinand were good Catholics who did not like the Reformation, but neither was sufficiently strong to take consistent action. In 1526 Sigismund interfered when the Reformation in Danzig threatened to overthrow ordered government there, and for a short time he tried to enforce edicts against heretics; but the Lutherans enjoyed some protection from Prussia, from Erasmian Cracow, and also from the queen, Bona Sforza. Ferdinand sensibly put the preservation of some measure of political unity and the enlarging of monarchic influence before a bigoted enforcement of heresy laws, but in the circumstances that meant leaving the Reformation alone. Aristocratic constitutions, royal weakness, war against foreign foes protected the steady but private and unaggressive progress of reformed ideas. In the east, as in France, the crisis came later, when a more stringent Protestantism and a reformed Church of Rome came to the grip of death. Here, where there were no powerful princes either to impose or destroy the Reformation, it neither took hold nor departed. It lingered, among individuals and little groups. In this way, the eastern kingdoms underlined negatively what elsewhere had been demonstrated positively. The progress and spread of reformed Churches might originate with intellectual and spiritual doubts and aspirations; it might involve and be assisted by stresses in society and economic difficulties; it might be fertilised by direct missionary activity from the German fountain-head; but for its ultimate fate it depended in the last resort on one thing only—the secular politics of principalities and powers.

Chapter 6

The Formation of Parties

1 The Emergence of Protestantism

In 1529, Germany awaited the arrival of its emperor. Since he had departed from it eight years before, he had changed both in himself and in his circumstances. In the place of the uncertain and untried young man, a dim figure by the side of the splendid kings of France and England, whose Spanish subjects were in revolt while his credit stood pledged to the merchant princes of Augsburg, there now approached a warrior-king victorious over his only possible rival, conqueror of Italy and protector of the pope, the assured ruler of Castile and its unimaginable, expanding dominions, the emperor of the West. Charles pointed the contrast by having himself crowned by Clement VII at Bologna (1530), before crossing the Alps to Augsburg to deal—as it was generally supposed he intended—with those troublesome heretics in his German lands. And if the emperor seemed to stand on a pinnacle of power, the Protestants were markedly ill-prepared to face him. The Marburg Colloquy had not only confirmed instead of dissipating the differences between Lutherans and Zwinglians; it had also led to a formulation of doctrine in the Schwabach Articles of 1529 which sharpened disagreement by defining the points at issue. Throughout 1529, Philip of Hesse tried in vain to create a solid front for the forthcoming crisis. All his efforts, assisted by the shrewd and active leader of Strassburg, Jacob Sturm, to bring together the Saxons, the South Germans, the Swiss, and the greater enemies of Habsburg abroad (Francis I, John Zapolyai), broke down over the theological differences on the one hand, and on the other over the conservative reluctance of Saxony and Nuremberg to contemplate political action against the emperor. By 1530 Luther himself had ceased to hope for anything from Charles V, but in political matters Luther, despite his conviction that he did not understand them, was usually more clear-sighted than the professionals blinded by their belief in the possibility of endless negotiation, or the lawyers tied by their formalism. The city of Nuremberg in particular had throughout the 1520s sought imperial endorsement of the Reformation, a hopeless and quite mistaken policy which nevertheless testifies to the honourable reluctance of such men to destroy for destruction's sake.

In this situation Charles might well expect to succeed in his own policy of reunion by a little pressure: despite the Protestation of Speyer, the schism did not as yet seem all that irreparable. Charles's error lay in underestimating the religious conviction behind the revolt. Like many since, he supposed that political or economic ambitions—particularism and the confiscation of Church lands—were more prominent in the actions of the dissident princes than issues of faith. He soon discovered that this was too simple a view. At the Diet of Augsburg the Protestant princes attended Lutheran sermons, a practice which scandalised the emperor who demanded that it should cease. "Sir," said the old margrave of Brandenburg-Ansbach, "rather than that I would leave off the Word of God, I will kneel here on the spot and lose my head." Badly taken aback by this unsophisticated statement of principle at a time when diplomacy demanded words of peace, Charles could only stammer, in his broken German: "My dear lord, no heads off."

However, if the Lutherans were determined to save the gospel, they also had no policy. The Catholic princes, led by that pair of dark and equivocal self-seekers, the two joint dukes of Bavaria, were in little better case. The Wittelsbachs of Bavaria found small difficulty in preferring their traditional opposition to the Habsburgs to their traditional belief in the old religion. They would welcome an end to the schism but not if it involved increasing the power of an emperor who had achieved so many triumphs elsewhere that he looked capable of making a reality of the imperial position in Germany. The only man who had a genuine policy to put forward was, in fact, Charles himself. He came to Augsburg with three aims in mind. He wanted to secure the election by the Estates of his brother Ferdinand as king of the Romans, the title given to the prospective emperor elect. He wished to obtain unity by the suppression of the schism. And he sought German aid against the Turks. Indeed—though Ferdinand's election was also a necessary part of the Habsburg dynastic programme—the first two aims were really preconditions of the last and real aim. In 1530, the problem of Islam, complicated by the Habsburg claim to Hungary, overshadowed even the problem of the Lutherans. To Charles, and to others, the Turkish danger appeared the foremost issue of the day, and he needed united support from Germany if he was to deal with it. Therefore he preferred to bring the Lutherans back to the fold by peaceful means and wished to see the united will of the Holy Roman Empire expressed in unanimous support for Ferdinand and a free offer of ample assistance, in men and money, from the Diet. Throughout the negotiations, while the Lutherans thought of the gospel and the Catholic princes of Habsburg power, the emperor thought rather more urgently of the sultan.

Before looking at the events of Augsburg it will therefore be advisable to enquire both why the Turkish threat should at this time have seemed so immediate and whether it was as real as was so widely supposed. It appeared immediate because the events of the 1520s had removed the old buffer between Europe and Asia, the kingdom of Hungary which in the fifteenth century had held off the infidel almost single-handed. Though in 1529 the sultan had retreated from Vienna, there was nothing to stop him returning. And the fear of the Turks was based not only on their undoubted successes but also on an understanding of their remarkable organisation to which many sound observers of the century paid respectful tribute.

The Ottoman Turks did not attempt to displace or foot out the peoples they conquered; they formed a ruling layer of feudal land-owners imposed on subject races. The only real distinction between the two lay in religion, and converts to Islam could easily move into the governing sort. Indeed, there is no evidence that Turkish rule was at this time resented by the Slavs and Greeks of Anatolia and the Balkans; in many respects it was an improvement on what had gone before. The very peculiar organisation of the Ottoman empire offered exceptional prospects precisely to the subject peoples. The feudal levies of Turkish horsemen—the regular sipahi and the irregular akinji—contributed to the army, and an organisation of departments (sanjaks) grouped in the two provinces of Rumelia (Europe) and Anatolia, ruled by governors called beglerbegs, provided some structure in the empire. But the real government and military force lay elsewhere, in the vast slave household (kullar) of the sultan which included not only his domestic establishment and harem, but also the civil administration from the grand vizier downwards and the standing army of janissaries (infantry) and sipahi of the Porte (cavalry). This unique institution, some 80,000 strong, was entirely recruited from non-Turks by means of a levy of Christian children collected at intervals and brought up within the kullar to either civil or military employment. Every member of it was a true slave, a chattel of the sultan's. The most powerful ministers and commanders, lording it over all the people whether Turk or Christian, had no life except what the ruler allowed them. This intensive and coherent élite centring upon the sultan gave the Turkish empire great political vigour, especially in war. Inferior to the best western armies in equipment, the Turkish army, and especially the janissaries, won victories by dint of their devoted professionalism. Though prohibited from marrying and compelled to live in barracks, they enjoyed much honour and many privileges, and their organisation as a true standing army gave to the Ottoman empire a permanent and most formidable striking force.

Even in an age of personal monarchy, such a system naturally depended quite exceptionally on the qualities of the one man who controlled it, and the fortunes of the empire fluctuated predictably with the personality of the sultan. Sulaiman the Magnificent represented the race of Osman at its characteristic peak. The tall, slender figure of the sultan, with his hawk-nose and flashing eye, his stern sense of justice but frequent mercy and generosity, emerges vividly from the reports of Venetian envoys, men who were cynics by profession and rarely allowed themselves to be impressed. Sulaiman was, of course, manifestly a warrior; despite the help of some remarkable grand viziers, he really had to be present in person at the scene of action if success was to be assured and the troops were to fight loyally, a fact which limited the expansive potential of an empire fighting on three fronts. But in the Ottoman tradition he is even better remembered as a law-giver, as the organiser of a realm so suddenly enlarged by his father Selim. The sultan was a despot in this, too: his word was law. Yet whereas in the field of government or war he had no rival, in that of law he was compelled to heed the advice of the only institution not comprehended within the kullar. This was the ulema or Muslim Institution, a cross between a Church, a University and a supreme court, staffed by the muftis (legal advisers to imperial officials at all levels) and kazis (judges). The ulema were the guardians of the Koran, with respect to both theology and law; they could adjudge all edicts as correct or false by the prophet's Book. The mufti of Constantinople (sheik-ul-islam) acted as adviser to the sultan; though he spoke only if consulted, consultation was customary, and once he had spoken there was no appeal from his verdict. Thus in the making of law, the sultan was subject to a powerful and conservatively inclined restraint which often operated to minimise the ill effects of despotic wilfulness.

Nevertheless, the Ottoman ruler exercised more untrammelled power than any king in Europe had ever known, and European statesmen, while fearing the consequences, can also be found expressing envy of such autocratic possibilities. This personal despotism, however, could easily collapse in sloth, incompetence, or madness, as it was to do after Sulaiman's death. Even the great sultan demonstrated in his last years, when under the influence of his chief wife Khurrem (or Roxolana) he executed his ablest son Mustafa, how easily a system could be perverted which rested on one man's will and shoulders. But through most of his reign he proved the advantages of a purposeful and competent despotism.

He was greatly helped by an income enviable in its size and independence, for he could tax without seeking consent and in so large and populous a realm could tax without imposing undue burdens. The wealth of the country lay in its raw materials and its trade; there were no manufacturers, and even textiles were practically all imported, mainly by Venice. The sultan therefore protected and promoted trade. Untroubled by nationalist or racialist prejudice, he welcomed foreigners into his service, paid them well, and encouraged contact with those who would buy the empire's produce (in the main grain) and supply the necessities and luxuries which a purely peasant economy could not provide. Despite a characteristic distrust of foreign diplomats, who were thought to be spies, this need for trade therefore opened up the Turkish empire to visitors and observers from abroad. To the long-established Venetians, the French were added in 1536, by an agreement very like a trade treaty. So far from destroying the trade of the Levant, as used once to be thought, the Turks even involved themselves in a trade war with the Portuguese in the Red Sea (1551-2), in an attempt to redirect the flow of spices through the Middle East; but despite great efforts to maintain a fleet and naval bases in the Yemen and the Persian Gulf, this proved on the whole a failure. The Turks had no maritime traditions and no navy to compare with their remarkable army, and when they became a Mediterranean power they found it necessary to employ the corsairs of North Africa, acquiring a fleet at the cost of permitting depredations on the trade on which they so much depended.

This highly organised and highly dynamic power naturally looked like a constantly looming threat to the only power that seemed capable of resisting it. But whether Charles V, and his age, were right in thinking the Turks such a menace is not clear. In Europe it was, of course, taken for granted that the main Turkish thrust was north-westwards. In this they were mistaken. In 1530 the sultan had held Egypt for only thirteen years, and though the power of the Mamluks was broken the conquest of that rich and vital part of the empire still needed consolidating. Egypt also led the Turks along the North African littoral, while the threatening presence of Persia, dominated by a schismatic heresy, concentrated attention on the eastern borders. From his point of view, Sulaiman in turn regarded the Habsburg power in central Europe as a threat to his northern frontier which he naturally wanted to secure by holding Hungary, Moldavia and Wallachia. But it is significant that for fifteen years after Mohács he avoided direct occupation of Hungary, and that his campaigns in Europe always looked much more like giant raids than like wars of conquest of the sort which had established

Turkish power in the Balkans in the preceding 150 years. The more recent expansion into Syria and Egypt had tilted his empire towards Asia and Africa; so far as Europe was concerned, the real clash was to be with Spain in the Mediterranean, not with Austria on the plains of Hungary. Yet while we may now recognise this truth, we must also understand that it could hardly appear thus to Charles V. When the banners of Islam waved round the ramshackle ramparts of Vienna, when the decimated nobility of Hungary followed a feeble Turkish client, and when the whole of Christendom seemed mortally threatened by this revival of aggressive Mohammedanism, the emperor of the West was bound to put the defeat of Turkey in Europe at the head of his long list of preoccupations.

Thus Charles went to Augsburg in 1530 with the intention of securing unity and preparing a force against the sultan. Germany was to be made to see the danger and offer help against it. The Lutherans had, rather tactlessly, thought to prepare the ground by sending the Schwabach Articles, to show where they stood, but Charles waved these aside and began proceedings at the Diet by demanding a new statement of the Protestant position from the dissident Estates, so that the debate, which was to lead to reconciliation, could begin. The result of this was the famous Confession of Augsburg, a document so manifestly designed to facilitate peace that it frightened the men of conviction. It was the work, in the main, of Melanchthon who led the Lutheran theologians at Augsburg; Luther himself, still an outlaw and therefore unable to attend, fretted in his impatience at the castle of the Coburg, the nearest he could approach, because he thought that Master Philip was selling the gospel down the river. He warned the negotiators that the Catholics "will accept our concessions largely, more largely still, and most largely of all, but make their own narrow and very narrow"; but he need not have worried. The Confession omitted such controversial topics as purgatory and transubstantiation, and though it stressed justification by faith it said nothing of the priesthood of all believers; but, pacific as it was, it could not succeed while the problem of the papal supremacy remained to divide the sides. As Luther told Melanchthon: "Agreement on doctrine is plainly impossible, unless the pope will abolish his popedom." The papal representative, Cardinal Campeggio, worked hard to prevent the emperor from coming to terms with the Lutherans, and French diplomacy, operating through the Bavarian interest, assisted him. The emperor, who saw some hope in the mildness of the Confession, instructed the Catholic theologians to produce a reply (*Confutatio*), and this document attacked points of difference rather than sought points of agreement. The Catholics were naturally even less enamoured of the alternative Tetrapolitan Confession, prepared by Bucer and subscribed to by four south

German cities; this contained touches of Zwinglianism. The peace moves had failed; Charles regretted his tentative concessions; in September, as the Catholic majority prepared for a savagely anti-Lutheran decision, the Protestants withdrew from the Diet. In November 1530, the Catholic remnant passed a recess which confirmed the Edict of Worms, reorganised the supreme court (Imperial Chamber) so as to be more effective against secularisers of Church lands, and demanded that the Protestants should return to the Church by April 1531. In January they gratified Charles by electing Ferdinand king of the Romans.

The Diet of Augsburg had been called to bring peace; instead it proclaimed the need for separatist defence and protection. The extremer elements had been proved right: Strassburg and Hesse, with their warnings against the emperor's intentions, had clearly understood the situation better than Saxony and Nuremberg with their trust that he would prove a good lord to them. Luther had been right—and Melanchthon wrong—in thinking that Rome would accept no compromise. The Protestants remained unrecognised and virtually outlawed; and now they were to be further threatened by process out of the Imperial Chamber over the lands taken from the Church, and by military action if they did not surrender within a few months. On the other hand, the emperor had also failed of his major purposes. Some of the more important princes had not yet recognised Ferdinand's claim to the imperial succession, and Charles had got very little more than partial promises of aid against the Turks—no substance. In part he had been thwarted by the pope whom he had thought safely tucked away in his pocket, even though his own rigid orthodoxy had also in the end forced him to retreat from accommodation with any part of the Lutheran position. Enough voices were encouraging him to enforce the Edict of Worms by military action, but he knew better that as things stood, with the Turk rumbling, Zapolyai in the ascendant and France intriguing, he had no chance of the rapid success which would be needed.

In particular, the Catholic princes of Germany, willing enough to denounce their Lutheran brethren, were entirely unwilling to assist the emperor in turning denunciation into suppression. The years 1530–2 witnessed a series of obscure manœuvres, directed by France and involving a Polish agent of Zapolyai's, Jerome Laski, which tried to create an anti-imperial alliance and in the process to protect the Protestants.[1] In 1533 Clement VII even managed to drift towards Francis I in an endeavour to escape from Charles's domination. One way and another, the situation was so complex—so perverted by cross-currents of interest—that the brave words of the Augsburg recess had little meaning. Still determined to secure general adherence to Ferdinand's election, still aware of the Turkish danger, still unable to free himself for decisive action against any of his widely assorted opponents, the emperor seemed to have lost the power of decision. In truth, however, he was being sensible, not weak. Since he could not conquer, he determined, with that incredible and patient tenacity which was his chief characteristic, to resume the policy of reunion along a new tack. The imperial Diet had failed; there remained the General Council of the Church.

The idea of calling such a Council was not, of course, new in 1531, but it was to be a major issue in European affairs throughout the 1530's and after. When the ordinary authorities of the Church, especially the pope, had failed in the face of abuses or disunity, a general assembly of this sort had always been the only way out. In the early fifteenth century, a powerful movement in the Church had nearly succeeded in establishing conciliar constitutionalism in place of the papal monarchy, but its impetus soon failed and by about 1460 the popes had restored their grip. Thereafter they remained inexorably opposed to any Council which might in any way trench upon their authority, in particular to any called by someone other than themselves. Yet while Rome remembered the conciliar ideas and practices with horror, others with equally good memories recalled them with hope. From the first days after Worms, when it had become apparent that Luther could not be simply destroyed, the notion of using a General Council to restore unity had been repeatedly and wistfully urged. The 1523 Diet of Nuremberg made the demand for one the essence of the German Catholics' position, while that of 1524 asked for a national Council for Germany alone. This last idea Charles had rejected with vigour, but at the same time, under the inspiration of Gattinara, he began to think of the Council as a solution for the Church's troubles. In 1526 he first pressed the idea upon Clement VII, and from 1529, when he again had time to turn to the problem of Protestantism, he made the Council a main plank in his programme. Gattinara regarded the Council as a political move and was prepared to encourage Charles to call one himself, ignoring the pope, but this the emperor himself never favoured. He always wanted a universal Council called by the pope, omnicompetent to reform the Church and restore concord; nothing short of this either suited his concept of the *res publica Christiana* or would assure general acceptance. Unfortunately his aim implied a common purpose between emperor and pope which simply did not exist. Since Clement had no intention at all of risking a revival of constitutional ideas in the Church, or of permitting the reform of abuses by such a body, it was futile for Charles to demand a Council from him; but since Clement was weak he could only procrastinate, lament, avoid action, all of which he did with competence and success. However, Charles was not a man to be put off by delay; from 1531 the calling of a General Council became the cornerstone of his policy towards the Church, and he pursued his purpose inflexibly through all the difficulties raised by Rome, and through the refusals successively of Henry VIII and Francis I to permit a meeting which could only result in advantage to the emperor.

The problem of the Council was further complicated by the newly defined vigour of Protestant organisation which resulted from the Augsburg debacle. The threat that force would be used to bring them back to their allegiance finally persuaded even the Saxon elector and his council that they must prepare for defence, and late in 1530 they began to negotiate with Hesse and other like-minded territories for a mutual alliance. In February 1531 this emerged as the League of Schmalkalden, named after a town on the borders of Hesse and Saxony where the foundation and later meetings were usually held. Eight princes of the empire and eleven cities (including not only Magdeburg, Bremen and Lübeck, but thanks to Bucer's conciliatory activities also Strassburg and others from the more Zwinglian south) agreed to assist one another if any of them should be attacked "on account of the Word of God and the doctrine of the Gospel". Though the first effect was not large—Charles's inability to enforce the Augsburg recess suspended the immediate cause of the alliance—the implications were enormous. For the first time a section of the Holy Roman Empire, affirming the right of a minority to follow its own will, had declared open resistance to emperor and Diets. The League effectively demonstrated the end of German unity, the end of Charles's hopes, the end of policies which had used the imperial Diet as an instrument of national government. Deprived of positive means of power, the emperor had to suffer its existence.

Worse still, he had to come to terms with it. By early 1532 it was plain that Sulaiman was once more moving up-Danube in order to resume the business abandoned outside Vienna in 1529 and also to punish Ferdinand for a somewhat foolhardy excursion against Zapolyai in the previous autumn. Charles needed immediate help, but in April the Diet of Regensburg, attended only by the Catholics, refused to admit the reality of the threat. Charles therefore had to turn to the Protestants with whom he entered into private negotiations in July. It says something for their still sensible and deferential minds that the members of the League should have recognised the truth of the Turkish danger and been prepared to offer aid in return for only a verbal promise from the emperor; but it also speaks well for Charles that he should have stood by his word. In effect he surrendered the Augsburg recess for men and money.[2] The Religious Truce of Nuremberg proclaimed peace in the Empire, suspended the suits pending before the Imperial Chamber, and allowed the existing Protestant territories toleration until the meeting of a General Council.

As it turned out, these concessions need not have been made. In August, Sulaiman's armies reached the small Hungarian town of Güns, near the Austrian border, only to be held up for three weeks by the desperate and quite incredible defence of its tiny garrison. Knowing that the emperor was approaching in person with a force of 80,000 men, that the summer was nearly over, and that his presence was required in the east, the sultan abandoned this campaign also and once more withdrew from Hungary. Charles's splendid armament never saw action. The ridicule he thereby earned was no doubt misplaced, but he himself felt very depressed at yet again missing the chance of distinguishing himself in battle. In June 1533 a temporary peace of exhaustion descended upon Hungary, with Zapolyai controlling the bulk of the country under Turkish protection, while Ferdinand held on to his foothold in the north and west. Charles departed from Germany, having achieved little enough. The pope's temporary defection to France, urgent demands for his presence from other parts of his dominions, and above all lack of money forced him once more to leave the Lutherans to themselves. For the moment, only the General Council remained as a means of healing the schism, and in the intervals of consolidating his position in Italy and preparing to meet the Turk in the Mediterranean he continued, in and out of season, to urge its assembly on Clement VII.

The nine years which elapsed before Charles next felt free to visit Germany thus offered a second breathing space which the Protestants were not slow to exploit. The expansion of the 1520's had been spontaneous and explosive; the territorially even more impressive expansion of the 1530s, with the League of Schmalkalden acting as a centre of attraction and an agent of control, was more political and deliberate. In the years 1532–6, Lutheranism once again seemed to carry all before it. Zwingli's death in 1531 had removed a disruptive rival influence; the defeat of Zürich ended its expansive policy in Switzerland and south Germany; the Upper German regions of necessity turned to Wittenberg. The League had adopted the Augsburg Confession as its doctrinal basis, and since this was both moderate and vague it proved acceptable even to some of the more delicate spirits. Behind the politics of the day, behind the constant addition of new members (mostly cities), the theologians were busy negotiating and quarrelling. Finally, Bucer's unremitting efforts to bring about unity in the evangelical ranks yielded success in the Wittenberg Concord of 1536 in which the South Germans virtually accepted Luther's determined stand on his own position, especially with regard to the eucharist. In these years Luther was changing. He had never been exactly the easiest of men; had he been, there would have been no Reformation. But as the years advanced, success and the near-papal position into which, despite himself, he was elevated by his followers made him more abrupt and offensively dogmatic; some of the spiritual refinement of his youth coarsened into something very like arrogance and pettish intolerance. He was never less than great— a rolling, rushing giant—but he increasingly inclined to treat opponents as enemies and friends as disciples. The constant practice of controversy soured a naturally unkind pen still further. Nevertheless, despite some growing deficiencies of temper, his mind retained its creative power and his personality its magnetic attraction. Much as it had expanded, the Reformation was still essentially identified with Martin Luther.

Late in 1531, the League of Schmalkalden received a workable organisation to provide money and armed forces in case of need. Its moving spirit was rather the vigorous landgrave of Hesse than the cautious elector of Saxony—John Frederick who in 1532 succeeded his father John whom he greatly resembled both in his slow temper and his real devotion to the gospel. Philip of Hesse, in whom political ambition and religious conviction mingled so inextricably that it is anybody's guess what it really was that drove him on, eagerly promoted the admission of new members, though it had been part of the Nuremberg understanding that the League should not expand; most of these were in the north, but in 1534 the League scored a resounding success in the south-German duchy of Württemberg. Since 1520, that important territory had been administered by an Austrian governor. Its duke, Ulrich, had fallen foul both of the law and of his order by murdering a knight in order to possess his victim's wife, and he had been driven into exile by the Swabian League.[3] The fact that he was an early and ardent convert to Lutheranism played no part in that story but now grew important. For Ulrich had never ceased to intrigue for his return; and his absence, assisted by the Austrian occupation, had turned him from a well-hated tyrant into a romantic dream to the people of the duchy. In 1534 Philip of Hesse decided to use the case of Württemberg as a demonstration of Protestant strength. By ceding a small county to Francis I he obtained French money with which to equip a formidable army, and the restoration of Ulrich was a walk-over. The Swabian League, disrupted by the religious split, stood aside, with the result that in 1536 it ceased to exist even formally. At the peace of Kadan in June 1534, Ferdinand accepted the accomplished fact and also agreed once more to suspend the activities of the Imperial Chamber against the Schmalkaldeners.

The Württemberg affair was a frightful blow to Habsburg prestige, a blow which the emperor and his brother bore with a curious air of total resignation. There was, admittedly, little they could do about it, especially as Bavaria, too, welcomed the end of Austrian control in the duchy, though at Munich there had been hopes of restoring Ulrich's Catholic son Christopher rather than the Protestant father.

Still, the Habsburgs had suffered a public humiliation and had allowed a Lutheran enclave to be established between their Austrian and Swabian possessions. Kadan in effect marked the end of the last attempt at imperial government in Germany, though the Chamber continued to institute processes and attack secularisers of Church lands; the Protestants, proclaiming the court a partisan body, professed to ignore it, though time and again they made its actions matter for complaint in the many negotiations which followed in the next six years. One thing Ferdinand did obtain by the treaty: the Saxon elector formally recognised him as king of the Romans. Contrary to usual practice, positive dynastic interests were sacrificed to the prospect of a permanent Habsburg lien on the imperial title.

Württemberg was at once reformed, somewhat oddly because its situation ensured a conflict of Lutheran and Zwinglian penetration. Thus the northern half was committed to Erhard Schnepfen, who looked to Wittenberg, while the south fell to Ambrosius Blaurer who held with Zürich. The consequent friction led to several attempts to settle the long-standing eucharistic dispute; in the end, another leader emerged in John Brenz who introduced a modified Lutheranism and thus helped towards the elimination of these distracting differences. When Christopher succeeded Ulrich (1550), the duke and not his duchy changed religions; indeed, Württemberg survived the Counter-Reformation and has been a strongly Lutheran territory ever since. The landgrave's bold action bore the fruit for which he had hoped; cities and territories all over Germany hastened to introduce the Reformation and join the League of Schmalkalden, though it was very doubtful whether the terms of the Peace of Nuremberg protected newcomers. But for the moment there was nothing and nobody to stop the progress of the new religion, and more and more what had started as a modest defensive alliance turned into a power of European importance and with European policies. In 1534, the League had dealt, through Philip of Hesse, with France; by 1536 it was as a visible unit negotiating with Henry VIII of England and playing its part in the politics of Scandinavia. Its activities in suppressing the Münster kingdom of heaven in 1535 also reflected its true character. The League of Schmalkalden clearly inherited something from earlier associations like the Swabian League by means of which some order had been introduced into the fragmentation of Germany. But the old leagues had carried imperial approval and acted as agents of such central control as there was; the new one could be nothing but an instrument of disruption.

While the Lutheran Reformation thus continued its expansion among territories and, more ominously for the authorities, also among the people of territories which so far had not changed their official colour, it also made progress with its internal organisation as a Church. Bishops continued to be replaced by disciplinary organs in which pastors and secular officials co-operated. In the cities, it was usual to appoint one of the clergy as superintendent over the rest, with responsibility to the town council. In the lands, the Saxon Visitation was the model generally adopted. After 1532, Saxony itself underwent some further reorganisation when another survey, undertaken by Justus Jonas (1493–1555), now Luther's chief assistant in the management of that territorial Church, revealed the need for closer control. The work was planned by the theologians, but enforcement, of course, depended entirely on the co-operation of the elector. The reformers reorganised the parishes to suit changes in population, confiscated Church revenues, and applied the money to such characteristically evangelical uses as the maintenance of pastors, relief of the poor and provision of schools. The problem of the Church courts was also solved. It had already been settled that matrimonial cases—that is, the supervision, in great part, of the laity's morals—should be committed to the civil courts, afforced for the occasion by a clerical assessor called a superintendent. Now the episcopal consistory courts, the chief instrument of the old ecclesiastical jurisdiction, were refurbished for the Lutheran situation, a process completed by 1542. By then Saxony contained three courts, each composed of two lay lawyers and two theologians, which supervised the spiritual and moral welfare of the people, enforced uniformity of doctrine and worship, and generally acted as the ecclesiastical arm of the secular government. The model was adopted, with modifications depending on the whim of the prince, in all other Lutheran territories; even Hesse, which in 1526 had introduced a more democratic system, fell into line in the general consolidation of Luther's ascendancy over all Protestant communities which marked the 1530's, with the death of Zwingli and the suppression of Anabaptism. In fact, while he lived, Luther's person did more than any organisation to provide united leadership, and his untiring and determined efforts to keep matters of the spirit free of secular preoccupations helped to modify the worst features of a system in which the state controlled religion. But Luther could not live for ever; and in any case, something had to be done both to reform the Church in structure and manners—after all, the demand for that had started it all—and to counter the charge that Protestantism meant anarchy. By 1542 the Lutheran Churches were efficiently and sufficiently organised on a territorial basis, itself a recognition that the schism would be permanent.

These were, no doubt, in part the fruits of the neglect which was all that the emperor could bestow upon his German charge during these years. But the neglect did not grow from idleness. Charles had left Germany in 1532, immediately after the Nuremberg agreement and

the fizzling out of the Turkish campaign; passing through Vienna—
his first visit, celebrated by an enthusiastic reception—he crossed into
Italy, tried to get some co-operation out of Clement VII, and moved
on into Spain. Settled and peaceful as things were in that peninsula,
Charles knew well enough that his long absence caused resentment
and might revive the refractory days of 1521; he simply had to leave
the German problem to itself and turn to another sector of his
commitments. In any case, matters had recently grown more serious
in the Mediterranean. The Barbary pirates, based mainly on La
Goletta near Tunis, had for long been a nuisance at best, a real
disaster to trade and communications as a rule. Occasional raids
against them had never done more than hold them off for a little
while, and by about 1530 they represented, under their leader Khair
ad-Din Barbarossa, a genuine maritime power in the western Mediterranean. Barbarossa controlled Algiers before 1529 and captured
Tunis in 1534. In 1532 he was appointed admiral of the Ottoman
empire—no longer a mere pirate but the naval commander of a
power which had in twenty years become the dominant power in
the eastern Mediterranean. In 1534, Francis I, concerned as ever only
with doing down the Habsburgs, concluded an alliance with him.
Not that the pirate chief changed character; his corsair activities
continued unabated. From the emperor's point of view they now
represented not only a general menace to the welfare of his dominions but a major aspect of that surging Ottoman aggression which he
so passionately wished to repel.

Matters came to a head in the summer of 1534 when Barbarossa
carried out a large destructive raid on the Adriatic coast of Italy. Even
Clement VII, scared beyond measure, began to wonder if he had been
wise to seek freedom from Spanish domination by playing with the
Valois allies of such fiends and added his feeble pipe to Charles's call
for a crusade. In 1535 the emperor crossed the sea at the head of a
large and splendid armament comprising men from all his dominions
but predominantly Spanish. In a brilliant campaign he captured both
La Goletta and Tunis, destroyed the corsairs' bases, and drove Barbarossa to seek refuge in Constantinople. Even though he put a
permanent garrison into La Goletta, the victory was far less complete
than it at first appeared. The corsair raids resumed almost at once:
such enemies cannot be destroyed by depriving them of one base if
they can transfer to another instead. But Charles's triumph was
nevertheless real enough. At last he had proved himself in battle,
the leader of a true crusade, fighting not Christians, as did the rest of
Europe's princes, but the enemy of Christendom himself. Not even
the fact that the whole story has an air of romantic and chivalric
improbability about it, and not even the rapid revival of Turkish
naval power, should detract from the achievement. It had its uses,

too, in practical terms. When Charles returned to Europe he was no longer the man who had so pitifully failed in Germany but the knight and hero who had conquered the seemingly invincible. When, once again, he turned to the question of bringing peace to Christendom through the calling of a General Council, he did so with a new weight of authority. It also seemed as though the situation had at long last changed in his favour.

II   The Search for a Solution

Clement VII died in September 1534. It is a useful reminder of the papacy's continued importance (a fact too readily overlooked in the tempests of the Reformation) that this event and the election of his particular successor should have had notable repercussions in European politics. Alexander Farnese (1468–1549), who took the name of Paul III, was sixty-six at the time of his elevation and had been a cardinal for forty-one years. He owed his election in part to his eminence and reputation, in part to his predecessor's expressed preference, but in no small part also to his advanced age and indifferent health: nobody thought he would last very long.[4] In fact he occupied the Holy See for fifteen strenuous years and saw off a good number of the men whom he himself promoted to the cardinalate. Altogether, he was a much more formidable man than the ever lamenting but rarely lamented Clement: a stubborn, shrewd negotiator, a man who knew his mind, a man of sufficient character to restore both respect and purpose to the papacy. For himself he recognised the justice of the universal complaints against the unreformed Church of Rome and from the first demonstrated his readiness to tackle quite thorny thistles.[5] His professed and over-riding purpose was the creation of a united Christian front against the Turk, so that Charles and he had much common ground. To this end, Paul III, wishing to bring about peace in the Church, accepted the imperial view that a General Council should be called; unlike Clement VII, he did not evade that issue, but like Clement he remained determined that the Council must in no way threaten the papal supremacy.

Paul also hoped to make lasting peace between the emperor and the king of France, but in this he was frustrated by Valois ambition and irresponsibility. In consequence, his policy of peace necessarily became one of neutrality between the contending powers, much to Charles V's anger: since France was holding hands with the common enemy in Constantinople, papal neutrality seemed to the emperor remarkably like treason to Christendom. But though Paul III's tenacious determination to stand above the secular quarrels involved him in frequent disagreements with the emperor, he could not avoid the consequences of two less exalted facts. Charles continued to dominate Italy, and no pope could for long be at odds with him without reviving memories of 1527. And secondly, Paul had his Achilles heel in his family devotion. No pope ever practised nepotism more ferociously than this tough and usually unsentimental old man who meant to put his putative nephew Pier-Luigi Farnese and a brood of relatives in possession of lands and wealth. This reduced the arbiter among princes to a schemer for scraps of Italian soil, forced him time and again into deference to Spain, and disastrously lowered his moral standing. No more than any other pope of the century was Paul III prepared to distinguish between the interests of the papacy and the Church, or to put the second before the first; and more than any other did he confuse those interests with those of his own family.

Nevertheless, the new pope's willingness to consider the calling of a Council transformed the European scene and seemed to offer a chance of ending the deadlock between Catholics and Protestants which, especially since the latter continued to advance and had formed an armed league, was bringing religious war dangerously near. Paul began his pontificate by making several well known reformers cardinals and by sending nuncios round Europe to discover how good the prospects were for a General Council. He met a rebuff from England and marked coolness from France, but the most important embassy was that of Pietro Paolo Vergerio who went to Germany. Ferdinand was eager: not only did he hope for a restoration of peace, but he underlined the need for a Council by rather tactlessly stressing the insufficiencies of the clergy in his own dominions which, he said, made it difficult for him to find a confessor not tainted by notable sin. Unfortunately, no one else responded favourably. The Lutherans made no secret of their total distrust: as they were to state repeatedly, they could not attend a papal Council and were offered nothing else. But even the German Catholics, led by the Bavarian dukes, refused to have anything to do with Vergerio's proposals; they, too, demanded a Council of the German Nation and wished to avoid a situation in which support of their religion would force them to support their emperor. It thus became plain that the General Council, so often and so recklessly appealed to by all sides, had serious meaning only for Charles V with whose imperial policy and position it well agreed.

In any case, before Paul could follow up these beginnings, the prospects darkened with a renewal of the Habsburg-Valois conflict, dormant since 1529. In November 1535, Francesco Sforza, the imperial puppet-duke of Milan, died, and Francis I, who in his own mind had never given up his claims to the duchy, at once demanded his supposed rights. The position had altered since the great days when the French first started invading Italy; Savoy, traditionally pro-French and a gateway to Milan, had since 1529 been drawn into the imperial connection, so that this time the way had to be cleared. The duke of Savoy (the duchy included Piedmont) was already involved in war with the aggressive city of Bern which, ostensibly to assist the Reformation in Geneva but not a little concerned with its trade-routes into the Rhône valley, early in 1536 overran the province of Vaud and added it to its growing territory. Without even bothering to look for a formal *casus belli*, Francis joined in, and in March 1536, French troops occupied all Savoy and Piedmont, thereby announcing the return of the Valois to the Italian scene.

Charles, who at the time was engaged in setting his kingdom of Naples to rights, had to accept the challenge; indeed, in his anger at broken promises he offered to settle the issue by personal combat with his rival, a quixotic gesture which he meant seriously and which astonished rather than amused Europe. For a start he set about securing the pope. In April he arrived in Rome where he spent three months in neighbourly residence and often less than neighbourly exchanges with Paul III. Nothing he could do moved the pope to abandon his formal neutrality, even though Charles at this juncture held the whiphand over Paul's tortuous attempts to extend Farnese power to the north of the papal states. Pope and emperor did, however, agree on the General Council, and in June Paul at last issued the order summoning it to meet at Mantua in May 1537. Mantua was chosen because it might solve one persistent problem of the Council, its venue. The Germans always said that any Council would have to meet in Germany, and Ferdinand supported this view. The pope would not consider a meeting place outside Italy. Mantua, though Italian, was independent and, it was hoped, sufficiently near the Alpine passes to be considered a compromise.

Nothing at all, however, came of it. The war went badly for Charles; having apparently learned nothing from Bourbon's failure in 1523, he attempted yet another invasion of southern France which ended in ignominy. A small incursion into Picardy fared no better, while the French counter-invasion of the Netherlands in the spring of 1537 proved pretty successful; the regent, Mary of Hungary, was in despair, her treasury empty and the French occupying Hesdin and pushing into Artois. The French king's Turkish allies also took a hand when their fleet once more descended on the eastern shores of Italy. Venice now joined pope and emperor in an unusual alliance which showed that her privileged position at Constantinople was passing away; but she came to regret this step when in September 1538 the allied fleets were defeated by Khair ad-Din Barbarossa in the battle of Prevesa. The imperial admiral, Andrea Doria, must bear the brunt of the blame for what was in itself a minor reverse but had serious consequences; determined to keep his ships intact and (a man of Genoa) distrustful of Venice, he left the fighting to half the allied forces. Prevesa undid Charles's Tunisian triumph, revived Barbarossa's reputation, and secured the eastern Mediterranean to the Turkish navy, until the battle of Lepanto (1571) reversed the decision.

Even before Prevesa was fought, Charles had decided to put a stop to the war with France. Paul III eagerly acted as mediator, and in May-June 1538 the two monarchs concluded a ten years' truce at Nice. This left Francis possessed of Savoy and Charles in direct control of Milan. Nice also set the seal, for the time being, on the abandonment of the General Council. In 1537 French pressure had forced the pope to use a transparent pretence—the duke of Mantua's regret that he could not provide adequate protection for the assembled fathers—to adjourn the Council to Vicenza; when it actually opened there in April 1538 it was attended by only a few Italian bishops, and Paul resolved the fiasco by adjourning it again, this time *ad beneplacitum papae*, without date. A reforming Council was not so easily come by. Soon after Nice, Francis and Charles met in person at Aigues Mortes in one of those much publicised conferences in which the age believed, to agree, in their amity, on action against infidels of various sorts—Turks, Lutherans, Henry VIII. Prevesa put a stop to any move against the most infidel enemy of all, but the English and the Protestants remained to be dealt with.

The Protestants had, in fact, undergone a variety of experiences since early in 1536 when the emperor's renewed prestige and the pope's renewed vigour terminated a phase during which they had had it all their own way. After Paul had summoned the Council to Mantua, Charles had thought to try one more attempt to secure Protestant participation, but he picked the wrong man for the mission. The imperial vice-chancellor Matthew Held was not only a bitter opponent of the schism and a stiff-necked, discourteous man; he had also been the notorious leader in the campaign conducted by the Imperial Chamber against the Lutheran princes and cities. When sent, in October 1536, to negotiate with the League of Schmalkalden concerning the Council and, as usual, the aid against the Turks, he went well beyond even his secret instructions and, instead of persuading the Protestants, tried first to browbeat them and then to organise Catholic resistance. The League's leaders reacted according to temperament: Philip of Hesse told him frankly what he thought of him and his papal Council, while John Frederick of Saxony prudently refused to see either him or the papal nuncio but had his council convey a general refusal. Ferdinand protested to his brother about Held's proceedings, but the chance of a Protestant appearance at the Council was in any case nil.

However, the Protestants now faced for the first time the possibility that such a Council might actually meet and therefore the need to prepare their position. The Wittenberg Concord of 1536 had at least given a reasonable measure of unity to the various streams of opinion; Luther and Bucer were for the moment agreed on the Lord's Supper, and Melanchthon's policy of moderation and peace seemed to stand a chance. The princes instructed their theologians to produce a statement of faith, and Luther responded with the Schmalkalden Articles of 1537. These not only reasserted all the crucial points of doctrine but also justified resistance, even to the emperor, in the cause of the gospel. Though the Articles were not adopted officially and nothing else much came of all the negotiations, they demonstrated that peace moves within the Protestant camp did not extend to accommodation with the enemy at Rome. The princes refused the invitation to the Council, but even before they thus announced their resolute adherence to the schism, Francis I's opposition had put paid to the Council and rendered their deliberations out of date. Held abandoned his mission and instead organised the Catholic League of Nuremberg (Charles, Ferdinand, the archbishops of Mainz and Salzburg, the dukes of Bavaria and Saxony, and two Brunswickers) which, though meant as a counterweight to that of Schmalkalden, lacked political and military reality. All it did was to confirm the division of Germany; it never played any part in the policy of the emperor who most reluctantly accepted its existence.

Charles was still far from convinced that war must come; quite apart from the circumstances restraining him, he was himself very disinclined to put matters to the test of the sword. Reverses and disappointments never caused him to abandon a line of thought once grasped, and ever since Augsburg he had held to a policy of reunion by negotiation, with pressure, of course, upon the Protestants, but pressure short of war. In this he was steadily encouraged by Ferdinand, ever conscious both of the German Catholics' resistance to Habsburg ambitions and of his own Hungarian problems. Yet from the Protestant point of view, the situation looked grim in the autumn of 1538. Nice and Aigues Mortes had freed Charles of his French incubus; more, they had proclaimed the long dreaded alliance of the great Catholic powers against all schismatics. In the summer, Ferdinand had also at long last come to terms with Zapolyai in the Treaty of Grosswardein. The *voivode*, still unmarried and not expected to live long, had there agreed that the king of the Romans should inherit after him; if the Turks could be ignored—rather a large if—it looked as though the Habsburg claim to Hungary would soon be a reality.

In any case, the treaty freed time, men and money for the concerns of Germany. The progress of Protestantism had admittedly continued, but not either with the vigour or in quite so satisfactory a way as had been the case in the splendid days after the conquest of Württemberg. Thus the orthodox elector Joachim I of Brandenburg

had in 1535 been succeeded by his reformist son Joachim II, but the
new elector had been very cautious indeed in introducing the Reformation in his dominions and had avoided involvement with the
League of Schmalkalden. More ominously, Protestantism had been
used as a weapon of burgher democracy and rebellion in the brief
and violent career of Jürgen Wullenwever, burgomaster of Lübeck
from 1533 to his execution in 1537, who had combined a vigorous
promotion of the Reformation with imperialist ambitions in Denmark and the Baltic, and with an anti-aristocratic policy in the
northern towns. Wullenwever came to grief, but the Lutheran princes
could never relish any reminder that Reformation and revolution
could easily ally. In 1539, the Reformation gained a last notable
advantage with the death of Duke George of Saxony.[6] In him
departed the most upright and uncomplicated defender of the old
order, leaving the Catholic cause among the princes in the devious
hands of the Bavarian dukes, the uncertain hands of the Elector
Palatine, and the reckless hands of Duke Henry of Brunswick.
Duke George was succeeded by his brother Henry, a good Protestant,
and the people of the duchy soon demonstrated that only the old
duke had kept them from joining the religion of Wittenberg, just
across the artificial border. Yet this important accession of strength
could not disguise the fact that by 1539 the League of Schmalkalden
was uneasy, its position uncertain, war only too probable—and likely
to find the Protestants unready to face a final showdown.

Once again, however, the immediate threat evaporated because yet
some other part of Charles V's dominions effectively, if unintentionally, came to the rescue of the Reformation. No sooner was peace
made with France, the Turk quiescent, and the Hungarian problem
apparently brought near to solution, than trouble broke out in the
Netherlands. In 1539 there occurred the last of those popular upris-
ings in the ancient city of Ghent which had so often troubled the
counts of Flanders, and though Charles proved victorious it needed
his personal presence and a sizable army to overcome the rebellion.[7]
This was not the moment to put the resolutions of Nice into effect.
An even more serious threat developed in the duchy of Cleves. The
death of Duke John in 1539 brought to the throne his son William
who also inherited from his mother the territories of Jülich and Berg,
while a year earlier his claim on Guelders, in succession to the
childless Charles of Egmont, had been recognised by the Estates of
that county. Thus William of Cleves had succeeded, by methods
familiar enough to the Habsburgs, in creating a powerful state in
the north-west of Germany, astride the Lower Rhine and therefore
astride the vital route which linked the emperor's Italian and south
German possessions with the Netherlands. Guelders had been a
standing problem to the Burgundian complex when its count was a

man of few resources: now, backed by the position and resources of Cleves, it represented a major and immediate threat.

In addition, though not Lutheran, Cleves was also not orthodox. Since 1532 it had enjoyed a peculiar Church order of its own in which the duke ruled as spiritual head. Duke William was an Erasmian, and the religion of the duchy was a mildly reforming compromise between Rome and Wittenberg. In its constitution as well as its *via media*, it bore some resemblance to Henry VIII's Church of England. The presence of this powerful and dissident new state had immediate repercussions on the religious situation in the north and necessarily affected the political situation to the emperor's detriment. Cleves now pressed upon the ecclesiastical electorates of the Rhine and threatened their adherence to Rome. The duke also made no bones about continuing the anti-Habsburg traditions of Guelders. He at once established contacts with the Schmalkaldic League one of whose leaders, the elector of Saxony, was his brother-in-law; he welcomed advances from England—one of the countries threatened by the truce of Nice—and early in 1540 married another sister, Anne, to Henry VIII. Throughout 1539 the League negotiated with England. The prospects of a general Protestant alliance, promoted by Thomas Cromwell, William of Cleves, and the Schmalkaldeners, grew quite large. In fact, the plan collapsed as quickly as it had grown. As soon as Henry VIII found his fourth wife distasteful and at the same time realised that he could protect himself better by an understanding with France, whose tenuous amity with Charles V showed early signs of cracking, he abandoned both Cromwell and the Protestants. In the end, the ambitions of Cleves proved to be excessive; in 1543, the duke was defeated by the emperor and lost Guelders to the Habsburgs. But down to Cromwell's fall in June 1540 the situation around the Lower Rhine was much too uncertain for Charles V to contemplate the drastic action against the Protestants which Nice had foreshadowed and which the League expected.

Thus in 1539, the emperor, once more and for the last time, decided on a policy of conciliation and reunion by treaty. Joachim II of Brandenburg offered to mediate. By this time he had made his adherence to the Reformation plain, but he would neither join the League of Schmalkalden nor accept the spiritual guidance of Wittenberg. Brandenburg was reformed with great moderation, the elector attempting to set up something like a separatist Church under his own control. On the face of it, the princely power was here so manifestly the chief beneficiary that Joachim has often been charged with looking only for secular and personal advantage; however, it seems clear that he was honestly troubled by the schism and honestly disinclined to commit himself firmly to either side. His mediation was well meant and so taken by Charles who early in 1539 replaced the relentless Held by a new and more accommodating envoy, John of Weza, the exiled archbishop of Lund. In April, Lund came to terms with the Protestants in the Frankfurt Interim. Once again, a final settlement was deferred till the assembly of an acceptable General Council, though after the Protestant reaction to the summons to Mantua this equalled the Greek Calends. The threats uttered at Nice were dropped; the League of Nuremberg was played down, though not dissolved; it was agreed to hold exploratory discussions between the religious parties with a view to finding a formula which would resolve the doctrinal difficulties. This promised colloquy began at Hagenau in June 1540, was adjourned to Worms in November, and finally was deferred to the Diet called to meet at Regensburg in April 1541, so that the expected settlement might be arrived at in the emperor's presence. The pope watched these proceedings with misgivings much encouraged by the opposition to Lund of the nuncio in Germany, Giovanni Morone. Nevertheless, he not only gave in to the emperor by sending a legate to Regensburg but chose in Gasparo Contarini a man of notoriously liberal sympathies.

By the time that Charles, fresh from his victory over Ghent (February 1540), reached Regensburg, he had been presented with an unexpected trump card. The Protestants had suffered their worst setback since Luther published his theses. What imperial power and papal traditions could not procure, the lechery of Philip of Hesse achieved in short order. The landgrave had never been a continent or a moral man; indeed, his early adherence to Lutheranism had been encouraged by the scruples of conscience and frequent remorse which are common in violently sensual temperaments. His religion was perfectly sincere, so sincere that by a suitable irony it led to his downfall. He could not bear his wife; he could not do without women; he must have the grace of God in the sacrament which was not available to him while adultery kept him in a state of sin. Thus he wished to solve his dilemma by marrying again and appealed to the Lutheran theologians for help in the matter. Divorce being out of the question and the first marriage manifestly valid (so that Henry VIII's way out was closed), they counselled bigamy which they justified by reference to Old Testament precedents. Apparently convinced that he was aiding a truly troubled conscience, Luther gave him a species of dispensation but insisted that it be kept secret. In March 1540 Philip obtained his rejected wife's consent to marry a second time, but, of course, the business could not be hidden from the world. Of the compliant theologians Melanchthon was "like to die of shame" and Bucer stood bewildered; Luther talked of the seal of the confessional and advised "good strong lies" by way of denial. Needless to say, this did not work. The Catholic world rejoiced in self-righteous ribaldry; the friends of the Reformation were utterly dismayed. What made the scandal so serious was not so much the fact of bigamy—though this in itself naturally served to revive the charge that Lutheranism meant the dissolution of all law and morals—as the discreditable twists and evasions produced by the discovery of the truth.

Even more serious than the scandal itself were its consequences on Philip of Hesse's politics. Unhappily for himself, para. 121 of Charles V's criminal code, promulgated in 1532 and accepted by the landgrave, had for the first time made bigamy a punishable offence in the imperial courts; the penalty was death. The landgrave had every reason to be frightened: Charles would have been more than human and less than dexterous if he had not taken advantage of so splendid an opening given by a determined old enemy. Thus Philip saw no hope except in surrender and began to treat for the imperial pardon. Charles left him to tremble in the trap, until in June 1541 he condescended to a treaty with the landgrave by which the bright star of the Schmalkaldic League at long last accepted Ferdinand as king of the Romans, abandoned the Cleves alliance, and submitted in all matters to the emperor. The man who in the years 1534–6 had led the Lutherans to their remarkable triumphs was now instrumental in wrecking their public credit and the united purpose of their defensive league.

Though Philip's final surrender came after the Regensburg Diet, the scandal broke before it; it speaks well for the sincerity of Charles V's desire to see peace restored that he should have made no attempt to exploit the situation until the negotiations had failed. At first they promised well. Charles in person opened the proceedings and urged the participants to work in a spirit of peace. The papal legate, Contarini, lived up to his reputation as a reasonable man and to his education as an Erasmian reformer.[8] Even before the meeting, moderates on both sides had prepared the ground, and the committee charged with drawing up articles of agreement included almost only moderates. On the Catholic side, the chancellor of Cologne, John Gropper (1503–59), took the lead. Trained as an ecclesiastical lawyer, he had not long been a theologian when, in 1538, he published his *Enchiridion* or *Manual of Christian Doctrine*, a clear but conciliatory statement of orthodoxy whose reforming tendencies caused it towards the end of the century to be placed on the papal Index of Forbidden Books.[9] Gropper had the unswerving support of Contarini, while on the other side Bucer and Melanchthon were also sincerely determined to find common ground rather than seek points of disagreement.

The result, to everyone's understandable amazement, was a joint definition of the doctrine of justification, one of the really thorny problems because it involved not only the theology of the fall and of grace but also the nature and powers of the Church. Concord was achieved by means of a formula (*duplex iustitia*, double justification) which, though variously attributed to Contarini and Gropper, ultimately derived from Erasmus' last contribution to the religious controversy, his *Repair of Christian Unity* of 1533.[10] When even Eck and Calvin could see nothing wrong with the formula, Charles had cause to think the religious split at an end. But the achievement also proved to be the only one of note, and even it was quickly repudiated outside the Diet. Luther thought the article dangerous because he held that it left the way open for justification by works; he abandoned Melanchthon. Paul III, and especially the fierce Cardinal Carafa, refused all concessions on points of doctrine; they abandoned Contarini. Like all previous attempts at peace, Regensburg ended in total failure. By the side of the one agreed article stood many unresolved problems, with the insoluble problem of the papal claim to supremacy overshadowing everything else. The recess of the Diet could do no more than once again refer the decision to a General Council.

This recess issued in July 1541, at a time when the international situation was once more turning against the emperor. Zapolyai died in July 1540, but the Treaty of Grosswardein never came into effect. After its conclusion the bachelor *voivode* had married, crowning the joke by siring a totally unexpected heir. After his death, his ambitious widow contested Ferdinand's claim to the succession and appealed to the sultan. By early 1541, the Ottoman armies were on the move; in August they took Buda, and the policy of maintaining a client kingdom was replaced by conquest and occupation. The subsequent war was long and intermittent, peace being made in 1547; the immediate point was that for Charles aid against the Turks had again to come before any settlement by force of the German problem. Despite pressure from the few remaining determined Catholics among the German princes, at long last resigned to supporting the emperor against the heretics, Charles could only stall. For the French war, too, revived. In the month which saw the end of Regensburg and the climax of the Turkish advance, two French envoys were treacherously murdered in the Milanese. Full war broke out in 1542. Once again, Charles V turned away from the question of Lutheranism; once again, the activities of his enemies saved the Reformation from having to face the facts of political life.[11]

The decade between the Diets of Augsburg and Regensburg thus had a curiously inconclusive air. Though much happened, the historian is left with a sense of running on the spot. Protestantism made considerable progress territorially, gained cohesion and military backing, but lost spiritual impetus. The period was bracketed between two perfectly genuine but also perfectly futile attempts to bring back peace by religious debate and the discovery of compromise formulae. The first attempt only produced a specific statement of Lutheran doctrine in the Augsburg Confession, moderate and halting enough but sufficient to act as the basis of a schismatic denomination. The second could not undo the *Augustana*, even though it tried to proceed without reference to it. Regensburg forcefully testified to the sincere peace policy of Charles V, and it will not do to regard this only as a product of his multiple problems. Of course, these affected his decisions and action, but they did not create his main and fundamental way of thinking. Though he remained throughout determined to end the schism, there is nothing to show before 1541 that he regarded war as either inevitable or necessary. The emperor of Christendom did not want to fight Christians in the name of religion. He continued to believe in the possibility of reconciliation by various means of which a universal General Council was both the most satisfactory and the most difficult to arrange. Such colloquies as that of Regensburg were to Charles a second best. Unfortunately he judged the situation less with the clear eye of the politician than with hopes born of long-suffering.

Among the Protestants some theologians continued to believe in discussion and academic committees. If the 1520s belonged to Luther and Zwingli, if Augsburg was Melanchthon's day, the later 1530s saw the temporary ascendancy of Bucer, giving voice to the fears of those who saw the schism widening, possibly beyond hope of repair, certainly beyond all intent. In Bucer and Contarini, the voice of Erasmus, the voice of reason, was once more heard. But it was crying in the wilderness. Nearly all the men concerned—especially the pope and Luther himself, but in the last resort even the emperor—would not contemplate any genuine compromise; these were matters of faith, not policy, and they all held firmly to essentials in their respective positions which made concord impossible. But if opinions were extreme, deeds could not be. A variety of concerns, mostly political, prevented the pursuit of any incisive line of action. The pope did almost as much as anyone to hamper Charles V; the ambitions of German princes kept even Catholics from supporting vigorous policies against the Protestants and made any consistent policy difficult in Germany; while France stood by to exploit any one of Charles's embarrassments. As for the Turks, they had no interests in these squabbles. To the sultan, Lutherans were also Christians, which is more than can be said of the pope; the Protestants in fact expressed more frequent and more sincere appreciation of the Muslim threat to the Church than ever came out of Catholic France. Yet it was the Protestants who benefited most from the threat, and Ottoman pressure did more than anything else to take the heat off them at critical moments.

The truth is that though the 1530s witnessed one attempt after another to end the schism by agreement, and though they even witnessed at long last the first abortive calling of a General Council, the split really became unbridgeable during these years. Protestant-ism expanded; new forms of deviation appeared in England, Cleves and Brandenburg; Rome was being steadily pushed back. Princes and potentates invested their futures in a self-interested break-up of the illusory unity of Christendom, and peoples and nations either led or followed in the stampede from orthodoxy. Charles stood for a losing cause. Against him, Luther recognised the truth and gave up all hope of accommodation. If his first concern was still the gospel, he also now accepted the political consequences, threw in his lot with the separatist princes, and abandoned his earlier belief in the obedience due to the emperor. The magistrate who must be obeyed was now quite definitely the territorial ruler. This opposition from the schis-matics was obvious and totally to be expected. It was more surprising that Charles's aims should also be frustrated by the pope. Side by side with the steady advance of the schism, the 1530s also witnessed the first signs of recovery at Rome, and before the fortunes of Charles's policy are further considered we must see how it came about that the organised Protestant party was shortly to be faced, not by a variety of interests vaguely allied or plainly conflicting, but by a vigorous body of Catholic opinion reorganised to meet the shock of Luther's assault.

Chapter 7

The Revival of Rome

I Catholic Reform

In the revolutionary turmoil excited by Luther it is easy to forget that the Protestant success was never more than partial. Loud though he blew his trumpet, the paper walls of Rome (of which he spoke so eloquently in his *Address to the Christian Nobility*) refused to fall. However badly shaken, the papacy proved surprisingly resistant. Indeed, it is one of the ironies of the age that when the dust settled the pope was found in more undisputed control of the reduced territory left to him than his predecessors had exercised over the whole Latin Church. The Reformation split the Church, but it forced Rome to organise for war, and organisation for war naturally meant giving fresh powers to the commander-in-chief. The process took time. It was affected by the continued hopes for reunion, particularly strong in Charles V, by the division in the Catholic ranks between the fanatics and the moderates—those who could see only the heresy of Protestantism and those who could not help admitting the justice of some of its charges—and by the fundamental difficulty of reforming an ancient and long corrupted institution. Nevertheless, among the more astonishing phenomena of this sufficiently astounding half-century is the revival and renewal of the papacy.

That the old faith should not everywhere surrender before the evangelism of the Protestants is understandable enough. The Reformation brought to many a message of hope and spiritual joy, but it also deprived many others, perhaps the more earth-bound, of certain reassuring instruments of grace—pilgrimages, worship of the saints, the performance of those little concrete acts that are so much easier than the strains of inner regeneration—instruments which, one cannot help thinking, are essential to the *mobile vulgus* if any religion is to be made supportable which stresses the prospect of hell as graphically as medieval Christianity did. Habit, need, conviction would ensure that the customs grown over 1500 years should not be swept aside overnight. But that the papacy should emerge more strengthened, that papacy for which in the age of Leo X and Clement VII even orthodox believers could at best apologise, causes rather more surprise. The resilience of Rome is a greater wonder than the resilience of the Church of Rome, until one realises that those who attacked the old Church were themselves very largely responsible for identifying tradition so indissolubly with the papacy. In fact, the history of the Reformation proves rather pressingly that the universal Church cannot be separated from the papal claim to universal supremacy. As things were, and as they are to-day, the two cannot but go together.

Of course, the ultimate issues did not all become clear from the first. Luther's attack unleashed a vigorous warfare of the pen. If, on the whole, the Protestant writings are the more familiar and the more important, that reflects not only literary quality and the fact that of all these writers, many of them learned and able, Luther himself was the only propagandist of genius, but also the truth that novelty is usually more successful than mere defence of an existing order. Yet the anti-Lutheran writings demonstrate the continued vigour of the old theology. Germany, naturally, produced the largest number of controversialists, four of whom stood out. John Eck (1486–1543) was the first and the most persistent of Luther's adversaries. A passionate and eloquent man, he pursued Luther steadily—always trailing—from the Leipzig Disputation of 1519 to the Regensburg Colloquy of 1541. There is much to admire about Eck. An eminent theologian, he made his chair at Ingolstadt in Bavaria as much a centre of orthodoxy as Wittenberg became the centre of heterodoxy: even as Luther owed much to his elector's protection, so Eck may be seen as the academic manifestation of Wittelsbach Catholicism. But apart from being a professor, Eck was also an active pastor and preacher, a four-square figure who stood in the world of action as much as in that of books. One odd aspect of him was his defence of commercial capitalism: closely linked with the merchant princes of Augsburg, he advocated the justice of taking interest on loans (five per cent. seemed right to him) and was accused of representing the Fuggers rather than the Church of Rome. Even more prolific than Eck was John Cochlaeus (1479–1552), a humanist who turned against the Reformation as early as 1520; the higher journalist of the controversy, he displayed no originality in theological argument but great assiduity in repeating established arguments and in taking up every turn of the game. His sizable compilation on the character and person of Luther prevented for centuries a just appreciation of the reformer, even among his followers. John Fabri (1487–1541) and Frederick Nausea (1480–1552), successively bishops of

Vienna, may also be mentioned as active writers and preachers who used their humanist training in the service of the old religion; both were taken up by Ferdinand of Austria and in effect acted both as official Habsburg propagandists in religion and as conscientious reformers, in the Catholic interest, of the Church in the Austrian territories.

Outside Germany, Luther's eruption also provoked replies, ranging from the official condemnations by Louvain and Paris[1] to the book with which Henry VIII obtained the title of Defender of the Faith from Clement VII (*Assertio Septem Sacramentorum Adversus Martinum Lutherum*, 1521). Henry's pamphlet is noteworthy not only because it was written (tolerably well) by a king, but also because it defended tradition on empirical grounds rather than fundamental principle. Henry supported the papacy because it had always been accepted, not because it was God's only way for the government of His Church on earth. The ablest theologian who laboured against Luther was English, too: Bishop John Fisher of Rochester (1459–1535), the later victim of Henry VIII's political Reformation, whose work secured European attention. Thomas More, on the other hand, confined his controversies to English followers of Luther, especially William Tyndale. There was some writing in Italy; Jacopo Sadoleto (1477–1547) in particular, an eminent Platonist and a conscientious bishop of Carpentras near Nice, attempted to find common ground while preserving the essentials of the Catholic faith. Neither France nor Spain, later to be so very active in producing defenders of the Church of Rome, took any important part in this first reaction to the Reformation.

The champions of tradition had no easy time of it. In Germany, only Austria and Bavaria offered them a safe refuge; everywhere else, civic and academic authorities looked on them with doubt and dislike. Fabri had to flee from Basel and Nausea from Frankfurt. The English Catholics ran into the upheaval produced by Henry VIII's divorce from Catherine of Aragon. But apart from these political difficulties there were at this juncture inherent weaknesses in the Catholic controversial position. For one thing, a mere defence of tradition—a mere repetition of dogma—is never a very satisfactory way of winning over doubters, and for a long time the writers were too easily content with such a negative approach, with denying the Lutheran assertions. In due course, the error of this came to be recognised, and from the late 1530s we find them turn from mere refutation to positive instruction. Gropper's *Enchiridion*[2] was characteristic of this more fruitful attitude, and its success in the book market proved how right he was to provide guidance rather than theological controversy. A growing mass of catechisms and books of edification showed how well the Catholics had learned the lesson taught by Luther who had always put positive teaching before mere controversy.

More important still than errors of method were uncertainties of position. After all, Luther did not assail a well-ordered society but one in the throes of moral decay and spiritual doubt; and he was not alone in recognising these weaknesses. Even those who did not wish to follow him had difficulty in defending that which he denounced. We have already seen how the humanist tradition inspired by Erasmus helped to spread reformed ideas all over Europe. If Erasmus himself did not favour this, and if most of his avowed followers remained with the Church, neither he nor they could forget the abuses which they had so often attacked. Indeed, the attack on abuses—the desire for reform—was present in the Church long before Luther. Whether the Catholic revival should be called the Counter-Reformation or the movement for Catholic Reform has become something of a dispute among historians; and we shall say something more about this in the course of this chapter.

However, it is clear that there were traditions of protest and renewal that went back well into the fifteenth century and in themselves owed nothing to the Protestant revolution. The reform of the Church, in head and members, had been demanded from many sides for at least 150 years before Luther made his appearance: the Conciliar movement, late-medieval mysticism, the ethical demands of Platonist humanists, revivalist outbursts like that of Savonarola at Florence, all represented different manifestations of the widespread recognition of problems and the widespread determination to do something about them. Leo X had called a Lateran Council which sat for five years (1512–17) and produced a few sensible suggestions for reform. Individuals had led holy lives—often, by way of example, ostentatiously holy lives—and had inspired followers. In 1517, some fifty Italian clergy got together at Rome in the Oratory of Divine Love, a voluntary association dedicated to austerity of life and charitable occupations which struck observers of Medicean Rome as somewhat incongruous and (according to temperament) as risible or impressive. The group included names soon to be famous as active reformers: Matteo Giberti, Gaetono di Thiene, Gian Piero Carafa, Sadoleto. The most notable of all these high-minded and distressed spirits, Gasparo Contarini (1483–1542), experienced spiritual conversion in 1511, before anyone had heard of Luther. Contarini came from a leading aristocratic family of Venice. He studied philosophy and natural science at Padua before he turned to theology. It is significant that despite his experience of direct revelation he remained a layman: the order of the clergy in Renaissance Italy held no attraction for his generous, sensible, devout and eirenic spirit. There was also the pull of his hereditary career. From 1518

he served Venice as ambassador abroad, acquiring a wide understanding of politics and political man, especially at Rome and at
the imperial court. His spiritual excellence and intellectual distinction
made him the natural leader of the group of Italians who sought to
regenerate the Church from within, somewhat in the spirit of Erasmus. Reason and plain decency, rather than spiritual passion, distinguished these reformers, though Contarini, having passed in some
respects through an experience very like Luther's, always showed a
better understanding of what Protestantism meant.

Unquestionably, therefore, these traditions of protest and reform
within the old framework went back to pre-Lutheran days and mark
an independent line of development within the Church. Yet it is also
obvious that under the impact of the Reformation the movement
changed character: it became at once more purposeful and gradually
more intolerant. Giberti (1495–1543) was a member of the Oratory,
but he was also secretary and chief adviser to Clement VII, the maker
of that pope's anti-Spanish policy, and the protagonist of the policy of
using France to liberate Italy from foreign domination (libertas Ita-
liae). It took the Lutheran Reformation on the one hand and the Sack
of Rome on the other to drive Giberti out of public affairs; from 1528
he retired to his bishopric of Verona and became the model bishop of
tradition, reforming his clergy and restoring spiritual life among the
laity, all within a strictly orthodox setting. Other bishops pursued this
policy of self-help in the absence of papal leadership: Sadoleto at
Carpentras, Carafa (1476–1559) at Chieti, Giovanni Morone (1509–
80) at Modena. Their ideas were in no sense new, but it is hard to
avoid the conclusion that only the pressure of the great upheaval
precipitated such positive action as there was. In this sense, even
these early signs of reform were in some ways already a Counter-
Reformation. The point is even clearer in the few non-Italian dioceses
where systematic reforms were undertaken. Briçonnet's work at
Meaux, more Lutheran than anti-Lutheran, has already been
noted;[3] between 1526 and 1536 Gropper reformed Cologne under
the benevolent eye of its elderly archbishop, Hermann von Wied; at
Liège, Eberhard de la Marque combined reform and the repression of
heresy in equal measure. Unlike Ximenes in Spain before them, these
men acted because the need for action had become imperative after
the German revolt.

The same mixture of old and new appears in another striking
feature of the time, the revival of the religious orders. Since, with
reservations, it would be fair to say that medieval Christianity,
always hostile to this world and always impressed by withdrawal
from it, found in the orders its most distinguished and most characteristic expression, the health of the regulars (those living under a
rule) was always a good barometer of the general health of the

Church. By that test, too, the fifteenth century did not emerge very well; worldliness, indifference, declining numbers mark monastic history at the time, and straightforward corruption was common enough, if not so common as the scurrilous legend suggests. Even the orders of friars had participated in the general decline for which the growth of offshoots favouring a more rigorous adherence to the rule furnishes proof rather than disproof. These "observants", distinguishing themselves from the laxer "conventuals", testified in fact to the widespread departure from the mendicants' original purpose as well as from their supposed austerity. In part because they came into more frequent contact with the laity—but only in part for this reason—the friars rather than the monks provided the main targets for the pens of satirists and vilifiers. By the early sixteenth century, even the observant communities were beginning to languish, and it says something for their condition that so many of the early reformers, Luther included, should have been ex-friars.

Then, as so often, a few individuals restored morale and purpose by the example of their lives. Here, too, Italy led the way. A peculiar movement began in the small community of Camaldoli in the south; under the leadership of men like Paolo Giustiniani (d. 1528), settlements of tiny reformed groups or individual hermits began to spread all over the peninsula and to bring Christianity to the people. These Camaldolese were particularly active in pastoral work, and the same was true of a new order which in these years branched off from the Franciscans. Reviving the austerity, simplicity and determination (if not always the saintliness) of the founder, these Capuchins (so called after their hood) existed as a separate body by 1529 and, after a good deal of opposition, were confirmed by Paul III in 1536. They laboured especially among the destitute, diseased and lost masses of Italy, a work of charity deserving the highest praise as much as it fulfilled the highest need. Fortunately for themselves, they also attracted friends in high places, especially that earnest protector of high aspirations, Vittoria Colonna. The Capuchins needed friends. They naturally excited the usual distrust and dislike felt by the worldly and secure, but also the rational and cool, for uncomfortably sincere and generally rather wild men who find it impossible to hide their conviction of their own rightness behind the forms of proper modesty. Worse, they nearly came to an early end in 1542 when their superior, Bernardino Ochino, defected to the Protestants.[4] The event lost them not only papal trust but popular support as well; but in the end Paul III declared himself satisfied with their orthodoxy, and they continued.

These Camaldolese and Capuchin movements were essentially traditional—spontaneous revivals within existing orders—even though in their work they naturally faced the particular conditions created by secularism and the Reformation. Other developments were more novel and pointed more manifestly towards a break with the past. The old orders had been distinguished by ostentatious peculiarity; even if, like the friars, they worked in the world, they were not of it, wore distinctive clothing, and jealously guarded privileges which exempted them from the control of the diocesan organisation. The new orders, called orders of clerks regular, were associations of ordinary clergy and laity who lived together, took some or all of the monastic vows, but formed no houses and did precisely the same work as ordinary parish priests. The idea grew from such groups as the Oratory of Divine Love, and the first of the new type of order were the Theatines, founded in 1524 by two leading members of the Oratory—Gaetano di Thiene (1480–1547) and Gian Piero Carafa, from whose bishopric of Chieti they took their name. Both were men of aristocratic descent; Gaetano came from Vicenza and Carafa from the neighbourhood of Naples. The former, later canonised as St. Cajetan, was gentle and spiritual, with the powers of persuasion and organisation so often found in his kind; the latter violently impatient, but at this time genuinely dedicated to reform above all else. The Theatines, transferred to Venice in 1528 after escaping from the Sack of Rome, were a purposely small order designed to set an example, and the example was in fact followed by two similar new orders in whose foundation Carafa had a hand—the Sommaschi in 1532 and the Barnabites in 1533. A new order for women also emerged with the creation of the Ursulines (1535), at first devoted to spiritual regeneration and charitable works, but by the end of the century noted for their work in the education of girls. These new orders always retained something of the semi-organised condition of their foundation, rejecting monastic enclosure and the monastic ideal in so far as it specialised in the service of God rather than in man's needs. They were a promising response to the condition of the people and gained their reputation less by the unquestioned holiness of their members' lives than by their manifest labours among the poor and suffering. Although the older orders—that is, the friars—had by no means neglected these aspects of life, they had put the stress elsewhere; the clerks regular did not say offices or offer prayers, but preached, taught, nursed and succoured. However much the ideal itself of an order obeying a rule emerged from the past, Gaetano's and Carafa's interpretation of it was novel. The new orders, culminating in due course in the Society of Jesus, are no manifestation of pre-Reformation Christianity.

There was thus a good deal going on in the Church throughout the 1520s. Reform was in the air, and some of it even happened. Italy made the chief contribution to this stage of the movement, and a quite small group of eminent and influential men gathered there to promote it. Some, like Contarini, Morone, and the Englishman Reginald Pole (1500–1558), a cousin of Henry VIII, were primarily pious humanists, whose religion, though orthodox, owed a good deal to Plato, whose temper remained conciliatory, and whose chief guide was inspired reason. Others, like Giustiniani or Matteo da Bascio, founder of the Capuchins, were more like holy fools. Others again— and here the signs of the future are stronger—followed Carafa in believing that heresy could not be brought to see sense but must be stamped out; for them, the war had begun and had to be won, even while Contarini was still anxious to negotiate treaties. But all were agreed that the Church needed reform, that abuses, especially in the papal Curia, must be remedied, and that the worldly taint hanging about papacy and Church must be removed by the practice of a rigorous, austere puritanism. Contarini and Pole so far saw no problem in reconciling their orthodoxy with their humanism; unlike the northern humanists they had never been true Erasmians and escaped the condemnation which Erasmus' teaching suffered in 1527. Nor were they necessarily the more unworldly or politically less competent of the group. Pole, indeed, never seems to have developed much understanding of the world; he never really saw the point of Thomas Cromwell's remark to him, in 1528, that the political teaching of Plato was all very well for the schools but did not have much meaning in life. But Contarini spent seventeen successful years in the best diplomatic service of the day, and Giberti passed through a long experience of administration and international intrigue before applying his very practical genius to the creation of a model bishopric. Both these men were abler and more sensible in ordinary things than the embittered Carafa; both they and Carafa were abler and understood the needs of the Church much better than the deplorable Clement VII. However, while Clement lived they worked privately, piecemeal, without a chance of taking the lead in the Church. That chance came in 1534, with the election of Paul III, and it is by the use they made of it that the true character of this movement for "Catholic Reform" must be judged.

II   Counter-Reformation

What are we to think of Paul III? Are we to agree with the lively English scholar that he was "one of the select band of really great personalities among the popes", or with the solemn Austrian that "he cannot be acquitted of the charge that he devoted himself frequently to worldly things which did not suit those serious times... It was to be a long time yet before it became impossible for men to occupy the papal throne to whom there clung so much of an unspiritual character"?[5] Father Hughes supports his high estimate only by praise for the pope's diplomatic ability, intelligence, will, experience and judgement, all of which qualities he manifestly possessed. Is that enough to make a great pope? Quite apart from the nepotism of which mention has already been made, Paul III never attempted to free himself from the political preoccupations pressed upon him both as an Italian ruler and as a factor in European affairs. Whether one blames him, as Pastor does,[6] for being "in many things a child of the Renaissance", or regrets that his successors could not combine fervour and uprightness with a readier tolerance of intelligence and harmless amusement may be a matter of taste, but that this subtle, slow, prolix, ailing man pursued too often a devious and discreditable course clean contrary to the interests of his spiritual charge is plain enough and hardly qualifies him for a high place among popes in general. The favourable estimate would seem to rest on what he did for the papacy rather than the Church.

At the same time, it is true that Paul III appreciated the need for reform and laboured to do something about it. When soon after his election he nominated two adolescent grandsons as cardinals, it seemed that nothing had changed for the better; but when at the same time he added Contarini, still a layman, the cynical world of Rome stood amazed. (Incidentally, one of those juvenile cardinals, another Alexander Farnese, came to be quite a star of the Counter-Reformation.) In the following year (1536), the pope indicated further that during his rule the proponents of reform would get their chance by conferring the red hat on Carafa, Sadoleto, Pole and others of a like mind. Though, true to his cautious temper and divided purpose, Paul always combined these promotions with equal honours for the conservative administrators and lawyers of the Curia, there was cause to wonder at a pope who filled the sacred college with notorious critics. And in the summer of 1536, Paul took a seemingly decisive step when he appointed a commission of nine leading reformers, headed by Contarini and including the others just mentioned, to investigate the causes of notorious abuse and recommend remedies. The commission were ordered to speak without fear or prevarication, and in March 1537 they produced their report, the famous *Consilium de emendenda ecclesia* ("Advice on the Reform of the Church").

To come to the *Consilium* after reading the eulogies of Catholic historians and those cautious sitters on fences who follow the current fashion is to experience some disappointment. True, the preface is firm, courageous and outspoken. The cause of all the trouble, it says, lies in the popes themselves who have allowed their desires to rule them and have listened to false counsellors, with the result that they believed themselves so fully owners of all the Church that they were

entitled to buy and sell its offices, appointments and benefices without any danger of sin. "From that spring, Holy Father, as from the
Trojan horse, have erupted into the Church so many abuses and such
grave diseases...that because of us—us ourselves, we say, Christ's
name is blasphemed among the nations." Nothing could be plainer,
or more true. But when one comes to look at the remedies proposed,
one must recognise that these "Catholic reformers" still had not
grasped the realities of the situation. The particular abuses which
they specify and demand to see removed are familiar enough: ordina-
tion of unsatisfactory priests and even infants, sale or reservation of
benefices, pluralism, non-residence (especially by bishops), dishon-
esty and idleness in the Curia, corruption in monastic houses aggravated by their freedom from episcopal discipline, dispensations
granted too readily and merely for money, compounding the sin of
simony, the pope's failure to put his own diocese of Rome into order,
and so forth. These were all longstanding complaints, often enough
denounced by both schismatics and good sons of the Church, and it
is possible that their cure might have helped to keep some men more
safely in the fold. Those who too readily regard Contarini and his
friends as liberal intellectuals should note the article which attacks
free speculation in the Italian universities (the teaching of "impiety"),
demands a censorship and a ban on uncontrolled public disputation,
and asks for the removal from the grammar schools of Erasmus'
Colloquia, the best-selling schoolbook of the day, "in which there is
much to teach impiety to untrained minds".

Even if Carafa rather than Contarini may have been responsible
for this attack on the freedom of the mind, it tells one a good deal
about these men. They were themselves conservatives, sincerely
troubled by the insufficiencies of the Church but convinced that
reform meant no more than a cleansing of the stables. There is no
sign at all of positive reform in the document: no indication that the
commission recognised the spiritual shortcomings, the lack of faith
and inspiration in the Church, which were driving men all over
Europe to seek solace and nourishment in the teaching of the Protestant Reformation. Did they even begin to understand what a doctrine
like that of the priesthood of all believers had meant to men hitherto
led to think that they could not find God except through intermediaries? The men who composed the *Consilium* still thought that if
only the Church put its house formally in order the schism would
end. Four years later, at Regensburg, Contarini could still therefore
act as though agreement might easily be just around the corner. In
some ways, this blindness is to their credit. If they failed to diagnose
the spiritual malaise it was in part at least because they were men of
reason and charity who could not fully understand the revolt against
reason which underlay so much of the Lutheran explosion. And if

they contented themselves with drawing attention to outward abuses, they also at least displayed no particle of the embittered dogmatism and persecuting bigotry which were in fact to be chief weapons in the restoration of Rome's ascendancy over many lost parts of Christendom. But all this adds up to saying that the *Consilium,* and therefore the early movement for Catholic Reform, quite missed the point and in no sense led forward to the true Counter-Reformation. It was the voice of the past, and later in the century the new papacy proved this when it put the document, commissioned by a pope and composed by a body of cardinals and papal theologians, on the Index of Prohibited Books.

In any case, the commission's labours were pretty much in vain. The shocked conservatives and the staff of the Curia eagerly seized on the fact that Lutheran propaganda made much play with these revelations from the fountain-head itself; if the enemy got comfort from the document, it clearly deserved no credit. The Catholic reformers suffered the usual fate of men who in the middle of a war dare point out that there are serious shortcomings on their own side. Paul III did try to carry some of the proposals into effect; in 1537 and 1539 serious efforts were made to reform the administrative departments of the Curia, especially the Datary and Penitentiary responsible for issuing dispensations and grants. But the pope was in a very difficult position. Reform would inevitably mean a decline in revenue: after all, the abuses had arisen from the need for money. And Paul had inherited a very unsatisfactory exchequer. At a time when prices were rising rapidly and his recognition of the Turkish danger was increasing his commitments, his income of 200,000 ducats a year represented only two fifths of that available to his predecessor in 1526, before the Sack of Rome had virtually wiped out its chief source, the Roman excise (*dogana*), and ruined the yield of the papal lands. In 1537 more than half the papal income came from those sales of licences and exemptions which the *Consilium* so rightly condemned. It is thus no wonder that all attempts at reform soon turned out to be half-hearted. Something was done to improve the morals and education of the clergy, to insist on residence and pastoral care, and to follow up the decisions of Leo X's Lateran Council which had tried to subject the religious orders to diocesan discipline; but neither in these matters nor especially in the reform of the Curia did Paul III's pontificate achieve anything of note. The reform in head and members, talked of for so very long, was once again evaded, and the movement for Catholic Reform petered out.

At the same time, however, there were quite different stirrings of a new kind, but little connected with the spontaneous self-criticism of the past and quite consciously designed for counter-attack on the Protestant Reformation. If Paul III's rule witnessed the running down of Contarini's Reform, it also witnessed the beginnings of the real Counter-Reformation (though elements of the two naturally mingled for a while) and thus merits the description often given of it as an age of transition, from one state of the Church to another. The disappointment of Regensburg may have helped to kill Contarini who returned to find himself distrusted for his willingness to seek an accommodation; he died in 1542. Giberti followed the year after. The leadership, if it can be so called, of the philosophic moderates passed to Pole, quite as high-minded as the Venetian aristocrat but neither so authoritative nor so able. In any case, Regensburg altered the balance of forces at Rome and brought Carafa into the ascendant. With him, the spirit of relentless persecution entered papal policy.

In July 1542, Carafa secured from Paul III the Bull *Licet ab initio* which created a totally reformed Inquisition for Italy. The Bull superseded episcopal powers by concentrating the fight against heresy at Rome; it made Carafa inquisitor-general with authority over all men everywhere in the peninsula, irrespective of their social standing; and it gave him full power to inquire, imprison, punish, and confiscate goods, *prout iuris fuerit*. Assisted by a group of like-minded men, he could appoint deputies where he pleased, could call on the secular arm to help him, and was given sway even over all religious orders, a provision which underlined the vigorous new papal policy of reducing these privileged bodies to obedience. Modelled on the successful Spanish Inquisition, the reformed Holy Office was really something quite new in the papal armoury, and in Carafa's energetic hands it achieved devastating success in rooting out Lutheran and other deviation among the Italian laity and clergy. As was only to be expected, the attack did not confine itself to those who genuinely broke with the old Church and really adopted Protestant, Anabaptist or Antitrinitarian views, but also looked with some suspicion upon the orthodox reformers, the men of the *Consilium* and their like. While Paul III lived, his hesitancy and humanity kept the tribunal from their throats, but when Carafa became pope as Paul IV (1555–9) he gave his hatreds free play. Morone was actually accused of heresy and imprisoned by the Inquisition, and Pole would have suffered the same fate if by then he had not gone to England to assist his cousin, Queen Mary, in restoring the papal obedience there. Even so, he was deprived of his office as legate and his actions were denounced by the pope they benefited. These were extravagances, but the consistent activity of the Holy Office brought to death or disaster a great many lesser men whose crime was often not heresy at all but merely reasoned doubt of the absolute perfection of Church and papacy.

Within a surprisingly short time the many signs in Italy of a vigorous intellectual and spiritual life, which to some extent had

diverged from strict orthodoxy, were destroyed; the survivors chose
either forced conformity or exile; Italy lapsed into mental stagnation.
The Inquisition rather than the Sack of Rome put an end to the
Italian Renaissance, even though, of course, isolated examples still
occurred of men willing to think and speculate. It is significant that
the most famous of these were those like Giordano Bruno or Galileo
Galilei who fell among the victims of the Inquisition. The tribunal
was assisted by the control it exercised over the press. The papacy
was not alone in its concern at the spate of books with possibly
dangerous implications; we have seen that the *Consilium* also had
asked for some form of censorship, and all European governments
were beginning to wake up to the consequences which the invention
of printing could have for public order and obedience to constituted
authority. But the papacy developed its weapons first. Individual
books had often been condemned and sometimes burned. Henry
VIII burned Luther's books in 1531, even as Luther had burned the
books of the canon law in 1520; the Sorbonne's list of dangerous
works was given legal force by a decree of the Paris *Parlement* in
1524; in 1527, Clement VII issued the oft-repeated Bull *In coena
domini*, an attack on heretical books and their readers; in 1543,
Carafa, as inquisitor-general, published a comprehensive order
against books and printers of which he disapproved. The full inau-
guration of the *Index Librorum Prohibitorum* (1559) awaited his
pontificate. Its first edition was enormous and full of solecisms, and
the Index, often varied in the sixteenth century and since, has
remained a revealing indication of the changing attitudes of the
Church of Rome to intellectual developments in the world at large.

The weapons of repression were, however, only one side to the
reconstruction of the Church. Above all, if heterodoxy was to be
wiped out, it would be really necessary to have a clear idea where
orthodoxy lay. Medieval theology had rarely been monolithic, and in
the later middle ages in particular the variety of possible views on
leading problems of the faith was distinctly bewildering. After all,
some modern scholars have demonstrated, to their own satisfaction,
that Luther had absolutely nothing new to say but got all his doctrines from the past; though, if this was so, it is not easy to see what
all the fuss was about.[7] The learned often differed widely on crucial
points, and one may distinguish four major schools surviving into the
sixteenth century: the pure Thomism of St. Thomas Aquinas himself,
mainly professed by his own order, the Dominicans; the modified
dissent from Thomism of Duns Scotus (*via antiqua*) which was very
influential in many universities; the sceptical and often antirational
attack on Thomism called Nominalism (*via moderna*) derived from
William of Occam and possessed of affinities with late-medieval
mysticism; and the rigorous tradition of St. Augustine which

Aquinas' synthesis of theology and Aristotelian philosophy had pushed into the shadows, but which not only survived especially among the Augustinian friars but also came to be the chief weapon of sixteenth-century Protestantism against the stultified scholasticism of the dying middle ages. Apart from the profundities and subtleties which separated these schools, there was also a good variety of what has been called popular theology to confuse the issue: movements of Mariolatry, for instance, which came near to forgetting Christ in the adoration of His Mother, or perfectly genuine survivals of pagan worship of the natural elements which had taken on a Christian disguise. In the trial of Joan of Arc, for example, charges were made which prove her accusers to have been very well aware of "superstitious practices" continuing in country places which were directly descended from a pre-Christian, magic religion. One need not doubt that a good deal of such witch-worship went on all over Europe, without following the enthusiasts who see witchcraft and covens everywhere and would in effect deny the existence of any truly Christian religion in the middle ages at all. But even without these dark and often nasty places in popular religion, popular inter-pretations of the Church's teaching could be disconcerting enough, as the debased doctrine of indulgences shows plainly.

The Church had always been conscious of the problem, a problem which itself arises in great part from the fact that the sacred writings do not pretend to compose a consistent body of doctrine. The need to produce order out of historically so diverse books gave to the Church one of its primary tasks, that of defining the truth of religion and setting the stamp of its authority on that truth, though it might have helped erring mankind if that truth had not been quite so protean through the centuries. The first generation of the Reformation—when it became plain, in the controversies by books and disputations, that there was simply insufficient certainty on too many debatable points—made this ancient task suddenly very much more urgent. Dogmatic definition on the scale required was a matter best handled by a General Council and safely to be left to it even by popes fearful for their authority; and Paul III wished to call the Council in the main for that purpose. This brought him into conflict with the emperor who saw the Council chiefly as an instrument of reform, for the repair of the Church's organisation and the removal of abuses. Charles always demanded reform before discussion of doctrine because to him the Council remained a means for bringing the schism to an end. He saw clearly that any definition of points of faith would, on the contrary, throw into relief the differences between the con-tending denominations, a fear in which he proved correct. The pope had a double reason for taking the opposite line: he did not propose to allow the Council to interfere in the Curia or usurp the governmental functions of the Church, while the new policy of resisting rather than conciliating the schismatics demanded a clear statement of doctrine by way of defining the battle-lines.

The history of the Council, which from 1545 onwards met intermittently but actively at Trent,[8] was therefore determined by the tussle between the imperial demand for reforming decrees and the papal preference for doctrinal decrees. In this tussle the pope nearly always held the advantage and ultimately won hands down. The Council of Trent did occasionally deal with such problems as the residence of bishops and priests, the discipline of the orders, or the revision of the Vulgate in the light of modern scholarship, but in such matters it was always careful to reserve the powers of the Holy See. Competently guided by papal legates, it avoided with some ostentation any revival of the ambitions which had made the fifteenth-century Councils into rivals to the papal monarchy in the Church. The bulk of its enormous output of decrees concerned doctrine. The Church of Rome emerged from the Tridentum with a much clearer body of faith, a definition of orthodoxy on all disputed points which not only made possible the enforcement of a quite novel uniformity but also discarded a great deal of the vigorous diversity and disputing doubt of the past. Though it may be going too far to call the post-Tridentine Church a new Church, it is also wrong to ignore the incisive break made in the Church's history by the Council of Trent. In fact, if not in outward appearance, it marked the end of the old, universal, comprehensive Latin Church and the emergence of modern Roman Catholicism as one Christian denomination among several.

This was so because the definitions provided by the Council always—if often after much debate—swerved away from all concessions to Protestantism. The decisive work was done in the first set of meetings, in 1546–7, when Paul III succeeded in holding off the emperor's urgent demand for reform and instead got the Council going on the main theological issues raised by the Lutheran revolution. Nothing could have been more displeasing to Charles V in his continued search for unity, and nothing could have been more acceptable to the growing Counter-Reformation spirit in the Curia. In its fifth session (June 1546) the Council agreed on a definition of original sin which denied Luther's view of man's total depravity. Six months were then spent in discussing the really central issue of justification. In the process, the Regensburg compromise, with its concept of a double justification,[9] disappeared very quickly, but the debates were dragged out because there was deep disagreement even among the Catholics. The strict Thomism of the Dominicans, ascribing justification to God's grace but allowing for some efficacy in works, was contested by certain Jesuit theologians who would seem to have approached the heresy of Pelagius by stressing man's free will to receive grace and his power, by his own efforts, to attract the divine mercy. On the other side, the German Augustinians, led by their superior Girolamo Seripando (1493–1563), by stressing St. Augustine's predestinarian teaching on grace sought to find a formula acceptable to the Lutherans. The outcome was the decree of 13 January 1547 which embodied the victory of the most anti-Protestant point of view. Faith was defined as "the beginning of man's salvation, the ground and root of all justification, without which it is impossible to please God", but the Lutheran tenet that justification comes by faith alone (*sola fide*) was expressly denied. Free will was preserved by anathematising the opinion that grace operated entirely independent of man: he could, of his free will, accept or reject God's gift. Good works, and especially the work of penitent preparation for the sacrament (a crucial point: to the Protestants this exemplified the "buying" of grace) were described as necessary for salvation.

The decree on justification may stand as a typical example of the Council's work. By consistently and vigorously denouncing the opinions of the reformers, and by providing exclusive dogma on disputed points, the Council firmly shut the door on any form of compromise or conciliation. Though Protestant representatives attended the second group of meetings in 1551–2, the tone set from the beginning endured until the final meetings in 1562–3. The General Council of the Church, so often demanded as the one hope of reunion and peace, became instead, in the hands of popes determined to preserve their supremacy and of theologians insistent on dogmatic rigidity, the occasion for the consolidation of one party. Once again we see how a prominent ambition of the older Catholic Reform grew into a prominent weapon of the new Counter-Reformation.

III · The Jesuits and the New Papacy

The fact that by 1546 the deliberations of the Catholic Church were decisively influenced by representatives of a new organisation brings us to the foundation of the Jesuit order, the last, and perhaps the most important, of the reorganisations which turned the medieval Latin Church into the modern Church of Rome. The order was entirely the creation of its founder, Ignatius Loyola (1491–1556). Born of an old Basque family of the middle nobility, Iñigo was brought up to be a soldier, but was so badly wounded at the French siege of Pamplona in 1521 that his career came to an end. Hitherto his sole intellectual diet had been the popular knightly romances of the day which he swallowed whole and in quantity; but during his long convalescence he read devotional works for the first time and experienced conversion. As he saw it, he would now have to do some special service to God, and the only thing he could think of was a pilgrimage to the Holy Land. However, he got stuck for eight months at Manresa in Catalonia where he practised severe austerities, discovered his striking influence on other people, and underwent a variety of visionary experiences. Here also he wrestled with an acute and living consciousness of sin, fully justified by his earlier life. Desperate to find salvation and the assurance of God's acceptance of himself, he solved the problem in the end by deciding that all scruples of conscience and attacks of despair arising from sins already confessed and absolved were the devil's work and must thus be firmly ignored. At Manresa he also discovered the book which was to prove his main inspiration—à Kempis' *Imitation of Christ*—and began that systematic search within himself ending in complete understanding of his real nature, complete control over his natural self, and total surrender to God which he later embodied in his *Spiritual Exercises* and made the basis of the Jesuit training.

But the pilgrimage was not abandoned, and in 1523 Loyola succeeded in reaching Jerusalem after a journey marked by the ghastly hardships which beset all his travels, especially as he would never carry any money and relied on the world's charity. He was refused permission to stay in Jerusalem where at this time he wished to live out his life in contemplation of God, and on his return discovered within himself a new eagerness to bring others to the realisation of the truth as he himself had come to see it. Recognising that he lacked the training for such a purpose, he began to study at the universities of Alcalá, Burgos and Salamanca (1525–7). All this time, though still a layman, he attracted attention by a life of severe holiness and found himself giving spiritual counsel to troubled souls, mostly women. Not unnaturally, this brought him to the notice of the Inquisition, since both his unauthorised ministry and the character of his group (which included both noblewomen and ex-prostitutes, both given to manifestations of hysteria) raised totally unfounded suspicions of heterodoxy and immorality. Though temporarily imprisoned, he convinced the authorities that he was no *Alumbrado*;[10] but he had to give up some of his more distinctive austerities and practices. In 1527 he travelled to Paris, and his long stay there proved the turning point. Because of his advanced years, his studies were slow and not very successful, but they were accompanied by a search for others to whom he could communicate his own inner assurance of God and his missionary purpose. Here he also for the first time encountered Lutheranism and saw that he hated it. By 1534 he had gathered around him six disciples—Pierre Lefèvre, Diego Lainez, Alfonso Salmerón, Nicolas Bobadilla, Alonso Rodriguez and Francisco Xavier. This group of founding fathers, as they turned out to be, he chose with care, studied thoroughly, introduced to the *Spiritual Exercises*, and made his own to a quite astonishing degree.

The *Spiritual Exercises* are so remarkable a book that they need a word to themselves. On the face of it, the work is neither very original nor very inspiring. It derives from devotional books like the *Imitatio Christi* and manuals for the search for God like that of Garcia de Cisneros (d. 1510); but it altogether lacks the verbal beauty and emotional inspiration of its predecessors. Instead it possesses a total air of practicality, a kind of sober obviousness in an essentially mystic setting which is the secret of its impact on those who for several centuries have come to it prepared to listen and to follow. In form, it consists of a detailed and precise course of meditation and study, divided into four weeks (though these need not be literally seven-day weeks), which the aspirant must undergo in strict sequence and total obedience to the instructor. The student searches his soul for sins and defects, in the process acquires the means for ridding himself of them, meditates on Christ and His passion, and is quite literally made over. The evidence is overwhelming that many who have undergone this training felt themselves to be new men, possessed of a moral strength and capacity for religious experience which they did not know they possessed until the *Exercises* called forth the resources of their souls. The pedagogic purpose and success are equally patent; St. Ignatius' relationship to his disciple is that of teacher and pupil—even drill-sergeant and recruit—rather than that of mystical visionary and follower. For Loyola's concrete and practical mind—always aware of reality yet totally wrapped in the task of bringing men to God—had, by embodying the course of his own inner labours in a manual, solved the great problem of how to induce men to renounce the world without leaving it. He wanted men who would labour among the concerns of humanity; yet experience had shown that a man can be set free of the world only by exciting him to a pitch of religious exultation which results either in the unstable passion of the enthusiast (*Schwärmerei*) or the private contemplation of the mystic. The *Spiritual Exercises* bring the aspirant to a high point of mystic excitement halfway through the course but will not leave him there; instead they proceed to accustom him to his new-found "indifference" (a crucial term in the training) to the world while consolidating in him the determination to serve God in the service of mankind. The trained Jesuit thus combines assurance of righteousness, knowledge of God, controlled mystic experience, and practical resolve to a unique degree. It might be added that (as Loyola recognised from the first) the *Exercises* really work only with a man already well on the way to the end they intend.

In August 1534, the little group of seven took a vow at Montmartre by which they dedicated themselves to missionary work in the

Holy Land or, if this should prove impossible, to whatever work the pope might put upon them. After some more travels, and so far with no thought of forming a permanent society or order, the companions reached Venice in 1537, intending to take ship for the Levant. The Turkish war of that year frustrated them, but Loyola made some useful contacts especially in the Contarini family. He also made an enemy of Carafa by writing him a letter criticising the practices of the Theatines. Since Jerusalem was out of reach, the alternative of their vow came to apply, and in May 1538 they were at Rome. Only now was the decision taken to turn the small band of devout ascetics, all by this time ordained to the priesthood, into a standing order. Loyola drew up articles of foundation for submission to the pope. He called to "all those who want to fight under the banner of God in our Society, which we wish to designate with the name of Jesus, and who are willing to serve solely God and his vicar on earth". The purpose of the society was defined as "the propagation of the faith by the ministry of the Word, by spiritual exercises, and by works of charity", with a special stress on "teaching Christianity to children and the uneducated". The society was to be organised in total obedience to its elected "provost" or general, and Loyola repeated that they shall "serve as soldiers in faithful obedience to the most holy lord Paul III and his successors". Despite this last, the pope took some persuading before he gave his approval to the new foundation. The Curia was not unjustly suspicious of this kind of self-help which might conceal extravagances of unhealthy enthusiasm or dubious ambition. But Contarini vigorously supported the companions, and in September 1540 the Bull *Regimini militantis ecclesiae*, embodying a modified version of Loyola's draft, founded the Society of Jesus. With great difficulty the fathers persuaded Ignatius to accept election as the first general, and despite his chronic ill-health—for twenty years he suffered agonies from undiagnosed gallstones—he ruled the new order for fifteen decisive years.

The Society bore, for ever after, the imprint of one of the most remarkable but also most strange personalities of that age or any other. Short, slight, racked by illness, permanently lame after his wound at Pamplona, of limited intelligence and never a scholar, preacher or theologian, Loyola hardly looked like an inspiring figure. His passion for system and planning often deteriorated into pedantry and pettifogging regulation. Although he was from his young days addicted to fantasies, substituting after 1521 dreams of knightly service of Christ for dreams of knightly service of ladies without at first seeing any essential difference between the two, his imagination was always rather meagre; he entirely lacked all poetry in the soul. The visions which came to him so frequently during the last thirty-five years of his life, and which he learned to turn off and on at will, were nearly always of the simplest kind—mere phenomena of light such as discs or rays, all of which he unhesitatingly identified as some specific manifestation of the divine.

Though, therefore, a mystic, he was the coolest visionary that ever thought himself directly inspired by God. His attitude to his own night of the soul is instructive, especially when compared with Luther's. Loyola suffered his despair for a few months, Luther for seven years; where Luther could find help only in his sudden recognition of God's infinite mercy to the sinner who believed, Loyola more confidently exercised his judgement in distinguishing between what in his experiences came from God and what from the devil. The second lot he simply put aside. If Luther's stress on justification by faith alone sprang from personal experience, so did Loyola's conviction that man can actively seek God; and so, by logical extension, does the characteristic Jesuit theology of salvation which, of course, holds grace to be bestowed at God's sole will but leaves room, in the relationship with God, for human effort and volition. Loyola proved to himself and others that the sinner can contribute to his peace with God; he knew that grace was not simply imputed to man regardless of his own state. Luther, with equal conviction, proved to himself and others man's total helplessness in the face of God. It is arguable that all religious leaders only proclaim as absolute truth that which has happened to themselves personally; but that is by the way. Theologically, Luther in going back to St. Paul and St. Augustine was perhaps the more soundly based, but in practice St. Ignatius' prescription had the advantage of offering an active way out of spiritual difficulties. The *Spiritual Exercises* are a systematic training course in the cleansing and curing of the soul, and they have worked with many. It is, of course, true that many Protestants have found equally helpful the conviction of being saved in their faith.

Loyola's greatness lies in the practical, sober and singleminded application of a mystic vision to bring solace and help to men content to be saved under authority. The two qualities which distinguished him and redeemed other deficiencies were the quite incredible power of his will and his astonishing understanding of men. His will not only made him indifferent to the really frightful experiences of pain, disease and hardship which filled so much of his life, nor did it only enable him to carry out his purpose. Above all, it made it possible for him to, if one may so put it, regenerate himself and thus to create an order singularly active rather than contemplative, a society which was both the emanation and lasting embodiment of this one man's determination. The deep impression he made on his disciples owed most to this total elimination of self, this utter command over his own nature and the nature of others, qualities which in fact resulted in ability to command the course of events. His understanding of men—

always penetrating, concerned, just, often charitable, and constantly refined and improving—not only led him to choose the right assistants and to employ each man's attributes in precisely the right place, but, more important, was fundamental to his missionary purpose. He was always and intensely concerned to heal souls. Whatever else the Society of Jesus came to undertake, this remained its primary task. It was not founded specifically to attack Protestantism, and there can be no doubt that when the founding fathers pledged themselves to carry the gospel to the unbeliever they were thinking much more of the infidels of the east and the heathens of America than of the German heretics. But that they meant to be missionaries somewhere is equally clear. Loyola had come far from the time when he thought that the service of God consisted in doing some notable deed of asceticism or pilgrimage, in the manner of a knight-errant, and in so coming he was to do a more notable deed than any he could have contemplated in his youth.

The organisation of the Society owed as much to him as did its purpose. He had always believed in total obedience to superiors, a virtue which nowadays may be regarded as military but in sixteenth-century conditions reflects religious rather than soldierly attitudes.[11] Thus the Society consisted of a hierarchy of officers ultimately responsible and totally subjected to the general. All thought of self, all personal ambition, were eliminated by a prolonged course of apprenticeship; entry into the Society was extremely difficult, and the move from novice to fully professed member involved years of study, preparation and examination, which many failed. Those who lasted the pace were certainly new men: as Loyola had reached the point where he could make himself into anything he wished, so he bequeathed to his creation the machinery for turning out men cut to a particular and identifiable pattern. But while unhesitating obedience and unquestioning service wherever called for became the essence of the order's discipline, Loyola had long lost faith in outward austeri-ties; he saw no purpose in severe regulations for dress, food or daily life, in the manner of the older orders. Since the Jesuits were to live in the world, they should also live moderately like it in outward matters.

No doubt, this introduced obvious dangers, but none materialised in the sixteenth century. Ignatius himself was as frugal and austere as his life had made him, and his example was copied; but he saw no point in illtreating bodies which had to be fit for a very active missionary life, often involving long journeys in the wilderness. Secure in the dedicated regeneration produced by their training, the Jesuits were otherwise encouraged to think of things in a practical way—to consider how their ends might be achieved as the world wagged, never to turn their backs on the world. Except among a few, this did not make for holiness, but it made for success; and pastors and missionaries, fighters against heresy and heathendom need success as much as they need sanctity. In its understanding and acceptance of the world, the Jesuit order differed markedly not only from the old monastic foundations, but also from the friars and even from such clerks regular as the Theatines whom in their organisation they much resembled. In that important sense, they were truly "modern", an aspect of the new, Counter-Reformation Church of Rome. Whatever one may think of the often limited and bigoted ideas, the drastic attitudes, the twisting of the human mind into a single prepared shape, one must recognise the purpose of it all and the remarkable degree to which that purpose was fulfilled.

Success did not come too easily. Certainly many men in that age of spiritual turmoil and schism found the new order attractive; by the time that Loyola died, there were nearly 1000 members, and this although he had thrown out dozens and scores, often for trivial reasons. Naturally, the older orders felt resentful; there has never been much love lost between the Jesuits and the friars. Secular authorities distrusted a body of men so exclusively pledged to the support of the papal supremacy; in both Spain and France they met effective opposition, and Charles V would not admit them to the Netherlands. At first their chief successes lay in Italy where Ignatius at Rome, supported by Paul III, exercised a widespread reforming influence, and in Portugal which received Xavier and sent him out as the apostle of the East Indies (1542–52). Indeed, some of the Society's most remarkable work was to be done among non-Christian communities, in India, China, Japan, among the Hurons and Iroquois of New France. But more immediately the pope wanted their services in Germany: it was the pope and not the order who directed their steps into the battle against Protestantism.

Almost by accident their services came mainly to express themselves in education. The intellectual training of his followers was very important to Loyola, and in organising it he displayed to the full his eclectic genius for utilising the enemy's weapons. Much as he hated Erasmus (whom he never read), and traditional as his own theology was, he had in his Paris days come to admire the virtues of humanist schooling, and Jesuit education was distinguished by its modernity and excellence. It incorporated the classical curriculum devised by the humanists, and showed psychological good sense in preferring to stimulate interest and competition rather than to flog learning into unwilling children, so that it was ahead of most other teaching available; admittedly, its insistence on authoritative instruction and its opposition to free enquiry were before long to render it backward. So renowned did the Jesuit schools become that very soon the fathers were asked to accept boys who had no intention of entering the Society, and with some reluctance they embarked on this unexpected development. A rash of Jesuit schools and colleges sprang up, especially in Germany: Vienna in 1545, Cologne and Prague in 1555, Ingolstadt in 1556, and so forth. The so-called second apostle of Germany was a Jesuit, Peter Canisius (1521–97), who joined the order in 1543 and carried out his labours of recovering large parts of the country for Rome from Eck's old chair at Ingolstadt. This work of teaching tended to supersede the more purely pastoral work, especially as Jesuits, being liable to removal at a moment's notice, could not take cures of souls in parishes; however, the order continued also in the founder's original purposes of bringing aid to individuals, serving in hospitals and among the poor, and the other traditional works of mercy. In the first generation, struggling for recognition and acceptance among suspicious princes and jealous ecclesiastics, the Jesuits did not yet specialise in that attention, as confessors and spiritual advisers, to the powerful which was to give them such enormous influence in the century after 1560: but such work again embodied the eminently practical, even pragmatic, attitude to the task in hand which, together with its rigidly doctrinaire foundation, was Loyola's bequest to his order.

Nevertheless, revolutionary, far-flung and influential as the Society of Jesus soon became, by itself it represented only an instrument, not an original force. As the Church stood, such force could come from only one source, from the papacy itself. Others could provide its weapons, it alone could wield them; and Loyola, in tying his order quite exclusively to the papal obedience, had of course recognised this. Paul III's unexpectedly long pontificate provided at least some encouragement to reformers. Even though he never tried very hard to set his own house in order, and even though his family ambitions continued to plague the papacy and the Church, he initiated the Council which defined the Church's fighting faith, allowed Carafa to organise the repression of heresy, and welcomed the Jesuits. When he died in 1549, the betting was on Reginald Pole, in itself a sign that the Roman world had changed. Twenty years earlier, a man whose only assets were intellectual distinction, moral uprightness, and a longstanding connection with the cause of reform would not even have been considered. However, the pundits were wrong. Pole belonged to the cause of moderate, humanist reform, now as good as dead; temperamentally, he had a good deal more in common with Erasmus or Melanchthon than with Loyola or Carafa. It was also still out of the question for anyone but an Italian—even so acclimatised an Englishman—to be pope, and also, the cardinals were probably wise in passing over a candidate who never in his life showed much practical ability: *capax papatus quia non papavit*. The choice fell on Giovanni Maria del Monte, one of the legates at Trent in 1545–7, though the one who by his arrogance and obstinacy had nearly wrecked the Council. Under Julius III (1550–55) the trends of his predecessor's rule continued, though without any notable activity of the pope's; the earlier momentum sufficed, and at least he offered no opposition to such events as the re-convening of the Council in 1551 or the reconversion of England in 1553–5. His successor, Marcellus II, had as Marcello Cervini been the saving of Trent and promised fair; a man of both sound principle and diplomatic skill, he might have directed the Counter-Reformation into conciliatory and possibly even eirenic lines, but he lasted only a few weeks.

At his death, the cardinals could no longer avoid the election of Carafa, as Paul IV; the papacy changed character overnight, and its recovery was seriously threatened. Paul IV (1555–9) was seventy-nine years old when he ascended the throne of St. Peter. He had always been a violent and unrelenting man, and now he was filled only with an old man's etched-in hatreds. Above all he hated the Spaniards who ruled his native land of Naples. He therefore hated the Jesuits, many of them Spaniards and certainly dominated by Spanish ideas of Christianity, nor had he ever forgiven Loyola his tactless letter criticising the Theatines. He seriously considered abolishing the order and put a temporary stop to its successful expansion and its missionary activities; only the death of Ignatius in 1556 and the election as general of Lainez, who for some reason could get on with the pope, saved the Society. Paul imprisoned Morone, threatened Pole, and would have nothing to do with the successes of the Counter-Reformation because they were linked with Habsburg support. Finally, he involved himself in war with Spain,[12] at a time when it had become perfectly clear that only alliance with that country could give the Church of Rome the physical backing without which its revival stood no chance of political success. Thus, although he furiously cleansed the Curia and at long last produced some reform at the centre of the Church (making more enemies, of course, but at least in a good cause), he put the whole new dawn in plain jeopardy. In his character—his severity, anger at all weakness and corruption, faith in the reformed Church—Paul IV was the first true pope of the Counter-Reformation; in his politics and attitudes he nearly destroyed it. Only charity, to which even popes are entitled, can suppress the conviction that he was to all intents insane throughout his pontificate. His death came just in time, but it also closed an era.

From 1559 the papacy appeared, very differently. Pius IV (1559–65) was the first pope to live all his sentient life in the sixteenth century. The work of restoring the supremacy of Rome and of recovering lost territories could now proceed with consistent direction from a centre no longer distracted by Italian politics and dynastic ambitions to the detriment of the main task, the spiritual and ecclesiastical task. The Jesuits resumed their victorious career; in

Philip II, the papacy found, in due course and by and large, a readier helpmeet than his father had been with his imperial dreams of a universal Church reunited by agreement. The years 1540–60 were not strictly part of the real Counter-Reformation. They were the preparatory years, when the papacy gradually, and with difficulty, abandoned the predilections of the recent past, when it came to terms with the need for reform, and when it acquired and perfected the weapons for the war which its own unalterable adherence to traditions of monarchic supremacy made certain, despite the best endeavours of Charles V and the peacemakers everywhere. Reorganisation and requipment had come none too soon: by 1560 the chief enemy to be faced was no longer Lutheranism, with its relative respect for tradition and its relative readiness, under secular leadership, to contemplate accommodation, but the more uncompromising Protestantism of Calvin.

Chapter 8

Calvin

I The Meaning of Calvinism

John Calvin was born in 1509, the younger son of a small notary and agent at Noyon in Picardy. Twenty-six years younger than Luther, he definitely belonged to the second generation of the Reformation, and there is more significance in this fact than in his French birth which many historians, convinced that nationality is the decisive element in history, like to think determined his chief characteristics and his chief differences from the Saxon doctor. It must never be forgotten that the use of Latin and the awareness of a common Christian purpose did more to unite these scholars and reformers than their mother tongues or places of origin could ever achieve in dividing them. But that Calvin was eight years old when Luther published his theses is a fact of quite another order of importance. Unlike Luther and Zwingli he did not reach manhood before the unity of Christendom was broken and the possibility of a schism had to be faced; unlike Loyola, he did not see the authority of Church and papacy questioned when his own convictions were already settled. He grew up into a world which had become disrupted and in which sweeping victories for "heresy" had become commonplace. As Luther told his students in 1531:

> We old men, soaked in the pestilent doctrine of the papists which we have taken into our very bones and marrow...cannot even to-day, in the great light of the truth, cast that pernicious opinion out of our minds. For habits acquired in tender years cling with the utmost persistence. But young men like you, your heads still fresh and not infected by such pernicious teaching, will have less difficulty in learning about Christ purely than we that are old have in rooting out these blasphemies from our minds.

When the religion of his fathers ceased to satisfy Calvin, he found an alternative awaiting him. However much he, in his turn, may have helped to transmute and develop that alternative, there is no mistaking the calm and straightforward manner of his move into the reformed camp. Not spiritual stresses or revivalist passion turned Calvin Protestant, but intellectual convictions and a moral fervour which learned that the truth had been rediscovered and was available to him who sought it.

Calvin's early career was orthodox enough for the intelligent child of a lowly but ambitious father. In 1523 he matriculated at the University of Paris, his maintenance being found in two small benefices attached to Noyon Cathedral and bestowed on him in the expectation that he would enter the priesthood. However, in 1528, when he had graduated as master of arts, his father ordered him to change from theology to law: that study was more likely to yield profit, and the old man also needed a learned son to assist him out of certain legal difficulties with the clergy of Noyon into which he had blundered. Calvin—never a man to rail against authority—obediently changed course, attended lectures at Orléans and Bourges, and acquired some grounding (though no perceptible interest) in Roman law. Certainly it is a mistake to suppose him later much influenced by these two years, except that he was beginning to make contact with Lutherans and with men who looked to Lefèvre d'Étaples. In 1531 he returned to Paris, but now to attend Budé's new foundation, the humanist academy which was to become the *Collège de France*. Soon afterwards his father died, and Calvin at once dropped the law. Though in this same year he published his first book, a *Commentary on Seneca* which showed him to be a highly competent philologist of the usual humanist type, his real interests remained in religion and theology. His humanism made him hostile to scholastic philosophy; unlike Luther, he did not draw his ideas from this traditional reservoir but went straight to scripture, Paul and Augustine; and his whole nature was pragmatic rather than abstract. He never really liked Zwingli who seemed to him too fond of metaphysical argument where faith alone sufficed. Calvin was at this time a young, even precocious, intellectual of notable gifts (especially of memory and exposition), with that kind of youthful, ardent temperament which so often leads the aspiring theologian into evangelical rather than philosophical ways. In addition he already showed himself possessed of a strong and narrow moral sense; one hears of no peccadilloes or light touches. Calvin was always intensely serious and also, as he himself later put it, "timid and fearful". The greatest influence on him was his array of humanist and reformist friends, men like the Erasmian Nicolas Cop or his own cousin Pierre Olivétan who had embraced Luther's teaching.

The crisis came in 1533–34, and it seems to have been purely an external crisis. There are some indications that in 1533 Calvin underwent conversion in some form, but no signs of a deep struggle for righteousness, against temptations, or even simply for the truth. Calvin suddenly received a total conviction of God's omnipotence; from that moment he knew himself to be under orders, an instrument chosen by God to proclaim the truth, and he lived the rest of his life in that knowledge and for that purpose. Like everything about Calvin, his conversion (so far as we can tell) was sober, clear-cut, psychologically almost uninteresting, but its manner accounts in great part for his ultimate success. Calvin seems never thereafter to have had the slightest doubt of the grace of God, and his assurance of salvation stiffened his stern will and intellectual certainty to the point of irresistibility. The timid and fearful scholar, never really happy outside the study and by nature neither a pastor nor a statesman, accepted the inner guidance of God so unquestioningly and to such good purpose that he turned into the most single-minded and successful maker of a reformed Church among all these innovators. If he lacked Luther's passion, humanity and reckless courage, he also lacked his self-doubts and extravagances;[1] if he was inferior to Zwingli in speculative intelligence, he also avoided the superficiality and self-centred playing at politics which marred the reform at Zürich. He surpassed both his predecessors and lesser, if still notable, men like Bucer and Melanchthon in lucidity and learned precision.

Will-power, discipline and order were Calvin's particular watchwords, and he put his powerful mental and moral gifts at the service of a single purpose: the erection of God's kingdom in this world, the creation of a living Church on earth embodying his particular vision of the truth. Despite the apologists who earnestly stress his moderate enjoyment of wine or far from total disapprobation of dancing, the truth is that Calvin was a puritan intellectual, a man who found it easy to condemn some human weaknesses because he had never happened to share them. Certainly he was not the gloomy and black-avised killjoy of the legend, but he remains a man for whom it is difficult to feel much affection. Even his friends stood in awe of him. His outstanding weakness—one often enough found in puritanical spirits—was an ungovernable temper in the face of opposition. It is to his credit that he was aware of it and tried to hold himself in; but a man so utterly sure of divine inspiration could not help but equate opposition to himself with denial of God's omnipotence. His controversial writings frequently decline into abuse which, if not so crude and scatological as Luther's could be, is in its cold anger even more savage and harder to bear.

All this, however, though implicit in the young Calvin, lay well in the future when the day of decision arrived in 1533. Late in that year, Nicolas Cop, then rector of the university, got into serious trouble for preaching a sermon derived from Luther's teaching, and Calvin unhesitatingly chose the side of reform and, for the moment, suffering. At that juncture the conservatives had it all their own way, because Francis I, negotiating to marry his son Henry to Clement VII's niece Catherine de' Medici, withdrew his protection from the humanists and reformers whom he had seemed to favour during the preceding years; and in 1534 the day of the *placards* sealed the fate of the French "Lutherans".[2] Like many others, Calvin, who now surrendered his Noyon benefices, escaped the persecution by fleeing from Paris and travelling about France and elsewhere under an assumed name. His journeys took him to Ferrara, to the court of the French-born duchess Renée with her highflown but unreal reformed *salon*; they took him also to the Rhineland—to Bucer's Strassburg, and to Basel where he met a congenial group of like-minded men. Here, in 1536, he published the first edition of his great work, the *Institutes of the Christian Religion*.

The book at once made Calvin famous and demonstrated that a new leader of Protestantism had arisen. Throughout the rest of his life he laboured on it, till the final version appeared in 1559, but though he greatly added to its length and depth, the essential ideas were there from the first. Modern scholars agree that the *Institutes* are not a systematic theological treatise in the manner of a medieval *Summa*. Calvin conceived the work as an introduction to and instruction in the Christian faith, a commentary on the only authority (God's will as revealed in scripture), addressed not to fellow scholars but to the world. The appearance of a system embodying a clear-cut doctrine resulted from its superb lucidity of exposition and clarity of language. In fact, it left much contradiction and uncertainty unresolved, with the consequence that Calvinism developed after Calvin quite often by deviating from him rather than by following him. Nevertheless, there must be no doubting the book's immense influence and importance. In it, Protestantism received a solid statement which all could read, based on a breadth of scriptural and patristic learning astonishing in one so young who had only five years before finally abandoned the law for theology. The *Institutes* appeared to provide a total scheme of faith, resting solely on the truth of the bible.

The form of Protestantism fathered by Calvin has been even more fruitful than Luther's, and it is therefore of some importance to know what he taught. This has not been made easier by the manner in which his teaching was developed, and sometimes perverted, by his followers; within two generations it would have been necessary for Calvin, in the words of R. H. Tawney, to tell those who claimed his authority that he was not a Calvinist. The doctrine which dominated later Calvinism was that of predestination, but recent work on Calvin himself has certainly shown that this was not the core of his own religion.[3] The deceptive lucidity of the *Institutes* was easily turned into a system by stressing some of its comprehensive treatment at the expense of the rest. In particular it is not true that he was so over-whelmed by the Father that he forgot the Son. Yet it is impossible to agree with those who would have it that all his theology centred on Christ. Calvin's theology is, in fact, much less dominated by the problem of redemption than is Luther's or Zwingli's; he starts, as it were, further back, at the problem of the creation—its meaning and purpose and therefore, while getting more into his scheme of things, also lays the stress more heavily on the Creator than on the Redeemer. To put it plainly, he is much more concerned with God than with man. His starting point is the beginning of his own catechism: "What is the chief end of human life? To know God by whom men were created". To know, not as the Calvinist catechism of the Westminster Assembly (1646) was to put it, "to glorify God and to enjoy Him for ever". The stress is from the first, and throughout, on the overwhelming omnipotence and omnipresence of God who has created the world so that man may have knowledge of the Supreme Being. That man may thereby also achieve salvation and eternal life is a secondary point. The first purpose of the creation is to embody the fact of God. Calvin's God is a self-advertising God; in later Calvinist thought he becomes a God who uses man for the sole purpose of showing His justice and His mercy.

It should not, however, be thought that the knowledge of which Calvin speaks is intellectual knowledge, an exercise of the human senses and reason. If man were still in his unfallen state, he would, thought Calvin, know God in His works, that is in the natural creation. But to fallen man such knowledge is impossible: the fall has erected an insuperable barrier between man and God. The only way open is thus through God's single, knowable manifestation—through the incarnate divinity of Christ. In God made man, lost humanity can find the means to know the invisible God outside time and space. And the instrument for achieving this knowledge is offered in faith—not generalised faith as such, but faith with a special content and purposefully referred to a particular object (Christ). Like Loyola, Calvin rejected the mystic and contemplative ideal of a personal union with God achieved in the individual soul; he saw faith as an active principle directed to the Son as the sole means of grasping the reality of the Father. In this specialised sense his teaching was Christocentric; but to him, Christ was not primarily the saviour, He was the knowable fact, the evidence (as it were) of God. Calvin's thinking, like the universe he saw, was theocentric, overwhelmingly filled with the awareness of a supreme being outside all human experience. It was essentially an intellectual awareness, which is not to say that it was purely rational. Indeed, mere reason has nothing to do with Calvin's view of man's place or duty in this world and the next; the intellectuality of the vision consists in its being apprehended in thought rather than feeling. Calvinist theology found it easier to accommodate itself to the mechanistic universe described by seventeenth and eighteenth-century science than did the emotional salvation theology of Luther or the human pomp of baroque Catholicism. Calvin's God the Creator has affinities with the Prime Mover of Newton or the First Cause of the rationalists. The essential difference lies in Calvin's insistence that by his own efforts man cannot even know God, that is to say, come to total comprehension of creation. For that he needs faith in the insoluble mystery, and the faith must centre on Christ.

This redirection of theological thinking from the human problem of salvation to the transcendental problem of the universe is Calvin's chief contribution to Reformation theology. On salvation itself he is, on the whole, less original, if only because he here followed Luther whom he started by regarding as his teacher and for whom he always retained great respect and devotion, even when the older man bit the outstretched hand. Calvin agreed that man was justified by faith alone, that works contributed nothing, and that faith was God's gift to man—the manifestation of His mercy. However, his theocentric vision and his willingness to face the logic of his doctrines induced him to rephrase justification by faith alone into the much more rigorous form of predestination. His starting-point, as always, was God's omnipotence and omniscience. Before time had existed, God had created all things in full knowledge of them and of what would be. His plan for man—His "decree", as Calvinist theology has it—therefore involved knowledge of the fall, of the incarnation, of salvation for some and damnation for others. From before the beginning of time, God had predestined some men to be saved (election) and others to be condemned (reprobation); the means He had chosen for executing the decree was faith in Jesus Christ which, of His grace, He imputed to the elect and refused to the reprobate. This double predestination is the characteristic core of Calvinism, though Calvin did not stress it so much as his followers were to do. Not unnaturally, that part of his teaching which immediately concerned men's hopes of eternal life came to play a greater part for them than his primary concern with God as such—God apart from man. Predestination is not only a logical derivation from the concept of an omnipotent God fundamental to Christianity; it is found in St. Paul and St. Augustine, was adumbrated by Luther and more explicitly emphasised by Bucer. Calvin most certainly did not "invent" it. Modern theologians, while admitting that there is scriptural authority for election, accuse Calvin of introducing his double predestination without such warrant; but it is hard to see that there can be any meaning in election unless the

opposite is implied. If all are elect, the concept loses its meaning—
and besides, "few are chosen"; if all are not, what except reprobation
can follow for the rest?

The real problem of Calvinist predestination is not its scriptural
basis but its implications. It raises the difficult, probably insoluble,
questions of the existence of evil and of free will in man. God,
being good, cannot have willed the fall and the fact of sin; yet God,
being omnipotent, cannot have allowed them to happen without His
knowledge or contrary to His will. Is man in his sin—and Calvin held
that every human being is from birth guilty of sin in his own person,
not merely as the inheritor of Adam's sin—the victim of his own
insufficient nature or of God's decree; and is man capable of choos-
ing between good and evil, and is such choice relevant to salvation?
Calvin did not so much resolve these questions as push them on one
side. These are the mysteries of God which man has no means of
probing: he must humbly accept that he is born in sin, can become
pleasing to the God, Who has so decreed it, only if God will extend
His predestined mercy to him, and yet must always strive to come
nearer to God by living a moral life and by seeking to know God in
Christ. Calvin did not regard the elect as saints on earth, or think
that conviction of election was proof of it; only God knows whom
He has chosen, though the decree is irreversible and the elect cannot
fall from grace. But since no one knows which side of the coin he is
on, all men must live in hope rather than certainty of salvation.[4]
Their good behaviour cannot obtain it, and Calvin always vigorously
denied that an upright life and success in this world in any way imply
election, though he thought that the saints would inevitably live
morally: the "imitation of Christ" was a consequence of election,
but the reprobate might nevertheless do all that the moral law
demanded.

There is, once again, logic in the doctrine, and the stress on the
mystery—man's inability either to reason out or to understand the
decree—is fair, given the premise of a God whom man must seek to
know but never can know in this life. Calvin always rejected all
attempts at metaphysical speculation (what he called philosophy) in
regions in which unquestioning faith alone seemed to him appropriate; this was one of his objections to Zwingli, and one point in which
he came much closer to Luther. Yet it is also an essentially inhuman
doctrine—naturally enough, since it starts from God, not from
man—and in some ways a highly cerebral, even a bookish, doctrine.
Not surprisingly, it usually worked rather differently in practice. The
true Calvinist came to think that assurance of salvation was possible
on earth, that the saints knew they were saved and had God on their
side, and that success implied divine approval and favour. Calvin's
insistence that election was so entirely without merit in the elect, so

purely a matter of grace *ad solam Dei gloriam*, that the last thing the elect would evince was pride, got easily lost in the human predilection for identifying personal ends with the purposes of the universe. At the same time, even ardent Calvinists like the puritans of Elizabethan Cambridge tended to forget about double predestination when they went forth to serve the cure of souls in parishes. To the vulgar they stressed the love of God and the general promise of redemption in ways which should have horrified them in the days of their academic speculations.

Calvin's teaching in two essential aspects of the faith, the nature of the Church and the meaning of the sacraments, again followed logically enough from the Pauline, Augustinian and reformed basis of his predestination doctrine. He agreed with Luther that the Invisible Church is the communion of saints and that the Visible Church on earth necessarily (since the saints remain unknown) includes both the saved and the damned. He agreed with Zwingli that the Church on earth is the community of Christians and that its organisation must be relatively popular rather than hierarchical if it is to obey scripture. He agreed with everybody that the Church has powers of discipline, of enforcing proper behaviour as well as proper teaching. His peculiarity lay in the stress he placed on this last point: to him the Church became so overwhelmingly a disciplinary institution that one is sometimes in danger of forgetting that he also demanded of it the true preaching of the Word and the faithful administration of the sacraments. His views on the correct structure and duty of the Church informed his work at Geneva, as shall be shown in a moment. As for the Lord's Supper, he naturally denied the sacrifice of the mass and transubstantiation as "errors which the devil has sown to corrupt this holy ordinance". He would have nothing to do with Luther's doctrine of a bodily presence: "to fancy Jesus Christ enclosed under the bread and wine, or so to conjoin him with it as to amuse our understanding there without looking up to heaven, is a diabolical reverie." And he agreed that Zwingli had left himself open to Luther's charge that he reduced the elements to mere symbols, though he seems to have thought that both Luther and Zwingli were misled by the difficulty of contesting the erroneous views of the papists into extreme statements which they did not really mean. For himself, he taught a real but spiritual presence: there is no body or blood in the sacrament because Christ is in heaven, but to the believer Christ is spiritually present, having chosen the means of bread and wine in the communion to infuse grace into the redeemed soul. On the whole this has proved the doctrine most easily accepted by later Protestants: it avoids the nominalist complications and carnal imagery of Luther, while escaping the Zwinglian danger of reducing the sacrament from a means of grace to a commemorative occasion.

One other aspect of Calvinism deserves mention. In laying the stress on the sole authority of scripture, Calvin did no more than the other reformers, but more than they he held that the whole of scripture was authoritative. Like Luther he thought the New Testament superior to the Old; but where for Luther the gospel had superseded the law, for Calvin the New Testament reaffirmed the Old. In a characteristically beautiful passage, Luther, commenting on Gal. v. 4, asserts that "Christ, when the time of the law was accomplished, did abolish the same, and so brought liberty to those that were oppressed therewith". To him this liberation from the killing edicts of the law by faith in God's mercy revealed in Christ was the central fact of the Christian religion; and who is to say him nay? Commenting on the same passage, Calvin, in his bald fashion, can only say: "The exemption which Christ has procured for us does not imply that we no longer owe any obedience to the doctrine of the law." As he proved in other contexts, Luther was no less opposed to antinomianism than Calvin himself, but he regarded the Old Testament as almost irrelevant after the Incarnation. Calvin, a legalist if not a lawyer, wanted to keep it: for him, the covenant of Christ's promise of redemption is but a renewal of God's earlier covenant with the chosen people which had been broken by the Jews' failure to observe the law. Thus he laid a heavier stress on the Old Testament and on obedience to its law than any other reformer.

This characteristic emanation of Calvin's moralistic and censorious temperament was also to have considerable importance in the outcome. Even above other Protestants, the Calvinists were to be the people of the Book, and in the fullest flowering of Calvinism— Scottish presbyterianism and American puritanism—the Old Testament, with its often apocalyptic note, its triumphing over sinners, and its positive interest in justice now rather than salvation another time, was at times to play a greater part than the more spiritual and peaceful message of the New. It may not do Calvin justice to link him exclusively with the doctrine of predestination, puritan discipline, and Old Testament sentiments. These are assuredly not the whole of his theology and not even the whole of his practical ministry. Yet there is nevertheless some justice in this slightly perverted view. Calvin's life and work operated in narrow and deep-cut channels; his view of the world was quite unusually restricted and his vision of God imbued with terror of His mystery rather than love of His mercy. There is a constant girding of loins and stern assertion of discipline in Calvin's fight against sin: and sin is seen too ubiquitously. While one must certainly agree with those who have recovered Calvin's real message concerning the knowledge of God and faith in Christ from the distortions produced by history, one must also think that the disciples penetrated to the master's psychological reality when they made double predestination the essence of their theology and moral censorship the essence of their Church. Even in Calvin's hands, Calvinism was a stern, even a stark, faith well suited to war.

II   The Reformation in Geneva

In the long run, Calvin's *Institutes* were to exercise the widest and most diverse influence; their immediate importance was that they brought about Calvin's ministry in Geneva. The incalculably fruitful association of man and place began with that species of accident which to the Calvinist is clear proof of God's will. In June 1536 Calvin was once again leaving France after a short visit. He meant to go to Strassburg, but the war between Francis I and the emperor forced him to pass round to the south of Alsace. He stopped in Geneva, for a night as he thought. The city had recently been reformed by Guillaume Farel, late of the group of Meaux, who found the task greater than he could manage. When he heard that the author of the *Institutes* was in town he at once went to Calvin's lodging and pressed him to stay. Quite unwilling to exchange the scholar's life for that of the pastor and missionary, Calvin protested his unsuitability, but Farel, a man given to colourful rhetoric, got on his prophetic high horse and told the younger man that God's curse would be on him if he did not take up the burden. Calvin yielded: once again he felt he had heard the very demands of God. His ministry at Geneva, so unexpectedly undertaken, lasted, with inter-ruptions, for the remaining twenty-eight years of his life (he died in 1564). Many of these years were full of unhappiness and strife, for Calvin had assessed his own preferences correctly. He never really liked the politics and practical affairs in which he now became involved, and in the battles that followed he had deliberately to stiffen a naturally shrinking temperament with the resources of a firm will, in the assurance that he was doing God's work. Unlike Luther and Zwingli, who both rather rejoiced in a fight, Calvin always had to nerve himself painfully for each encounter. It says much for his character that despite his inclinations he endured the trials of his ministry with unswerving determination and even refused to take obvious opportunities for ending his work at Geneva. The Calvinist willingness to do one's duty with no thought of personal happiness could look back with confidence to the example of the founder. Few men have worked for so long and so successfully with such frequent distaste for the task.

The city of Geneva, French-speaking but not of France, was in some ways particularly well suited to become the seat of Calvin's true

Church. Subject to its bishop, it had experienced the usual difficulties of medieval towns with ecclesiastical overlords in obtaining freedom and self-government. A third party in the conflict were the dukes of Savoy who by the fifteenth century had secured a permanent hold on that particular episcopal mitre. From 1511 onwards, bishop and duke tried to restore their ascendancy by reducing the city's hardwon liberties, but their successes were cut short in 1525–6 when Geneva obtained the friendship and support of Bern and Fribourg. The bishop fled the city in 1527 and concerted military action with Savoy, so that the elected syndics of Geneva declared the see vacant in 1534. The town's armed resistance triumphed early in 1536 when Bernese troops dispersed the bishop's somewhat casual investment and went on to attack Savoy. Bern had hopes of establishing suzerainty over Geneva, but the citizens' desire for independence was greater than their fear of a Savoyard revival, and the aggressive neighbour city had to be content with an alliance. A town which had won its freedom in a battle with an episcopal lord was manifestly ready for the Reformation, and from 1533 evangelical preachers had been active there with much encouragement from the magistrates. In addition Geneva was in economic decline. It had been an important mart town in the later middle ages, commanding a crossing of the Alpine roads with the route down the Rhône into France. But in the later fifteenth century France and Savoy had begun to boycott its prosperous fairs, partly for political reasons and partly in order to promote the rising prosperity of Lyons. At the same time, Bern was overtaking the Rhône city as a centre for trade passing through Switzerland. Thus the Geneva of the Reformation was struggling against decay, its poor often unemployed and its richer merchants nothing so splendid as they had been. It would seem that declining prosperity expressed itself in a growing recklessness; sober trading gave way to speculative gambling, and the general uncertainty led to a somewhat feverish public and private life.

The reform had come to Geneva in 1533, with Farel's arrival there after a wandering ministry in the Pays de Vaud. With Bern pressing for him, Geneva rapidly accepted the new religion and expelled the remnants of both popery and episcopal authority. By 1536 Farel had triumphed, and in May that year a general assembly of citizens made a public declaration of their adherence to the gospel. Farel was an enthusiast, almost a *Schwärmer*, a preacher of great fire and power, but neither an organiser nor a man of constant purpose. Recognising his deficiencies, he found in Calvin the right man to supply the qualities needed. From September 1536, the two men, occupying places of no visible authority (Calvin did not even become a citizen of Geneva until 1556), guided the Reformation in the city. They undertook a double task. On the one hand they wished to introduce

Protestantism and establish a fully reformed Church; on the other, they meant to bring about a total moral reform and regeneration. Unreformed Geneva had a bad name for licence and excess; the morals especially of the leading citizens left a good deal to be desired, and gambling and drunkenness seem to have been widespread. Most modern historians of Calvinism lay the stress on this state of affairs, by way of contrast with the godly and puritanical society which Calvin's labours were to produce. Whether Geneva was in fact particularly bad is anybody's guess. Late-medieval Europe was not exactly representative of the bourgeois virtues; affronted moralists found plenty to complain of in Savonarola's Florence, Luther's Saxony, More's England or Zwingli's Zürich. Geneva's reputation seems to rest on Calvin's denunciations and on malicious comments from Bern, as well as on the struggle between Calvinist rigour and common worldliness which ensued after 1536. At any rate, the reformers regarded with horror the easy-going behaviour of all classes at Geneva—their failure to attend church, their cheerful improprieties, their ready sexual licence. Though Calvin was not, perhaps, a true misogynist—he married, happily enough, in 1540 but did not remarry when his wife died in 1549—his attitude to women recalls St. Paul's; and he was to find the female members of the upper class especially opposed to his efforts at a moral reform.

The first round in the struggle over Church discipline went to Calvin's opponents, those whom he later called the party of the "libertines", meaning that they were for greater freedom from clerical supervision. Patriotism played its part, too, in the face of Calvin's encouragement of French immigrants, and in 1538 Farel and Calvin were exiled by the city council. The next few years were among Calvin's happiest. He moved to Strassburg where he taught at John Sturm's celebrated academy, preached to the congregation of French exiles, developed his ideas on the structure and services of the Church, and learned from Bucer about the best way to organise a reformed community. He attended the religious colloquies of 1540–41 and began to make his name among the leaders of Protestantism. This peaceful existence was interrupted by a message from Geneva, now sunk in confusion and left without effective spiritual guidance. It took months to persuade Calvin to accept the recall, but in September 1541, having left pleasant Strassburg in tears, he returned to his difficult and obstreperous charge. He was received with humility and joy on all sides and at once secured the acceptance of a new Church Ordinance, the fundamental constitutional reform from which all Calvinist Churches were to derive; but, as he had suspected, he faced a long struggle to establish his ascendancy in full. In fact, it was to take him fourteen years to eliminate all opposition to his dominance.

The *Ordonnances Ecclésiastiques* of November 1541 embody Calvin's considered view of Church government, allegedly found in scripture and cleansed from later accretions. They begin by stating that four orders of office were instituted by Christ: pastors, doctors, elders and deacons. The pastors' or ministers' duty is to preach the Word, administer the sacraments, and admonish and censure those of insufficient lives. They are to nominate additions to their own number, but these must be accepted and confirmed by the city council; and they are to hold weekly meetings to discuss doctrine and argue out disputed points, unresolved difficulties being umpired by the elders. In the doctors, Calvin introduced a teaching order into ecclesiastical government, assigning to it the task of defining doctrine and instructing in it. Here he demonstrated his constant concern with education, explicitly adding, "we will call this the order of the schools". The elders were laymen, chosen—this was a concession forced upon Calvin—by the city magistrates; they were "to have oversight of the life of everyone, to admonish amicably those whom they see to be erring or to be living a disordered life, and...to enjoin fraternal corrections". In the deacons, Calvin revived the scriptural office whose name had long become attached to a mere stage in the clerical orders; they were made responsible for charitable provision and the care of the poor.

The Ordinance goes on to stress the task of enforcing ecclesiastical and moral discipline, the instrument provided being a court (consistory) of ministers and elders. In actual fact, the Genevan consistory had at first little effective power; only when the number of ministers came to exceed that of the elders did it take over the full enforcement of the social and moral legislation which distinguished the Genevan holy commonwealth. But from the first it used informers to bring cases of moral delinquency before its bar, showed itself no respecter of persons, and displayed the characteristic puritan concern with tiny detail as well as the equally characteristic failure to distinguish between serious matters and trivial. As its power grew, so it also demonstrated that the fraternal admonition of the Ordinance could only too readily deteriorate into a savage desire to humiliate and punish, with public penances and excommunication growing apace. However often he might enjoin charity, Calvin's own severe bigotry and his disapproval of anything casual or light-hearted contributed greatly to this increase of selfrighteous censoriousness and this delight in the discomfiture of the ungodly. Though Calvin fearlessly attacked the powerful, there is no sign at all that he ever thought of mobilising popular resentment to assist himself. The traditional families continued to rule the city, and Geneva never even looked like undergoing a social revolution.

The Genevan Church Order was not by any means entirely original, nor did Calvin, who claimed to be fulfilling scripture, think it was. He maintained that he was returning to the practice of the early Church. Zwingli's example played some part, but Bucer's Strassburg, which in its churchwardens (*Kirchenpfleger*) even possessed something like Calvin's elders, exercised the greatest influence. However, even as Calvin's theology gave to Protestantism a clearer and firmer shape, so did his Church government provide a simple, systematic and effective organisation for consolidating the Reformation and for securing the control of the clergy and the devout over the rest, an organisation superior to anything used elsewhere. It was also adaptable. It had popular, even democratic, possibilities well marked in it, with election rather than appointment from above as Calvin's principle of operation. This was so even though the conditions of Geneva—the power of the leading families, and the hold of syndics and council on affairs—compelled him to make concessions which reduced the autonomy of his Church as against the secular authorities. The crucial office was that of the elders. Intended, as lay administrators in ecclesiastical matters, to secure independence for the Church as well as to act as links with the governed laity, they were at first rather representatives of the magistracy in Church government; but as Calvin finally won control, they became the means by which the Church ruled the lives of all, and this role they were to fill from the first in the Calvinist communities which in due course developed all over Europe and America. The fullest growth of Calvinist organisation, Scottish presbyterianism and its offshoots, depended upon the functions of the lay elders rather than upon the minister who came to be effectively their appointee. This tightly-knit, potentially democratic organisation attracted reformers everywhere; Geneva rapidly became the pattern of a true Church to many Protestants—that "example of the best reformed Churches" to which the English puritans appealed so regularly from 1560 onwards.

In Geneva itself, the story of strife and struggle continued for years. Calvin encountered two kinds of opposition. In the first place he was determined to introduce total conformity to his religious Reformation. This ambition not only involved the development of the characteristic Genevan form of worship, with prayers, sermons and the singing of psalms forming the core of the service and holy communion being made a frequent, even a regular practice, but also conflict with men who denied some of his most cherished tenets. Seeing that Calvin relied in general on arrivals from outside—most of his assistants were Frenchmen for whom, to the annoyance of a chauvinist element in the city, he secured citizenship—it is ironical that his ecclesiastical opponents should also have been among the immigrants. In 1542 he quarrelled with Sebastian Castellio (1515–

63), a Savoyard whom he had appointed head of his school. A combative and ill-mannered man, Castellio raised a number of doctrinal points concerning the authority of scripture; in particular he denied that the Song of Songs was an inspired book—he thought it an erotic poem. This accurate perception got him into trouble, and in 1544 he was driven from Geneva. From Basel he continued to attack Calvin. His experiences taught him the need to protect liberty of conscience, and in 1554 he opened in his book *Whether Heretics should be Persecuted* the long debate on toleration which is one of the more reassuring signs of the second half of the century. In 1551 Calvin procured the banishment of the Frenchman Jean Bolsec (d. 1584) who had attacked his teaching on predestination, even though Bolsec had powerful protectors among Calvin's Genevan enemies; this victory, given special point when Bolsec promptly reverted to Rome, marked an important stage in Calvin's general triumph in the city. There were also occasional difficulties with Italian exiles among whom spirituals and antitrinitarians predominated; Calvin could not win the permanent adherence either of the wandering Bernardino Ochino or of that more surprising convert, Pietro Paolo Vergerio (papal nuncio to Germany in 1536), both of whom visited Geneva on their physical and spiritual pilgrimages. In these doctrinal battles Calvin proved a relentless and merciless fighter.

More immediately serious, however, were the difficulties consequent upon Calvin's determination to make Geneva a city of God obedient to the moral law. The magistrates raised little objection when Calvin demanded the suppression of prostitution or induced them to try the charming experiment of opening evangelical drinking shops in which moderate consumption was to be combined with religious propaganda. (The people would have nothing to do with these, and the closed down taverns had to be reopened.) But when Calvin attacked the manners of the great, resistance built up. His opponents, who formed a powerful party on the council, stood not only for a less stringent control of private lives but also for a narrowly Genevan policy and for hostility to the immigrant Protestants. When Calvin's consistory tangled with such powerful men as Francis Favre and his son-in-law Ami Perrin, the result was war to the knife. In 1547 a young patrician, Jacques Gruet, was executed for blasphemy and atheism, to Calvin's satisfaction; but in 1549 the "libertines" got the upper hand in the council. The Perrinists endeavoured to reduce Calvin to obedience rather than be rid of him; with the generality his influence remained great, and there was always the memory of the previous occasion on which he had had to be fetched back, cap in hand. Thus they dared do no more than subject him to insults and annoyances. Calvin felt unhappy and distressed, but it never occurred to him to give way or seek relief by abandoning his post.

The situation remained in this uneasy balance, until the case of Michael Servetus brought matters to a head in 1553.[5] The Spanish heretic, who before this had crossed swords with Calvin, in that year published his *Christianismi Restitutio*, a defence of his highly original views on the Trinity and other issues which was deliberately aimed at Calvin's *Institutes*. Angered beyond measure, Calvin revealed to the Catholic magistrates of Vienne who the Dr. Villeneuve practising in their town really was. Servetus was arrested and condemned, but managed to get away. For some reason that has never become clear he chose to visit Geneva on his way to Naples. When Calvin, at a low time in his fortunes, found his enemy in his city he jumped to the conclusion that the "libertines" had brought in Servetus to complete the destruction of the Calvinist system. In any case, Servetus had had years of warning that if the chance offered Calvin would not let so pernicious a heretic get alive from Geneva. The unhappy man was arrested, tried and sentenced to burning, a fate he suffered despite Calvin's plea that the sentence be commuted for the more merciful one of beheading. It is perfectly true that all denominations of the day united in abhorrence of Servetus' views, that Servetus was tactless and violent and, in coming to Geneva, very foolish; but none of this reduces the guilt of Calvin in denouncing him and pursuing him to the death. In any case, Servetus, though the most notable, was not the only victim of Calvin's iron determination to root out diversity of opinion and his willingness to use the sword in the interests of God.

In his death Servetus achieved his enemy's triumph. Perrin had taken the Spaniard's part, and Calvin's victory undid all the successes which the libertines had won in the previous six years. In 1555 Perrin and his leading supporters fled from Geneva; the council at last surrendered totally to the reformer; and for the remaining nine years of his life Calvin ruled the city without hindrance. After his death his disciple Theodore Beza inherited his near-papal position, and Geneva was to preserve Calvin's constitution and principles unaltered for some 150 years. The more democratic institutions in the city's civil government disappeared, and the surviving top council came in effect to be an agent of the now all-powerful consistory. Laws of mounting severity were passed—against blasphemy and adultery, for attendance at church and compulsory schooling, concerning cleanliness and public health. Many of them were sensible and necessary, others bigoted and stultifying; all were the same to Calvin. Enforcement grew more savage, too, with banishments and whippings more frequent than one might expect in that supposedly purified city. The devil still took some driving out. Nevertheless, in his last years when he had a free hand, Calvin showed what could be done: the easy-going, dissolute, unstable city of the past emerged as a grim, solid, elevated community of psalm-singing church-goers, reporting each other to the ever-watchful consistory and anxiously exchanging "fraternal correction" in public meetings. To the many earnest visitors of evangelical leanings, the sight was edifying and glorious; here, at last, was a Church where God was truly worshipped by men's whole lives and not mocked by their delinquencies. In those early days the passion for godliness was genuine enough; hypocrisy came later. Calvin's Geneva should not be disbelieved or despised: it should be treated seriously, as an awful warning.

III   The Spread of Calvinism

Geneva became Calvin's scene of operations by an accident, nor did he ever restrict his interests to that one city. Indeed, it is clear that he conceived himself to be doing for the French what Luther had done for the Germans. The early editions of the *Institutes* carried a preface addressed to Francis I which reveals Calvin's hope that he might persuade all his nation of his message. When it became apparent that nothing could be expected from the Valois king, Calvin only intensified his efforts to reach the people. In 1541 he published the first French translation of his great work, a landmark in the history of French prose as well as French Protestantism; and thereafter every Latin edition of the *Institutes* was followed by a vernacular version. In the 1540s Calvin came to be accepted by Protestants everywhere as one of the outstanding leaders of the reform, and his influence began to penetrate widely. Bitter quarrels with Luther's heirs prevented the formation of a united front. Calvin had to be content with the Zürich Agreement of 1549 which set up a single Helvetic Church; within the Protestant camp, and especially in Germany, "evangelical" (Lutheran) and "reformed" (Calvinist) soon opposed each other with a ferocity born of family resemblance, leaving the Counter-Reformation to score spectacular successes of recovery. Outside Germany and Scandinavia, however, Calvin replaced Luther as the guiding star of active reform, and in Western Europe in particular Calvinist congregations proliferated.

   When one notes that this second wave of the Reformation did not anywhere enjoy the advantages which so helped Luther—nationwide and nationalist fervour, and the support of princes—it becomes something of a problem to understand the success of Calvinism. Although its main expansive phase lies outside the confines of this book, the reasons for its success are found in the essential character of Calvin's achievement and need investigating. In the past, the problem has too often been solved by theories which saw some kind of inevitability in Geneva's advance. When it ceased to be fashionable to see the hand of God in this—or the devil's, if the writer was in the other camp—economic determinism came to the aid of the historian. However, neither the view that a rising bourgeois middle class adopted Calvin's Protestantism as a means of fighting free of feudal and clerical predominance, nor the theory which attributed the attraction of Calvinism to the desire for a religion which would suit the practices of a capitalist society, will any longer do. Outside the doctrinaire fold of Marxist historiography no one now believes the first; and the second has taken sufficient knocks to look remarkably unhappy.[6] The theories have been particularly unfortunate because they distort the true picture of Calvinist expansion. According to them, Calvinism should have sought out the "middle classes", the commercially advanced and active communities and individuals, but there is no evidence that it did this.

In France, which naturally felt Calvin's influence before any other country (if only because he purposely directed it there), the more rigorous form of Protestantism edged out an earlier, vaguer attachment to Lutheran or even pre-Lutheran reform and attracted new recruits as much from the poorer sort as from any other layer of society. Persecution rarely let up after 1541; in 1545 the government promoted a massacre of the old-established Waldensians in the east, whose remnants fled to Switzerland; in 1547, the new king Henry II (1547–59) set up a special court, the *chambre ardente*, to destroy the spread of Protestantism. The court, which met much opposition from the *Parlement*, was abandoned in 1550, but it had done a good deal of bloody work. Though many died at the stake, the movement continued to advance steadily, proving everywhere that the religious impetus which had started the Reformation off was neither yet exhausted nor finding satisfaction in the gradually improving old Church. Though its followers came from all layers of society—artisans and peasants being prominent among converts—what kept it alive was the support it received from members of the nobility, especially the court of Navarre, not any particular attraction it exercised for the bourgeois. As elsewhere, the leading and successful capitalists naturally conformed rather than resisted; by definition, they could not be successful with the stake in the offing.

Calvinism gradually penetrated the Netherlands after the 1550's; here it took over from Lutheran and especially from Anabaptist predecessors and was strongest among the proletariate of the Walloon towns in the south and among the backward peasantry of the north-east. Its victory in Scotland after 1560 owed nothing to commercialism or a middle class, neither of which existed in that country of riotous nobles and a depressed peasantry. The movement affected Germany where certain princes, especially the Elector Palatine Frederick III (1559–76), adopted it in the second half of the century. In the 1550's it replaced Lutheranism among the Polish, Magyar and

Bohemian nobility, in part because it was less specifically linked with the German influence which in those regions could always rouse nationalist resentment. Nowhere did it owe its original reception or its wider successes to any connection with advanced economic ideas or to any imagined advantages for middle-class economic ambitions. In the west—especially in England, Scotland and the Netherlands, all later centres of advanced economies as well as Protestantism—it made its way among the poor rather than the rich; in the east it attracted the landowning ruling classes. There is the less need to seek a significant connection with capitalism because in fact such capitalists as there were adopted Calvinism only when the faith had triumphed and made conformity advisable.

The truth is that the impetus of the Reformation was not exhausted by the middle of the sixteenth century. There is no difficulty in explaining why more people and more countries should have continued to break with Rome in the years after 1550: all over Europe, the spiritual needs and social problems which had originally assisted the success of the Reformation were still present, and many countries had not yet experienced a major battle with the Church. The question which needs an answer is why the lead in this further growth should have been taken by the followers of Calvin rather than those of Luther. And that answer is to be found both in the weaknesses of Lutheranism after Luther's death (1546) and in the peculiar strengths of Calvinism. Even while Luther lived, serious controversies had arisen among his disciples. In the years 1537–40, he had had to struggle with his own pupil John Agricola (1499–1566) who had taken the doctrine of justification by faith to one logical conclusion by denying that true believers need obey any laws. This antinomianism smacked too much of the sectarian extravagances which Luther dreaded and detested, and Agricola was driven from Saxony. The ageing reformer began to see potential apostates everywhere, and even Melanchthon suffered his blows. Real trouble broke out after his death removed the one personality who could maintain some unity in the German Reformation. Two major parties developed at once: the moderate and accommodating Philippists who followed Melanchthon in his endeavour to bring peace among the Protestant sects, and the relentless Gnesiolutherans who found in Flacius Illyricus (1520–75) a leader to defend the supposed pure milk of Luther's teaching. Controversy succeeded controversy, and in the second half of the century Lutheranism became increasingly rigid, with a well defined orthodoxy and a devout hatred of Calvinism. Neither its divisions nor its growing absorption in theological disputes were likely to assist any further spread; the predominance of princely control in the Lutheran Churches made it an unsuitable faith for men struggling against unsympathetic secular authorities; and the earliest form of Protestantism was also too manifestly German by now to evoke a ready response in other countries. In many ways the Lutheran inspiration had slowed down; missionary zeal had been replaced by inward-looking consolidation and quibbling; by becoming respectable, the Lutheran Reformation had lost a good deal of its dynamic. All these departing qualities were revived in Calvin's teaching and precept, and the road was clear for him.

Calvinism in itself proved particularly suitable to be the main current of Protestant reform after the middle of the century because circumstances forced the reformers increasingly into the position of revolutionaries not only against ecclesiastical but also against civil rule. Calvinism expanded primarily in countries like France, the Netherlands and England where the Reformation had not yet got hold and where the powers that be had no intention at all of bowing down before Geneva. Thus it could not follow the Lutheran example of allying with rulers who would establish it by edict: tarrying for the magistrate, as the English puritans called such hopes, invariably proved a fruitless policy. Even in Scotland, the one country which turned decisively Calvinist in this period, the new faith was that of rebels against the existing Francophil government. Moreover, from the 1550s onwards, Protestant expansion encountered a Church of Rome revived, reformed and re-invigorated—a vastly more formidable enemy than that met in the spring time of the Reformation. In such a situation, Calvinism drew enormous strength from Calvin's two outstanding contributions. The theology of predestination— whatever its place in Calvin's own scheme of things—offered to ardent men an assurance of utter rightness and certain success: if God had chosen them, what matter if men rejected them? Under the pressure of persecution and resistance the Calvinists grew in self-reliance and contempt for all others; by no means sectarians in intent, they nevertheless acquired the sectarian's unshakable endurance in the face of adversity, an endurance born of their conviction that they were the Lord's elect. And the Calvinist system of Church government enabled them to translate this spirit into action. Based on the individual congregation with its tight order, its elective principles, and its active mixture of lay and clerical participation, Calvinist groups were extraordinarily difficult to root out and sometimes even difficult to detect.

In fact, Calvinism had all the advantages of a subversive movement organised in cells and filled with a total faith in its future. Its only difficulty lay in the need to extend an organisation designed for a single city and congregation to national movements composed of many separate congregations, a difficulty which hid the dangers of sectarian splintering. But the problem was solved, first in France (1559) and later in Scotland, by setting up provincial and national synods, meetings of elected or appointed representatives from the organisations lower down the scale. This system enlarged the moderately democratic potentialities of Calvinism and preserved initiative and vigour among members without losing the general guidance and cohesion of a national Church. Calvin's own view of the citizen's duties and the magistrate's rights had been very like Luther's. He held that secular government was instituted by God, must be obeyed except where it ordains anything against the faith, and even if disobeyed in obedience to God must never be resisted. Like every religious leader of the first half of the century, Calvin reserved the punishment of wicked rulers to God alone. Yet even before he died John Knox was preaching the right to overthrow false princes, and within fifteen years of Calvin's death the *Vindiciae contra Tyrannos* of Philippe Duplessis-Mornay proclaimed the subjection of kings to their peoples. In the hands of French Huguenots and English puritans, Calvinism became a source of anti-authoritarian and libertarian thinking. Despite himself, Calvin had founded a revolutionary faith.

He made two other contributions of note to the surprising expansion of a doctrine established not in a national state but in an obscure city. He himself acted as a true leader, exhorting and encouraging his followers everywhere, denouncing such weaknesses as willingness to compromise in externals for the sake of survival (what he called the "Nicodemism" especially of certain Italians who professed the faith in secret), and promising, from the safety of Geneva, future bliss for present disaster. His writings, tirelessly hammering home the clarity of his teaching and seemingly based on nothing but the inescapable authority of scripture, became to many a compelling body of doctrine in a manner never achieved by Luther's larger but much less systematic output. True, even with Calvinism ascendant, some men outside the Lutheran fold continued to find the poetry and humanity of Luther more attractive and more fulfilling, but on the whole the Protestants, especially in the west, received Calvin with the relief that in the middle of a fierce debate is provoked by the appearance of a clear-cut set of intellectually based tenets. Jesuits and Calvinists had this in common that they appealed to the bulk of the learned on their own side, seemed to provide all the answers within their given framework, and could out-argue all opponents in their own camps.

Calvin further resembled Loyola in his concern for schooling. The academy which he founded at Geneva (1558) was based on the example of John Sturm's institution at Strassburg but came to surpass it in influence. Consisting of a grammar school for boys and a university for adolescents, it adapted the educational reforms of the humanists to the production of highly trained and enthusiastic Calvinists. Many of its pupils came from abroad and went back to their countries to carry the message. Indeed, the amazing influence of

Geneva can only be understood if one remembers that it was exercised at short range, on the many who came there in search of the truth or in flight from persecution. From the 1540s Geneva became a chief city of refuge for suffering Protestants, especially after Charles V's victory over the Schmalkaldic League (1547) and the imposition of a rigorous Lutheranism at Strassburg (1548) ended the phase during which that latter city had acted as the main centre of residence and cross-fertilisation for many streams of opinion among the reformers. In the ten years after 1549, some 5000 refugees reached Geneva, all of course ardent Protestants escaping from the persecution which was the order of the day in France (1547–59), England (1553–58) and Scotland (1546–58). Even those refugee communities which established themselves in other tolerant cities, as at Frankfurt or Zürich, were in touch with Geneva and came under its influence. Calvin's Geneva rapidly replaced Luther's Wittenberg and Bucer's Strassburg as the high citadel of Protestantism. Calvin would never allow the variety and freedom of those earlier Jerusalems, but in the circumstances of the new age about to open—in view of the Counter-Reformation and the political struggles ahead—what was needed was a training camp for single-minded soldiers, and that Calvin's Geneva could supply. After Luther's death, the Reformation might have been worn down and overcome; as befits a leader of the second generation, John Calvin restored its aggressive and expanding energies.

Chapter 9

War and Peace

I The Triumph of Charles V

The Diet of Regensburg ended in July 1541, and with it went the last real hope of restoring unity and peace by negotiation.[1] Rome refused to contemplate any concessions: the era of Carafa's ascendancy had begun. On the Protestant side, despite the landgrave of Hesse's decline and defection, tempers were almost as unyielding. Contarini and Gropper, Bucer and Melanchthon, vacated the front ranks. And even the emperor had to admit that a change of methods could not now be avoided. He did not abate a jot of his basic policy: re-union in Germany continued to be his aim, in part because he believed in the single Christian commonwealth headed by the pope and guarded by himself, and in part because both Habsburg ambitions and the defeat of Islam could only be advanced if he had an undivided and obedient Holy Roman Empire at his back. Alone among the policy-makers (though strongly encouraged by his minister Granvelle), he still thought that a measure of compromise might be necessary, but he had also come to realise that even for himself the measure could be only nominal. Thus he spoke at intervals of allowing the Protestants their practices of clerical marriage and communion in both kinds, though these points were invariably rejected as surrender by the pope and invariably ridiculed as insufficient by the Lutherans.

However, while Charles remained convinced that the restoration of peace would require a little give and take, he so far agreed with Paul III that after Regensburg he was ready to use force in order to end the schism. There has been some discussion among historians about the date by which the emperor resolved on war; but it is reasonably clear that from 1541 he was prepared for it and believed it to be necessary. If his fundamental aims did not alter, his immediate policy did. From now on, negotiations would be less a sincere attempt to settle

differences without a fatal breach and more a screen behind which
the grimmer purpose went forward. He also re-arranged his order of
priorities. In 1530 he had looked for an understanding with the
princes in order to free himself for decisive action against the sultan,
and for a decade this reasoning had governed his policy. Now he
plainly decided that he first had to set his German house in order and
that the Turkish problem would have to take its chance until he
should be free to tackle it with his back secure. From 1541,
the emperor conducted affairs with a single eye to the defeat of the
Schmalkaldic League.

However, no more than in the 1530s was he a free agent in the
1540s, and the actual attack on the German schismatics—the dis-
rupters of imperial unity—was once again postponed by urgent pressure from other quarters. The year 1541 saw the revival of war with
Turkey and the renewal of the French claim to Milan. The Turks
invaded Hungary in the alleged interests of Zapolyai's infant son, and
this time they stayed, the bulk of the country in their hands and King
Ferdinand pressed extremely hard to retain his narrow foot-hold in
the north and west. As for Milan, Charles was, by the terms of the
truce of Nice, to administer it pending a final settlement, but early in
1541 he acted unilaterally by conferring it, as an imperial fief, on his
son Philip. Francis I reacted at once by preparing for a break in the
amity which had been steadily deteriorating since its inception in
1538. In July he sent agents to conclude an alliance with Sulaiman;
these foolishly crossed the Milanese; Philip's governor decided to
investigate their papers; his soldiers proved too thorough. The murder of envoys in time of peace was, even for the sixteenth century,
outside ordinary diplomatic practice, and war became certain. Francis was held back only by the emperor's apparent power and by the
delay, the result of the murder, in his treaty with the Turk. Both
obstacles were soon out of the way. In the autumn of 1541, Charles
thought to repeat his earlier triumph against the Barbary corsairs by
attacking Algiers; he started too late in the year, and his splendid fleet
was destroyed in a storm. Coming after Prevesa, the Algerian disaster
freed the Western Mediterranean for the Turkish fleet, and Barbarossa ranged about it at pleasure. The Franco-Turkish alliance, concluded late in 1541, grew to embrace all the enemies of the
Habsburgs—Cleves, Denmark, Sweden, Scotland—while both the
pope and the League of Schmalkalden remained neutral. And
the German army sent into Hungary in 1542 failed completely. This
expedition was the fruit of all those frequent appeals for aid against
the Turks and all those occasional promises of it; led by the incom-
petent Joachim II of Brandenburg, it only proved that left to itself
Germany had no hope of resisting Sulaiman any time he cared to
resume his march on Austria. Thus by the spring of 1542 Francis felt

safe to attack; and in the summer the French once more brought war and destruction, with varying fortunes, to the Netherlands.

The war went even worse for Charles in 1543, but it was at this point that he first showed clearly his new strategic thinking. There was, for the present, nothing he could do about the Turks, and he accepted that fact. Ferdinand was left to protect the eastern marches of the empire as best he might, while Sulaiman victoriously advanced all along the Hungarian front and consolidated his conquest. He made no further attempt on Vienna, which—since the chance did not offer again until 1683—was a mistake. In the Mediterranean the Franco-Turkish fleet did as it pleased, robbing and burning along the coasts of Italy, taking thousands of slaves, capturing Nice in August, wintering at Toulon. The treason to Christendom committed by Francis in allowing, even inviting, this fierce and unmanageable ally right into Europe was patent to all, and the success of the moment was certainly paid for in the hatred and lasting distrust which the Most Christian King brought upon his name and country. Charles left his viceroy in Naples to do what he could, which was very little. For himself, he concentrated on clearing the Netherlands, removing the threat in the north, and thus freeing himself for action in the empire. In February he concluded a long-negotiated alliance with Henry VIII, and by the summer English troops investing Boulogne (with, on the whole, less than sufficient competence) began to distract the French effort from Flanders and Luxemburg. At the same time, the emperor in person attended to the key point, the duchy of Cleves. Gathering troops in Italy he advanced rapidly down the Rhine, to enter Germany for only the third time in his life, though on this occasion he was not to leave for twelve years. In August-September 1543, in a campaign lasting a few weeks, he overwhelmed Duke William and forced him to accept the treaty of Venloo. The duke abandoned his French and Protestant alliances, surrendered Guelders, and restored the old religion in his territories.

Crushing Cleves was like touching the secret spring of a delicate lock: everything opened at once. The Netherlands were free of a pincer threat, the northern Protestant bloc fell apart, Charles was able to turn on France. Even a great French victory in Italy (Ceresole, April 1544) made no difference, especially as it was not followed up. The decision came in the north. While Henry VIII threatened Paris from Normandy, Charles attacked across the Marne. By August it looked as though France would at last suffer defeat on her own soil; not since the days of Joan of Arc had her peril been so real. But Charles did not drive his advantage home. As usual, money was running short; if, in assessing all these campaigns, one is to avoid the not uncommon error of expressing contempt for their alleged feebleness or fatuity, one must always remember that the plans and ambitions of all these commanders lacked the support of disciplined armies and the backing of efficient taxation. The mercenaries who won Charles's battles, as they won Francis's, fought well and often (since recruitment was by countries) even patriotically, but they fought only as long as they were paid.[2] Moreover, Charles was for the moment not concerned to crush France; he was all along thinking of finding time to deal with Germany. In addition he probably remembered his mistake after Pavia in 1525 when total success had gone to his head and had led him to overplay a temporary triumph. So he let Francis off the hook, on terms which looked very honourable but in fact prevented French assistance to the German Protestants for eight crucial years. By the peace of Crespy (September 1544) the two sovereigns confirmed the arrangements of that of Cambrai (1529): Charles gave up his claims to the duchy of Burgundy, and Francis his to Naples, Flanders and Artois. The renewed amity was to be sealed by marrying Francis's younger son, the duke of Orléans, to a Habsburg princess: if he married a daughter of Charles V, he was to get Milan for a dowry; if a daughter of Ferdinand, the Netherlands were to be his portion. Though the treaty insisted that neither territory must ever be united to France, this clause gave up such major dynastic interests that Charles's real purpose—the destruction of the German opposition—becomes very plain. It was underlined in the secret addition to the treaty by which Francis bound himself to assist Charles against all heretics and break off his Turkish alliance. As it happened, Orléans died the next year and the Habsburgs lost nothing. Henry VIII was left with the siege of Boulogne and a war in Scotland, deserted—as his inane policy deserved—by an ally who after the events of the 1530s had little cause to trust him.

Thus Charles won the major victory for his now single-minded policy by letting his enemies have their own way in secondary matters. The emperor was at the peak of his statesmanship, reaping the fruits of a long apprenticeship and a remarkable patience. He needed all his skills, for the two years of war, with the many defeats they had brought, had once again assisted the spread of Protestantism. Apart from Bavaria and the Habsburg family lands, only the northwest with its many ecclesiastical territories still preserved any notable allegiance to Rome; and now the Reformation attacked here, too. In 1542, the last Catholic prince in the north, Duke Henry of Brunswick-Wolfenbüttel, involved himself in a feud with Hesse over the imperial city of Goslar. Greed and dynastic ambitions alone provoked the quarrel, which was conducted with a thorough and salacious vigour by two enemies who could, and did, match each other's sins in handsome catalogues. But the landgrave called in the Schmalkaldic League, and in July the duke fled his territories which were at once handed over to Bugenhagen to reform. The archbishop of Magdeburg and the bishop of Halberstadt, squeezed between the rival ambitions of Saxony and Brandenburg, were showing signs of willingness to accept the Reformation as the price of survival.

Worse still for the emperor, the electorates of the Rhine began to waver. In 1542 Hermann von Wied, archbishop of Cologne, asked Bucer and Melanchthon to help him reform the Church in his territories. Charles was flabbergasted. As he later said to the landgrave: "How can that good lord make reform? He knows no Latin and in all his life has said no more than three masses." Philip replied that the old man (Hermann was sixty-five in 1542) read a lot in German and had a good understanding of religion; and indeed, the archbishop's motives seem to have been pure. He was a kindly, paternal ruler on whom spiritual office sat oddly, and a bit of a booby; but Bucer came, though Melanchthon contented himself with advice from afar, and the example of Cologne began to affect the neighbouring bishopric of Münster. From his office in Cologne Cathedral, Gropper strenuously resisted his episcopal superior, and the defeat of Cleves arrested the progress of the Reformation round the lower Rhine; but it was not until 1546 that Archbishop Hermann was forced out of his place, to retire into aristocratic and Protestant obscurity, while his successor brought the electorate back to the Roman obedience. In 1544 the Elector Frederick II of the Palatinate also began to welcome Lutheran preachers, and in 1546 he established friendly relations with the League of Schmalkalden. It looked at last as though in the near future all Germany would be Protestant; without actively resisting the emperor, the Reformation once again successfully exploited his preoccupations.

Charles dealt with the situation in a manner deserving high praise on political grounds, even though bigots then and later charged him with lack of principle. To him it was quite evident that he could not hope to win if he involved himself in indiscriminate hostility with all Protestants. The key to his problem was the League of Schmalkalden: destroy that, and the other reformed territories would soon come to heel. For the League by no means comprised all who had broken with Rome. Brandenburg, afraid of Saxon ascendancy, stood aside; and Brandenburg could be used. Another weakness in the Protestant ranks was a group of young rulers who did not remember the early struggle for the Reformation and who saw no prospects for themselves as long as Protestant politics were dominated by the elector of Saxony and the landgrave of Hesse, the latter having eased his way back into the League by 1544. Three of these young princes proved vulnerable to imperial diplomacy. The Margrave John of Brandenburg-Küstrin, a younger branch of the electoral house of Brandenburg, was a sincere Lutheran but opposed to the League because it limited the independence of the northern princes and seemed to pursue a

purely selfish policy. The Margrave Albert Alcibiades of Branden-
burg-Culmbach, of the Franconian branch of the Hohenzollern
family, entertained only personal ambitions in which religion played
no part: he wanted to found a territorial power and did not care how
he went about it. Above all, Maurice, duke of Saxony since 1541,
was ready to play politics for the sake of personal advancement.
Representing the junior, Albertine, line of the Saxon house of Wettin,
Maurice hankered after the electoral lands and title which the family
compact of 1485 had given to the senior, Ernestine, line. The two
branches of this family hated each other devotedly, even though both
the electorate and the duchy now followed the same religion.

The young princes sought personal greatness and power. They
never dreamt of abandoning the Reformation, but they no longer
saw German affairs in the light of the religious division only. While,
in general, they wished to exploit the confusion of the empire in the
interests of princely ascendancy, for the moment the emperor offered
a chance to break the hold of the older princes and to do oneself a
great deal of good without damaging one's honour by opposing one's
feudal overlord. John of Küstrin was an honest man who liked to be
made to feel important; Albert Alcibiades a reckless and deplorable
adventurer; only Maurice had the makings of a statesman. If moral
and religious principles did not enter into his machinations, he was
only applying the lessons of much recent history. When even the
pope, for the sake of family advantage, could overlook a French
alliance with Islam, a duke of Saxony intent on making something
of himself was wise to play the game by the prevalent rules. It is
arguable that in the whole period under review only the emperor
remained consistently true to his word and his principles; and it is
also arguable that he alone could afford this, though that rider would
be quite unfair to Charles V's highly developed sense of personal
honour.

In the years 1544–46, the emperor therefore set about preparing
the ground for his show-down with the Schmalkaldeners. It was a
tricky enough situation. He needed the neutrality, at least, of France,
and this he got at Crespy. He needed the alliance of the pope for a
war against Lutheranism, and the alliance or neutrality of many
German Lutherans in a war which to them had to be represented as
a punitive action against enemies to the imperial authority rather
than enemies to the universal Church. As it was, he played his hand
well, though he was assisted by the sluggish stupidity of the League.
In January 1544 he called a Diet at Speyer which he used to pull the
wool over their eyes. The recess spoke pacifically of letting things be
until (once again) the assembly of a "general, free and Christian
Council"; the main purpose of the meeting was to consolidate Charles's understanding with the middle party of Protestant non-Leaguers.

Only too willing to avoid conflict, and perilously sure of their strength, the Protestants at the Diet offered help against France and welcomed the promise of a Council. The pope did something to confirm this mood when he rejected the Speyer recess, only to be violently attacked by both Luther and Calvin—the leaders of Protestantism rushing to the defence of the emperor. Charles had his own ideas about Rome. With the Protestants caught in a net of false expectations and France reduced to peace, he opened negotiations with Paul III. Relations between emperor and pope had been very bad since 1541 when Paul refused to abandon his strict neutrality during the Habsburg-Valois war; nor did his reluctance to revive the General Council help matters. Using both the Farnese family programme and the new desire at Rome to suppress the schism by immediate war, Charles in May 1545 added the pope to his side. Parma and Piacenza were promised to Pier-Luigi Farnese; in return, Paul called the Council and offered armed assistance. The Council actually opened at Trent in December 1545 and really got down to business, even if it did not exactly proceed along the lines desired by the emperor. Trent was chosen as a meeting-place because it lay in the Holy Roman Empire and Charles had promised the Germans a location outside the papal dominions. At the same time, being in Italy, it was convenient for the assembling fathers all but one of whom (a Frenchman) came from Italy and Spain. No Germans attended at the first series of meetings which lasted until March 1547. In June 1546, pope and emperor concluded a formal alliance under which papal troops were to assist in the destruction of Lutheranism.

Thus all was ready by the middle of 1546. The League had been isolated from all possible allies; the pope offered help; a truce in Hungary (1545) had freed Ferdinand for the concerns of Germany; the unity of the German Protestants was fatally, if so far secretly, broken. The only quarter from which Charles could expect nothing were the Catholic princes of Germany; the new duke of Bavaria (Albert, who succeeded William in 1545) was a nonentity. All that remained was to start the war in such a way that the temporary disposition of forces could be properly deployed. This meant that the emperor had to avoid the appearance of a purely religious war while telling both the pope and his intimates that the ending of the schism was his true aim. Probably it was, but it is clear that the political motive—the creation of an irresistible imperial authority—was quite as important to him. It also meant that for preference the Schmalkaldeners must be induced to open hostilities. To this end Charles took the considerable risk of postponing the actual military preparations. As late as April 1546, he travelled to Regensburg, through a half-hostile country, with virtually no guard, to attend one more Diet at which yet another religious colloquy was proposed. But by now even the leaders of the League had begun to wake up to what was going on. At Regensburg the emperor was almost alone. He used the opportunity to conclude a defensive alliance with Bavaria and to make the final arrangements with Maurice of Saxony to whom he conceded the continued use of the Lutheran religion in his territories and held out vague promises of the great prize of Magdeburg. All this would last as long as he had need of the duke. In July, challenged to explain all these negotiations, he virtually came into the open: "His imperial majesty means to restore unity, peace and justice in the empire." The League of Schmalkalden, assured of support from Württemberg and the southern towns but unable to bring Nuremberg, Brandenburg and the Palatinate into its camp, mobilised its forces.

Before the crisis came, Luther died, on 18 February 1546, in his birth-place at Eisleben where he had gone to settle a political dispute between two counts of Mansfeld. Sixty-three years old, he was worn out and tired, broken down in the body by years of labour and illness. His mind remained clear to the last, and his spirit at the end returned to a more serene temper than he had commonly displayed in recent years. Over the sorrows of friends and the rejoicings of enemies, who at once spread tales of the devil's coming to fetch his own, his gentle and assured departure consolidated the triumph of his life. He had never meant to break the Church or bring turmoil to the world, but the thrust within himself of what he conceived to be the truth had not let him rest. Now it was done, and the work stood beyond undoing. No matter how one stands to the story—for or against or aside—only blind folly would deny his greatness and only blind partisanship forget the troubles he had brought. He had sought to serve his God. Being a man, he had both served and harmed mankind; and since he was a great man, both the service and possibly the harm were great beyond the ordinary.

The much delayed war did not last long. The Schmalkaldeners, led by divided counsels and unable to exploit their numerical superiority, did well to begin with. Their armies dominated the Danube and approached the Tyrol. But the advantage was not pressed; Charles at last received troops from Italy and the Netherlands; and his preparations bore fruit. In October 1546 Maurice of Saxony was forced to abandon his intention to act as broker between the parties. Ferdinand was preparing to invade the Saxon electorate from Bohemia, and the duke, fearful of losing the gains of his agreement with the emperor, had to come off the fence. He secured a promise of the electoral dignity for himself and fell upon the Ernestine lands. His treacherous attack—as it seemed to the Schmalkaldeners—was far from successful, but it drew off the League's armies which moved north to protect John Frederick's possessions. Charles promenaded along the Danube, reducing cities, imposing heavy indemnities, depriving but reinstating Duke Ulrich of Württemberg. Only in Augsburg, where the imperialist patricians used the situation to break the popular government, was the Reformation revoked; elsewhere the cities, though defeated and powerless, adhered to Protestantism and at most permitted the mass to be said again by those who wanted it. Then, in the spring of 1547, the emperor gathered his forces to follow the League's armies northwards. The decision came in April, at Mühlberg in Saxony. The battle was brief, the Spanish veterans shattering an army whose morale had sunk ever lower since the failure to exploit the earlier successes had allowed Charles to extricate himself from real danger. The Elector John Frederick was captured; his lands were overrun by Maurice and Ferdinand. Almost at once and in somewhat improper fashion, Charles had him tried for rebellion; after much hesitation he commuted the death sentence to imprisonment at the imperial pleasure. Maurice got the bulk of Saxony with the title of elector; since Charles had no wish to leave the ambitious young prince entirely unchecked in the region, the Ernestine line was paid off with a remnant of territory in Thuringia. A little later, the Landgrave Philip arrived, persuaded to seek Charles's mercy by his son-in-law Maurice who mistakenly thought that the emperor did not mean to be hard on the prematurely broken man who had taken no personal part in the war, though his troops had. But Charles, who had made no promises, added the landgrave to his prisoners. From the first he made it plain that the day of compromise and accommodation was over. He had won the war, and he meant to win the peace.

II   The Defeat of Charles V

This, however, was precisely what he signally failed to do. In the summer of 1547 he seemed utterly triumphant, with the Schmalkaldic League destroyed and gone, his leading opponents travelling under guard in his train, and no one to resist whatever settlement he chose to impose. Even the Turks, anxious to free their hands for a growing struggle with Persia, concluded peace in June 1547. The days of the Lutherans seemed numbered. Yet within a few months the situation was once more fluid, and thereafter it steadily deteriorated for Charles. Small wonder that he has been accused of personal failure. He is said to have overreached himself, to have been too vindictive, to have misread the signs, especially in believing that Protestantism would die when its political leaders were defeated. No doubt there is some truth in all this. Victory certainly brought out some unpleasing savagery and unreasonable stubbornness in him. He showed himself less flexible, less sensible, and less penetrating than he had been in his hours of adversity. His treatment of Philip of Hesse was not only needlessly harsh; it also turned out to be politic- ally unwise. Above all, there is little doubt that he overestimated the extent of his victory—an error, it must be said, which was shared by everybody else. Yet all northern Germany remained unaffected by the defeat of the League, and here the Reformation found a firm refuge among cities and princes. Virtually nowhere had Charles's victory made any difference to the religious frontier; he had ostensibly waged the war to suppress rebellion not schism, and now he could not easily switch to the repression of heresy without destroying the political alignment which had helped him to victory. The Lutheran faith, though without Luther and without the armed force of the League of Schmalkalden, proved very much tougher than Charles had fore- seen. Wittenberg and Melanchthon remained as active and secure under the Elector Maurice as they had been under the Elector John Frederick. The city of Magdeburg, refusing to accept the decision of Mühlberg, was left to continue in lonely resistance. Even in defeated Württemberg or Strassburg, so helplessly exposed to Habsburg power, the emperor's triumph did not bring back the pope.

If, therefore, it is true that Charles probably acted with an unjus- tified feeling of total success, one must also allow that he was nearer to such success than the outcome seemed to show. He had, after all, for the first time in his life overcome the particularist princes of Germany; there was no armed force left to resist him; things looked not so very different from Spain after the defeat of the *Comuneros*. It is understandable that for the moment he should have behaved as though he could settle things at his pleasure. Europe, too, was in no state to trouble him. Henry VIII had died in January 1547 and Francis I in March; Barbarossa had been dead a year or more. With England distracted by noble faction in the reign of a minor, and with France ruled by Henry II (1547–59), a sombre and slow man much less actively ambitious than his father, Charles seemed in command of the international scene. In view of this agglomeration of favourable circumstances he cannot, perhaps, be blamed for failing to see that general weaknesses remained implicit in his position: the difficulty, in the sixteenth century, of turning any victory, however complete, to permanent account, and the certainty that his sudden and dazzling preeminence would induce those fearful of his hegemony to work against it.

Characteristically, the first man to alter course in fear of Habsburg predominance was the pope who thus came to the rescue of the German Protestants. As early as January 1547 when the alliance of 1546 ran out, Paul III had grown doubtful of his wisdom in support-

ing an emperor whose total victory would be bound to reflect
adversely on Rome's independence of action. Ever since the Council
had assembled at Trent in December 1545 there had been nothing
but trouble between the imperial and papal policies, and therefore
between the papal legates presiding at Trent and the Spanish prelates
who worked under instruction from Charles. The dispute has already
been mentioned:[3] Charles wanted a reform of the Church, Paul a
settlement of doctrine, and the prolonged discussion of theological
issues which filled 1546 drove the emperor to distraction. This was
not the sort of Council for which even the Catholics of Germany had
asked; and the rigour of its dogma made it quite useless for bringing
back even defeated Protestants to the fold. Thus the understanding of
1545, on which Charles had rested his policy, worsened steadily
throughout the next two years; so far from renewing the alliance in
January 1547, the pope began to talk to France. Then, in March
1547, the legates at Trent inadvertently brought about a real break
between the two leaders of Catholic Christendom. Sick of the Council, sick of overwork, and especially sick of Trent, they took advantage of a threatening typhus epidemic to translate the Council to
Bologna, into the papal states. The pope had not been consulted,
nor had he specifically authorised the move, though many months
earlier he had given the legates a general power to do something of
the sort if it became necessary. Now he was both taken aback and
fearful of the consequences, but in the end stood by the move. The
translation of the Council wrecked the plan drawn up in 1545 by
which victory in war was to have been followed by the formal end of
the schism, achieved by a Council called by the pope, protected by
the emperor, and attended by the Germans. Charles was furious: there
could be no hope at all of using a papal Council in papal territory to
settle the religious problems of Germany. Relations grew worse when
in September the pope's son, Pier-Luigi Farnese, was murdered at
Piacenza in a conspiracy in which the Spanish authorities at Milan
were suspected of complicity. Pope and emperor stood further apart
than they had ever done, and Charles, outraged by what to him
seemed the desertion of the Christian cause, had to find his own
independent answer in Germany, not only without the pope but
against him. Though the pope kept the Council formally in being
until September 1549, he had in effect abandoned it early in 1547.

Thus Charles turned his attention to the settlement of Germany
and found it beyond him. The scene of his efforts was the "armed"
Diet which he summoned to Augsburg in September 1547 and which
sat until May the following year. There he appeared in triumph,
victor (as it seemed) not so much over Lutheranism as over princely
particularism. The princes and cities of Germany, great and small,
were either overwhelmed, or allied to him, or frightened out of any

hope of opposition. Yet the emperor did not really stand so unchallengeable even in the empire as for the moment it seemed. Though he meant to provide for his more effective rule, the one conclusive method—monarchical despotism of the sort that was building up in Spain—was not open to him. Whether a characteristic respect for established rights and traditions played a greater part than increasing poverty may be a moot point: by 1546 the Fuggers had warned him that he could not for ever hope to obtain loans which were never repaid. What is certain is that Charles's plans did not involve the complete subjugation of princely independence to himself but only a general assertion of imperial predominance in a realm remaining divided into territories. He wanted a general imperial league to provide an organisation and a standing army for the maintenance of peace and order. In other words, all the parts of the empire were to come together under his aegis and as agents of his rule. The plan derived ultimately from the old Habsburg connection with the defunct Swabian League; throughout his reign Charles had always shown a preference for such leagues rather than more direct methods of imperial administrations like the ineffective *Reichsregiment* of the 1520s, and several times he had tried to revive the Swabian League or something like it.[4] The three chambers of the Diet (towns, princes, electors) studied the proposal and produced memoranda varying in their degree of acceptance; Charles showed himself willing to concede points to territorial independence, even though he thereby undermined the principle of the reform; but in the end, opposition from Bavaria, the one state which even in 1547–8 retained some freedom from Habsburg predominance, put an end to the idea. It was allowed to run away in talk, and with it went the last chance of creating a real political unit in Central Europe and of bringing the Holy Roman Empire into the era of nation states. All that Charles could achieve in 1548 was the virtual separation of the Netherlands, as an effective sovereign unit, from the body of the Empire.

Charles was no more successful in solving the religious question. His original plan—to use the General Council—had been frustrated when Paul III set his reluctant seal on that body's removal to Bologna. In January 1548, the emperor formally protested against this. Determined to end the schism somehow, he now acted on his own, and in May the Diet proclaimed the so-called Augsburg Interim. These articles of the faith and worship, supposed to be a compromise but in fact little more than an assertion of Catholic orthodoxy with a few insignificant concessions to the Reformation,[5] he meant to impose on the realm until (that blessed and oft-repeated phrase) a General Council should settle all matters. The Interim failed pretty well everywhere, as did the alternative Leipzig Interim produced by Melanchthon at the request of the Elector Maurice. The pope, of course, denounced it as a settlement schismatically arrived at without his participation. The solidly Protestant regions of north Germany would not look at it. And even in the south and centre, where the war of 1546–7 had left the emperor in command, he could not secure its acceptance.

The opposition came from the people; it was an opposition of faith and principle. What baulked Charles V was not princely policy or love of secularised lands, but the deep hold of the reformed religion, something which he, unable to comprehend the genuineness of other people's beliefs, had never really considered. From his grave, Luther defeated his adversary on this one ground on which he would have taken his stand had he still been alive, ground on which by this time he was bound to win despite all defeats in battle. As broadsheets called on the faithful to resist, warning them:

> Do not trust the Interim;
> He has the Devil hind of him,

Charles's hopes of religious peace evaporated in the heat of contempt and ridicule. One may think these impassioned champions of points of the faith at the expense of political unity foolishly mistaken: that would be a view commonly encountered to-day, among historians and others. But those who would take such an attitude should reflect not only that the reaction to the Interim proved the existence of deep religious feeling and convictions which the historian, too ready to ask "who got what out of it?", will ignore at his peril, but also that Charles himself felt as strongly on the other side. For him the Interim was not some political counter but the furthest he could go in modifying traditional religion in order to bring about the hotly desired reunion.

League and Interim having failed, the emperor realised that he was no further in settling Germany than he had been before the war. Plainly only his own political and military power assured even the measure of obedience which he could command. And, as he saw quite clearly, his position owed little to the title to which he had been elected nearly thirty years before; it owed everything to the resources of his wide dominions. In 1547 he had, at the head of Spanish and Italian troops, defeated German particularism and asserted the Holy Roman Emperor's authority, though, of course, there were also Germans in his army. He could fight at all only because Spain and America supplied the assets on which German and Italian financiers advanced money; the taxes of Naples and Brabant did more to preserve the imperial peace than any "common penny" that might ultimately be voted by a reluctant Diet and prove impossible to collect even if it were. Germany would not help herself to unity behind the imperial crown, but she could be kept in subjection by an emperor who disposed of Charles V's sources of power.

Out of this realisation grew a fateful policy. In 1548 Charles began to think that the arrangements hitherto made for the succession to himself would not preserve Habsburg ascendancy in the empire. Ferdinand, for whose pre-election he had struggled so hard in the 1530s, could rely only on the meagre resources of Austria and Bohemia, and was moreover likely to remain embroiled with the Turks. The real centres of Charles's power in Spain, Italy and the Netherlands were designed to go to his son Philip. Would it not be best for Philip to step into all his father's shoes by also succeeding to the imperial title, after Ferdinand who could not be expected to survive his brother for long? The idea had a lot to recommend it, to everyone, that is, except Ferdinand and his son Maximilian; the latter, especially, a lively young man who sympathised with the Protestants and felt himself a German among all these Spaniards in his family, had little liking for either his uncle or his cousin. When Charles persisted in pressing the proposal, he succeeded in undermining one of the main pillars of his own success. Throughout his reign he had been able to keep hold of so scattered an empire only because all the Habsburgs stood together and because he could trust his relatives to govern for him, not for themselves. But this last demand was too much even for Ferdinand. He had always served his brother loyally, often in doubt and often at personal cost, but he could not relegate his own line to obscurity for the sake of a nephew whose qualities were quite unproven. Long family meetings settled nothing. There was no open split, no real quarrel, between the brothers, but Charles did not give up hopes of substituting Philip for the Austrian branch, and Ferdinand began to look out for himself. The solid Habsburg front, the controlling element in German politics since 1520, was broken; by 1549 Maurice of Saxony was aware of it, and all Germany knew it by 1550.

Thus the German problem remained for the moment unsolved, at the only time when Charles was free from outside distraction. On the other hand, late in 1549 hopes of bringing about the settlement of religion were revived by the death of Paul III and the election, in 1550, of Julius III. The new pope owed his elevation to the anti-imperialist interest whom he promptly repaid by turning imperialist. He was probably influenced by the continued Farnese hold on Parma, removed now by that family from the papal orbit and defended with French assistance against the Spaniards based on Milan, but the result, at any rate, was that the pope came to terms with Charles V and reconvened the Council at Trent. The second series of meetings lasted from May 1551 to April 1552 and was distinguished by the reluctant appearance of German representatives, both Lutheran and

Catholic.[6] Among the Protestants to come to Trent was a delegation from temporising Brandenburg, but there were also the theologians of Württemberg and Strassburg, and the envoys of Maurice of Saxony; the Wittenberg doctors, though expected, never turned up.

High though Charles's hopes naturally were, nothing could come of it. Indeed, the situation had been created out of deliberate misunderstandings. In fear of the emperor, the Protestant princes had agreed, at the two Augsburg Diets of 1547–48 and 1550, to send representatives to the Council; but they had always made the tacit reservation that it would have to be a "free and Christian" (non-papal) Council, while Charles had used their apparent commitment to press the renewal of the Council on the pope. At Trent the Protestants argued that all the decisions of the earlier meetings, taken in their absence, would have to be reviewed, while the papal legates refused to allow heretics to take part in the Council's business at all. Thus the Council continued from where it had left off, still an instrument for restoring the fighting power of Rome and not a measure to end the schism. But the resumed meetings had a fatal effect on the emperor's policy. Growingly conscious of his years and mounting weariness, Charles determined on one last all-out effort to achieve the end which he had always demanded of the Council. On this he now concentrated all his thought, took up residence at Innsbruck, across the Brenner from Trent, in order to keep the proceedings under his own eye, and while the situation in Germany was rapidly turning against him looked only south.

The crisis in the fate of Charles V's imperial policy, which filled the years 1549–52 and resulted in total defeat coming in the wake of seeming victory, revolved around the person and interests of the Elector Maurice who now displayed powers of unprincipled manœuvring that of their kind are hard to better even in the history of Renaissance Italy.[7] He was intent on only one thing: the preservation and consolidation of the gains he had made by his alliance with Charles V in 1546–48. As he saw it, these were threatened not by the apparent power of the emperor, but by the resentment and hatred which his tergiversation had evoked among the Protestant princes. The emperor tried to keep him controlled by preserving the Ernestine line of Saxony in a very weakened position: here there was desire for revenge. Charles also offended Maurice by keeping the Landgrave Philip imprisoned; Maurice had pledged his honour for his father-in-law's release, and the landgrave's son William, ruling Hesse for him, constantly demanded that that pledge should yield results. Then there was the problem of the imperial city of Magdeburg, never defeated in 1547, still defiant, and from 1548 under the imperial ban. Maurice wanted Magdeburg and could not allow anyone else (especially Brandenburg, which had its own ideas about the city) to execute the imperial edict; yet if he destroyed what had become a symbol of Protestant defiance, he would seal his doom with the north German princes and be totally dependent on the emperor. The manner in which he played a hand which, though it contained a few winners, was so mixed as to look impossible, is a testimony to his skill and intelligence, even if one cannot accuse him of devotion to either of the causes which he ultimately pretended to be defending: the Reformation, which he continued to protect in Saxony, and the liberty of the princes, which certainly gained from his activities. But his own purpose was simpler: he was looking after himself and his dynasty.

His problems were highlighted by the manifest decline in Charles's ascendancy—the failure of the League and Interim, and the growing differences within the house of Habsburg—and by the equally manifest revival of princely resistance to imperial control. Early in 1550, John of Küstrin allied with two other northern princes in defence of the Protestant religion and began to look to Henry II of France for possible support. Maurice saw himself as the target of any such combination; in particular, his relations with France, ally of the Schmalkaldeners, had always been bad, and it was hard to forget that he had accompanied Charles on his victorious campaign of 1544. The emperor was evidently no longer a safe protector, and the captive person of Philip of Hesse in any case threw a shadow over their relations. Maurice therefore determined to change allies—to ditch the emperor, make his peace with France, and turn the alliance of Protestant princes to his own use. Secondly, in order to ensure success for any such realignment, he proposed to exploit the disagreement between Charles and Ferdinand by directing his attack solely against the emperor while keeping in with the king. So tricky a series of operations naturally required elbow-room, and it would be wrong to suppose that the elector committed himself from the first to the precise result which in the end emerged. He played the game from hour to hour, keeping himself astonishingly free to revert to the imperial alliance if this should seem the better way, but in general following the plan outlined. What is more, it all worked like clockwork. In March 1550 he reduced his isolation by an agreement with the Margrave Albert Alcibiades, useful as a nominal Protestant and more useful as the commander of an army raised to aid England against the Scots which the Protector Somerset's victory in that war had rendered unemployed. At the same time he opened negotiations with France, accepted Henry II's reluctance, allowed himself to be told that he was the suppliant in the business, but kept the tenuous contact in being. All this while he held off representations from Hesse, improved relations with Ferdinand, and persuaded the emperor of his continued loyalty.

In the autumn of 1550 he was nearly forced off the fence when he had either to accept the imperial command against Magdeburg or open the emperor's eyes to his drift in the other direction. Once again he turned a difficulty into a brilliant success. He invested Magdeburg with an imperial army (paid for out of the reserves built up in 1548 to give Charles independent forces in Germany), but did not press the siege. Nevertheless, the northern princes went into sluggish action against him and began to raise a relieving army at Verden, some 120 miles to the north-west. In January 1551 Maurice appeared before that town, scattered the inept preparations, and, a crowning touch of impudent skill, took the better part of the forces mustered there into his own service. At one stroke he made himself the most powerful man north of the Main. John of Küstrin's little Protestant alliance had no choice but to come to terms with him, and a renewed approach to France could now be made from strength. In May 1551 the princes formed the League of Torgau by which they agreed to obtain the release of Philip of Hesse and to protect princely liberty against "the beastly, insufferable and everlasting servitude, as [it is practised] in Spain" which they charged the emperor with intending to impose on them.

Maurice, who secured the exclusion of Ferdinand's name from the list of those that might have to be fought, was for the moment more interested in eliminating his personal danger from the Protestant quarter; the League of Torgau guaranteed him against Ernestine revenge. At the same time he kept the siege of Magdeburg going, both to preserve his army in being and to have an excuse for not attending the emperor's court, while he told the city and the allies that it was all sham. Real action against Charles would need French support, and after prolonged negotiations this was finally secured in the treaty of Chambord (January 1552). In return for the imperial vicariate over the bishoprics of Metz, Toul and Verdun in Lorraine, Henry II promised money and armed assistance. Of course, the princes had not the remotest right to grant away imperial territory—the vicariate could be nothing but a euphemism for annexation—and German historians have never forgiven them for thus "betraying" the interests of the Empire. The princes were conscious of national feeling and expressly justified this surrender on the grounds that the regions involved had always been French in speech and habit; but otherwise they do not seem to have been aware of doing anything wildly out of the ordinary. The treaty really proves how little meaning the whole idea of the Holy Roman Empire had for this younger generation of princes. From their point of view, the Empire could bring only a restoration of central authority at their expense, and in the circumstances they stopped paying even lip-service to the ghostly notion.

Nevertheless, the alliance was not an easy one. Henry II would wage no war for the Reformation and made this plain; in consequence the more sincerely Protestant northern princes nearly all drew off. Albert Alcibiades was left out because he wished to be free to pursue personal ambitions, but he could be relied on to come into the war. Maurice's brother and heir Augustus was left out for a reason which will shortly become apparent. The important thing was that Henry and Maurice were agreed, but their aims differed so greatly that it was not too late for Charles to take action. Unhappily for himself, the emperor had steadfastly refused to see the truth. Throughout the long negotiations he had ignored every warning, had concentrated his attention on Trent, and had made no preparations to meet any possible threat in Germany. Charles was at a low point: now that he had grown prematurely old, his inveterate habit of slow care and procrastination had deteriorated into a genuine collapse of the will. Even when Maurice, in November 1551, raised the siege of Magdeburg without dismissing his army, Charles shut his ears to the urgent warnings which he received from Ferdinand and from his regent in the Netherlands. Maurice had put a spell on his decaying spirit, imprisoned in a pain-wracked body, worn out in thirty years of war and policy, and for the moment capable only of pursuing the vagrant dream of unity in the Church.

When the storm broke, the emperor had no armies and sat defenceless at Innsbruck. His Italian troops were tied up round Parma, the Netherlands too far away, his German reserves used up on the forces which Maurice had held at Magdeburg and was now to lead against him. Thus he fell into entire dependence on Ferdinand, a Ferdinand less unquestioningly loyal than he had been before the ill-starred succession dispute. Moreover, since the autumn of 1551 Ferdinand was once again involved in war with the Turk. He had thought to exploit a conspiracy in Transylvania to bring that part of Hungary under his control; but the business was mishandled, and in 1552 the sultan resumed energetic operations which engaged the Austrian forces to the full until peace was finally made in 1562. Its terms were those of 1547, but they settled the Hungarian situation for a hundred years, leaving only constant border skirmishing to remind the powers that Christendom and Islam shared a land frontier in the heart of Europe.

Thus when, in March 1552, Henry II opened the war in Lorraine and occupied the three bishoprics, Charles V was altogether helpless. In the same month, Maurice moved to the court of his ally, William of Hesse, and sent his defiance to the emperor. He explained that Charles's failure to release the landgrave compelled him to renounce his allegiance. Also, forced in consequence to go into Hessian captivity as hostage for Philip, he had ceased to be a free agent and had surrendered the government of Saxony to his brother Augustus. Since Augustus was no party to the treaty with France, Maurice trusted that the neutrality of the electorate would be respected! Once again he was backing himself both ways; even if no one could take these excuses seriously, they formed a strong hint to Ferdinand that, given the right terms, the elector would soon make peace. These right terms depended in the main on full security in his Saxon possessions: that was the meaning of keeping the electorate out of the war.

Meanwhile Maurice led his army south and in April 1552 invaded the Tyrol. Charles, who had simply been incapable of action, was left in imminent danger of capture; at the last moment he fled across the Alps to Villach in Carinthia. The Council of Trent, bereft of its guardian and seeing a Protestant army to the north of the Brenner, dispersed rapidly. At Villach Charles was joined by Anton Fugger, with a last great loan, and by Ferdinand, in tears. But Maurice did not mean to destroy Charles: he knew he could not hope for victory if he got involved in a major war. Even as he moved against the emperor, he resumed his carefully cultivated relations with Ferdinand and eased away from France. The emperor, temporarily quite shattered, remained obstinate enough to refuse to treat in person, but he allowed his brother to do so, and the negotiations which resulted in the treaty of Passau (July 1552) really demonstrated that Germany was now controlled by an alliance between the king of the Romans and the elector of Saxony. Charles would not accept the original agreement because it granted toleration to the Lutherans, but he signed a modified version which guaranteed Maurice all he had worked for and held out promises of a religious settlement. Philip of Hesse had been released—too late—in February; now the deposed elector, John Frederick, was also freed, though, deprived of any form of employment, he continued in voluntary attendance on his late jailer. Maurice, dominant in middle Germany and secure in his understanding with Ferdinand, knew that the Ernestines were finally vanquished. Almost by the way he had also demolished all plans for reducing the territorial independence of the princes, and assuredly by the way he had saved Protestantism from the consequences of the battle of Mühlberg.

But the conspiracy against the emperor left behind unsolved problems of which Charles's resentment was the least because in him the statesman once more asserted himself over the humiliated individual. Albert Alcibiades was still at large with an army, carrying death and destruction along the Rhine and into Franconia by way of carving out a personal principality for himself. More important, the French sat in Lorraine. By autumn, the emperor, lately so battered and decayed, once more displayed resilient powers of decision which amazed all who had seen him at Innsbruck and Villach. The succession of Mary

Tudor to the throne of England generated grandiose hopes in the old man: he would marry his Catholic cousin to his son Philip, bring England into alliance with Spain, and destroy France. Slowly he travelled up the Danube, scattering forgiveness and benison wherever he went. He even got Albert Alcibiades to join him, and by October 1552 he was laying siege to Metz. The city was brilliantly defended by Francis, duke of Guise, who here founded his reputation, and in January 1553 Charles had to give up. This failure really drained him; only will-power had kept him going so long. The distracted state of Germany, harrowed afresh by the rampant margrave, left Charles cold; others would have to deal with that. By a suitable irony, Maurice of Saxony found himself compelled to move against his own late ally whom he had unleashed on the unhappy land. In June 1553 he destroyed the margrave's army at Sievershausen—Albert Alcibiades shortly after fled to France—but himself died two days later of wounds received in the battle. So ended all his scheming and planning, no doubt a fitting conclusion in the eyes of the moralist. Unfortunately it must be said that Germany could ill spare a politician of his calibre, a man who had shown such clear recognition of feasible ends, such a grasp of the means, and such moderation in success. His double treachery has left him with a bad name, and in a sense deservedly so. Nevertheless, through it he had removed from Germany first the threat of a dominant selfish league and then the threat of Habsburg despotism; and if he had lived he might easily have been able to infuse more purpose into the loose grouping of territorial principalities than his successors were able to do.

By early 1555 all Germany was sick of trouble and longing for peace. Charles admitted the fact—which in the circumstances, meant final defeat for him—but could not bring himself to help. Again, he left things to Ferdinand while he moved to Brussels and prepared to divest himself of his power. The Diet of Augsburg, which sat from February to September 1555, presented a novel appearance. The emperor was absent and the pope not represented. Though Ferdinand came in person, few princes did so; and this assembly of envoys demonstrated clearly that the Holy Roman Empire had lost everything but its name. The prolonged negotiations produced a Religious Peace which was, with difficulty, to last for sixty-three years. As treaties go, this is a good record, and it is not easy to see why the work of this Diet should so often be regarded as futile. In effect, the parties agreed to tolerate both the Roman Catholic and Lutheran Churches in Germany, each territory to follow the religion of its prince,[8] while both confessions were to suffer each other in any city where they were both represented. Proselytising was forbidden, and ecclesiastical princes who changed to the Lutheran side were to abandon their territories and be succeeded by new prelates canonically elected. Anyone dissatisfied with the religion of his prince was to have full liberty to move into another's realm. It was perhaps unfortunate that toleration was expressly refused to any other form of the Christian religion. This clause, directed against the sects and Anabaptists, assumed serious importance with the spread of Calvinism; but of that there could be no suspicion in 1555. If the ostensible purport of the Peace was to accept the religious schism as inescapable, the fact of political splintering was even more obvious. The Peace of Augsburg closed the period during which Germany had been the boiling pot of Europe and set the scene for 300 years of German history in a back-water. By bringing peace to that much buffeted region, it also removed it from the place of first importance which it had occupied ever since the Diet of Worms; by ensuring the predominance of territorial independence, it reduced Germany to that condition of "petty-statery" (*Kleinstaaterei*) which characterised the region during the ascendancy of the great nation states.

Elsewhere, too, an age was coming to an end. In 1553, Duke Cosimo of Florence, the emperor's ally, settled a long dispute over Siena and confirmed one lesson of Charles V's reign—the triumph of Spain in Italy. In February 1556, the emperor and the king of France prepared for the final conclusion of their differences by signing the truce of Vaucelles. Charles's son Philip had married Mary of England in October 1553, but no immediate advantage was to be expected from this since Mary's government spent 1554–55 fighting rebellion and restoring the papal obedience in England. Charles was exceedingly tired. Only fifty-five years old, he had outlived his contemporaries and in a manner himself; he felt out of place and out of touch. His life had been one long struggle, devoted to duty and rarely eased by less strenuous employment. His health was very bad, and he was beginning to think seriously about his prospects in another world. Much of what he had striven for seemed in ruins—Germany divided, Lutheranism established, the General Council of the Church in abeyance, apparently for good. He was in no state to shoulder all these burdens again; the time seemed come to put a long-cherished intention into effect. In October 1555, in a solemn and touching ceremony at Brussels, the emperor resigned the rule of the Netherlands to Philip, reviewing his life's work in a speech which left speaker and audience in tears. In the following January he handed over his Spanish and Italian kingdoms, and gave up to Ferdinand the crown of the Holy Roman Empire. The Habsburg power was thus divided into its Austrian and Spanish parts; no more was heard of the plan to make Philip emperor. By easy stages, still at times yielding to entreaties to take a hand in affairs, Charles reached Spain and the house he had long built for such a retirement, close to the monastery of San Jeronimo de Yuste in Estremadura. Here he lived a peaceful life at last, still in touch with the great world which he alone, among so many potentates, had found it possible to leave, still giving advice, still capable of the kind of anger which in 1557 made him return the French order of St. Michael to Henry II with an insulting message denouncing Valois treachery. But in the main he prepared for his death, which came in September 1558.

III   The End of an Age

This should have been the end of it. That it was not—that the rounded drama should have to be burdened with an epilogue—was the fault of Pope Paul IV.[9] Carafa had no sooner been elected to the papacy (May 1555) than he reversed the imperialist policy of his immediate predecessors. His intention was straightforward. He meant to break the Spanish hold on Italy, based on Naples and Milan and secured by alliances with Genoa and Florence. Paul not only hated the Spaniards for occupying his native Naples, but sincerely believed that the revival of the papacy was hindered by Charles V's "monarchia", his universal claims. Whereas Charles regarded himself as the secular head of Christendom and the pope's equal, Paul IV reverted to the attitude of Gregory VII and Innocent III which had resulted in the overthrow of the medieval empire by the medieval papacy. He even reverted to the time-honoured device of calling in the French, the device which had destroyed the Hohenstaufen in the thirteenth century but, in the wars beginning in 1494, had only succeeded in ruining Italy. Misconceived as all this was, it must be admitted that Paul IV had a better chance than his predecessors of playing an active political part, for by his time the work of creating a consolidated state out of the disrupted papal dominions had advanced to something like success.[10] The process begun when Julius II captured Bologna and reoccupied the Romagna (1506–9) was continued even under Clement VII who brought Ancona to heel; and Paul III had contributed a good deal by subjugating Umbria in the "war of salt" (1540), destroying the Colonna, the pope's chief enemies in his own territories (1542), and restoring Camerino to the papal dominions (1545). Papal revenues had been improving steadily from the low point of the mid 1530s, and Rome was by now recovering from the disaster of 1527. Thus Paul IV seemed to dispose of power and resources which made an aggressive policy less unreasonable than once it had been; in particular, he was now the despotic and unchallenged ruler of the states of the Church across central Italy.

Hatred of Spain, though the chief motive, was not the only one. Like every sixteenth-century pope, Paul was burdened with relations;

like so many of them, he needed helping hands and preferred to use his family. At least his nepotism was extended to genuine, not putative, nephews, one of whom in particular became the leading figure of his pontificate. This was Carlo Carafa (1517–60) who had led a notably dubious life of adventure, mostly as an unsuccessful condottiere in both the imperial and French armies. His moral character was bad even for a man of his profession, and several straightforward crimes, including murder, can confidently be laid to his charge. This man, within a fortnight of succeeding Marcellus II, Paul IV made a cardinal, salving his conscience with a general absolution and dispensation. Even if Carafa's French friends put pressure on the old pope, it was an unprincipled thing to do for the enemy of corruption, the reformer of the Church, the ruthless inquisitor-general. It was also a mistake. The pope wished to free Italy of Spain; the cardinal was much more interested in carving out a principality for his brothers and himself. This difference of aim made for confusion, and the persons of uncle and nephew did not help. The pope, as has already been said, was near-insane and given to bouts of insensate rage which made it very difficult to have dealings with him and often prevented people from telling him things. The cardinal was cunning, precipitate and boastful. Their combination did not promise well in a situation requiring at least the sort of skill and secret ways manifested by Maurice of Saxony.

In October 1555, Paul IV declared war on the emperor, but before anything could come of this, the truce of Vaucelles put a stop to the fighting and frustrated papal policy. The year 1556 was therefore filled with the attempts of Rome to break the truce and bring France back into the war. It proved no easy task, in part because Philip II of Spain, who had now succeeded his father, adhered to a policy of extreme patience in the face of all provocations. A good son of the Church, he did not want to quarrel with the pope; a near-bankrupt, he could not afford war; a congenital procrastinator, he always tried to avoid irreversible decisions. Henry II of France, too, held back. His finances were in little better state than those of Spain, and his court was the scene of a struggle for power in which for the moment the peace party had the upper hand. This was led by the Constable of France, Anne de Montmorency, since the early 1520s a man of weight in the royal counsels, though in disgrace with Francis I after 1541 for opposing the renewal of war. On his accession Henry II called again on this old and experienced statesman who was greatly helped also by the alliance he managed to form with the king's all-powerful mistress, Diane de Poitiers. Opposed to him was the faction of the Guises, noblemen of France though cadets of the independent ducal house of Lorraine, whose leader, Duke Francis, favoured war for reasons of personal ambition. Carafa worked hard to bring

France round, while the pope did his best, by acts of aggression near the Neapolitan border and by imprisoning Spanish ambassadors, to provoke Philip into action. In the end, and very reluctantly, the duke of Alva, viceroy of Naples, invaded the papal territories, and even though he made not the slightest attempt to exploit his overwhelming superiority Henry II now listened to the war party and renounced the truce. The pope lost himself in remarkable dreams of a universal alliance against the Habsburgs; he was even perfectly willing to welcome the Turks as friends. In March 1557, Guise invaded Italy at the head of a powerful army. Meaning to attack Milan, he was instead persuaded by Paul IV to cross the papal states for an attack on Naples. His marauding forces did not endear the pope's war to the pope's subjects; but Alva retreated.

It was a flash in the pan. The war, renewed so that Spain might be overthrown, instead led to a Spanish triumph. In May 1557 Philip concluded offensive alliances with England, to deal with France, and with Florence, to control Italy. The English got nothing from the war except the loss of Calais, but in Italy Guise made no progress, and by the summer of 1557 the pope showed signs of recognition that he had made a mistake. The decisive moment came in August when an army brought up by Montmorency to relieve the fortress of St. Quentin in the Netherlands, besieged by Philip's general, the exiled duke of Savoy, was utterly destroyed. The Constable and many others, following the traditional practice of the French nobility, aggravated the defeat by falling into the enemy's hands. Guise was recalled, the pope defenceless; only Philip's and Alva's unchanged determination to deal gently saved the troublesome old man from the fate of Boniface VIII. In September he made peace; though Alva sought reconciliation on his knees, no one was deceived. Spain had confirmed her hold on Italy and her control over the papacy. The pope turned back to the more suitable task of reforming the Church.

However, the war which he and his nephew had so unwisely renewed continued for yet another year, though in 1557 both Spain and France repudiated their debts and declared themselves bankrupt. The crash shook the declining prosperity of Antwerp and ruined Augsburg, and though it could not stop the war at once it brought its end very near. The Netherlands government had borrowed so fantastically in 1555–56 that it had not only exhausted its credit but had also just about mopped up all available cash.[11] There was no more to be had, and only the convenient arrival of a consignment of American silver even made possible the conduct of one more campaign. Fortunately for Philip II it proved to be enough. Though Guise took Calais in eight days, thereby enhancing the reputation made at Metz in 1552, his invasion of the Netherlands was crushed by the count of Egmont at Gravelines (July 1558). France had had enough. After months of negotiations, peace was concluded at Cateau-Cambrésis in February 1559. The breakers of the truce of Vaucelles came to no good end. Paul IV broke with his nephew early in 1559, but this did not prevent his own death in August from letting loose a violent popular demonstration against him in which his services to the Church were buried and forgotten. His successor, Pius IV, did not scruple to institute a rigged trial for murder against the Carafa nephews which ended with their execution in June 1560. And Henry II died of a wound received in the tournament put on to celebrate the conclusion of peace.

The treaty of Cateau-Cambrésis really brought the age of Charles V to a close. Under its terms, France virtually abandoned two generations of ambitions in Italy, though she kept a few garrisons in Piedmont. She returned Corsica to Genoa and restored his territories to the duke of Savoy. She also gave up Navarre, contested since the days of Ferdinand the Catholic. There was an exchange of captured towns along the Netherlands border, and Philip, recently widowed by Mary Tudor's death, bound himself to marry Henry II's daughter Elizabeth. Nothing was said of the Lorraine bishoprics, and Ferdinand, the new emperor, took no part in the proceedings. As became the victor, Spain had the best of the bargain. It is usual to date an era of Spanish ascendancy from the treaty, and thought it should be remembered that her power was never unchallenged there is much truth in this. Perhaps her European predominance owed most to the accidental results of the peace, the death of Henry II which precipitated political chaos and religious war in France, so that Spain's chief rival was immeasurably weakened for nearly thirty years. But formally, for what it is worth, one may place the "century of Spain" between the treaties of Cateau-Cambrésis and Westphalia (1648).

At any rate, whatever the future, the treaty set a seal on the past, on the reign of Charles V. It is to-day commonly said that the emperor failed; he can be treated as a somewhat pathetic figure, which he certainly never was. True, if one looks at his own elevated notion of the imperial office, the fact of failure cannot be denied. As universal emperor, guarding and guiding Christendom, he not only failed but was bound to fail because he totally misjudged the possibilities. His power rested on no abstract concept but on his territorial dominions, and these dominions involved him in too many problems and conflicts to carry the programme of a universal empire into effect. Nor was he personally equipped for the task. With all his tenacity, determination, and sound judgement, he lacked the sweeping vigour of action and the depth of insight which might have made him a truly great ruler. Even if Luther had never been born, Charles V could never have been another Charlemagne. His failure is most patent in Germany where the religious split started and despite his best endeavour established itself in his lifetime. Since he spent the last twelve years of his rule on this problem, it is easy to see why he should sometimes be regarded as a failure all through. But the hegemony of Spain in the age of Philip II was the work of the father, not of the son. Charles had himself come to recognise that the reality of his power rested not on the empire and not even on the Netherlands, which he left in difficulties and decline, but on Spain with her two maritime empires in America and the Mediterranean. Spain herself never flourished more than in his time, before the weaknesses of her economy made themselves manifest; his reign was the great period of her colonial expansion. And even though his struggle against the Turk might at best appear a draw, one can see, in the light of later events, that by holding the line he had overcome the threat. Barbarossa had no real successor, and peace with France robbed the Ottomans of an ally and a base in the western part of the inland sea. There were to be no more descents on Italy, and the decisive deliverance of Lepanto (1571) is predictable in 1559. In short, one may say that though Kaiser Karl V may have failed, El Rey Carlos Primo had a prosperous and successful reign. If Luther triumphed from the grave at the Peace of Augsburg, Charles, from his grave, triumphed at Cateau-Cambrésis.

Chapter 10

The Age

I The Religious Revolution

The Reformation was a revolution. So much is plain, but it is easy to mistake the nature of that revolution. Too often Protestantism is regarded as simply an attack on abuses in the Church—on immoral popes, corrupt clergy, idle monks, a weak and vacillating Christianity. Especially to its enemies, the Lutheran movement appears to be concerned only with the outward behaviour of the Church, as though its quarrel with tradition turned solely upon those delinquencies and peccadilloes which all good opinion among the followers of the old religion agreed in denouncing. If this had been all, or even the main part of it, the Reformation could not be called either necessary or successful. Abuses among clergy and laity continued to trouble the earnest and sincere in the Protestant Churches quite as much as they had troubled them before the break, and at least from the later 1540s onwards internal revival within the Church did more to remedy these ancient troubles than anything achieved by the reformers. If Luther had really broken the unity of the Church only because he despised the mode of life, the absence of genuine devotion, the exploitation of popular piety for personal ends and for money, which marred the Church of the early sixteenth century, the common charge of Erasmian humanists and Catholic reformers, often echoed since, that he was recklessly jeopardising the essential for the sake of the accidental would have much truth in it. The failure of the Protestants to change human nature overnight and produce a "godly people"—that failure which made Calvin's Geneva such a model for those who believed in the possibility of holy commonwealths on earth—would then quite properly form part of the indictment. Not only had the reformers needlessly rent the seamless garment of Christ, merely because they magnified the importance of a few specks of dirt on it; in the process, they had not even cleaned the dirt from those bits of cloth which they had retained in their own hands.

However, this concentration on "abuses" quite misses the real issue and the real revolution, even though it is, of course, true that moral indignation played its part in driving many away from Rome. Luther, and Calvin after him, were deeply religious men, and trained theologians to boot, and their revolution took place in the realms of religion and theology. Whatever other effects and tributaries there may have been in the story, that is the point at which to start. Luther did not just quarrel with the Church because he thought it diseased and corrupt: he thought it unchristian and devilish. For in his view the popish religion would not "let God be God" (to use a phrase of his) but attempted to mould God to man's needs. The medieval scheme of religion proceeded from man to God, laying the stress on the human relationship to the divine and employing reason to discover God. Its theology described a universe comprehensible and useful to man. This is not only perfectly compatible with genuine piety but also, in many ways, sensible and consoling; but such a scheme may well be held to miss the essence of Christianity (that which forms both its strength and its weakness), namely its belief in a strictly non-human God. Luther started from the primacy of God and laid the stress on His relationship to man. He drew the logical conclusion from the Judaeo-Christian concept of God's omnipotence: man cannot influence, persuade, bribe, threaten God, but can only surrender to him. Salvation thus became the work not of a just God, rewarding man's efforts to avoid sin, or his repentance if the effort proved too great, but of a loving God who bestows His grace without regard to merit or endeavour, in an act of the only pure kind of love—that which has no taint of self-satisfaction in it[1]—of which God alone is capable but which He demands of men. The whole of Luther's complex, and often far from clear, theology, stems from the religious experience in which he had found the peace which he had vainly sought to win through "good works". He knew himself to be an incorrigible sinner, incapable of escaping what he called concupiscence (the sin of doing the right thing not merely to please God but with an eye to self). Yet God had assured him that he was "justified" and forgiven. Thus God must be pure love—irrational love, not repaying a debt or executing justice, but content to give eternal life to all who would open their souls to faith in Him. Thus ensued the total annihilation of the structure of the Catholic Church, an instrument of God the judge; the means it offered to man for the attainment of salvation Luther was bound to regard as expedients for coercing or bribing God into giving His love, and therefore as blasphemous.

How justified Luther was in regarding the late-medieval Church in this light is not here at issue: certainly, he had hit on some valid enough points. But that his concept of salvation, based on his vision of God, marked either a total innovation or the equally revolutionary return to a more primitive Christianity which he believed it to be, is certain. His preference for a simpler faith expressed itself in his distrust of philosophy. The Protestant Reformation developed its own dialectic and its own schoolmen, but it could never hope to equal the metaphysical and rational endeavour of Rome, past and to come. Luther was bound to denounce reason as presumptuous: in his theology of God and Christ—though not, it should be said, in his treatment of man and the world—reason could have no place because reason is human and because any attempt to argue about God at once forces God out of the centre of things. This restoration of God at the heart of religion and theology was the positive theological achievement of the Reformation, made possible by its treatment of God as love which removed the necessity, so much felt by the middle ages, for intermediaries and interceders. Thus the Reformation was bound to condemn all other cults, of the saints or of the Virgin Mary, as idolatrous because they detracted from God's single rule, and as blasphemous because they demonstrated lack of faith in God's immeasurable goodness. Luther was so confident of grace that he had neither need nor use for subsidiary supports; but this assurance has not always been available to everybody. Protestantism from the first was a more difficult religion than that from which it turned away.

Theology naturally affected also thought about the world as it is, the world of fallen men; and here the effects of the Reformation, in a way, operated in an opposite direction. In religion, Luther and his followers intensified, purified, and even spiritualised the fundamental problem of God's purpose and His relationship with man. In ordinary life, they removed the visible signs of the spiritual. Since all men were equidistant from God and equally dependent on His mercy— equally capable and incapable of reaching Him—there was no room in the Protestant scheme of things for a specially spiritual class of people. Not only are all believers priests, but no believers can be monks. All men can and should live the life of religion in whatever situation or vocation they find themselves, and they live such a life if they employ their "calling" (their place in the world) in works of love for others. Medieval religion had condemned the world and admired those who left it in their search for spiritual excellence: in the middle ages, a "religious" was a member of an ascetic order. Protestants did not, indeed, regard the world as good; for them, as for all others who call themselves Christians, it must be a product of the Fall. The new religion in fact adopted a rather lower view of man's natural perfectibility in comparison with the absolute goodness of the divine principle than that which can be accepted by a Church possessed of the power to bind and loose. But it treated the world as the proper abode of all men on their pilgrimage to the life after death, and one which no man can or should avoid. In addition, the denial of good works cut the ground from under the social service (if that is the correct term) performed by the medieval monks, with their prayers and masses, efficacious because by their renunciation of the world they had acquired merit. In short, Protestantism tried to diffuse religion through every aspect of life and, by the same token, to treat all life as an aspect of the life religious. To borrow Max Weber's famous phrase, its asceticism operated in this world, not out of it:[2] which is to say that a life pleasing to God and obedient to the divine law was to be lived in the ordinary avocations of men. The natural consequence of this, given human needs and tastes, was not so much to sanctify the world as to personalise and secularise religion; but at any rate, it helped to remove the formal asceticism, unaccompanied by spiritual truth or even by an upright life, which was the constant danger of the monastic ideal.

Altogether, the outcome of Luther's genuine revival of religion was not always what he had hoped. The institutionalised religion which he attacked suffered from its propensity to corruption, its readiness to accept human weakness a little too easily and to indulge in arrogant hierarchic pride. But it had its special strength in that it provided a visible organisation, a cloak to cover and a staff to support the uncertainties of men; moreover, by constituting a superior guide and positive standard it saved religion from the vagaries of the individual conscience. The outbursts of enthusiasm and mysticism which beset the Reformation from the first offered a warning (one which Luther, at any rate, heeded), but such extravagances could be overcome; it would be as improper to judge Protestantism solely by its Müntzers and Jans of Leyden as it would be to condemn the Church of Rome altogether for its time-serving prelates and women-hunting friars. A more serious problem lay in wait for a religion which placed complete confidence in the work of God upon the individual soul, and from the first the new Churches found themselves doing battle with the constant divisions which they had invited by rejecting the authority of the one universal Church. The danger, much publicised by their opponents, that men who believed themselves to be graced by God would ignore the moral law was never very real; at no time in this period or later did the mass of Protestants abandon the conventional morality of their day. Indeed, a bitter puritanism was always more popular among them than a regardless hedonism. What did happen was that the individual and his right to judge for himself were growingly stressed. Protestantism should not be too readily identified (as is commonly done) with the cult of the individual; mostly, the social bonds of the reformed societies proved quite as strong in ensuring uniformity as did the edicts of the Church in the older dispensation. Nevertheless, the very nature of Protestant belief encouraged self-reliance and self-determination, and there is some truth in the traditional view which associates movements of political freedom and social change with the Protestant religion. Such things are hard to assess: it is equally true that Protestantism had a special appeal for men and societies in which strong traditions of individual rights and free institutions existed. On balance one can say no more than that the failure of Luther and Calvin to capture all Christendom strengthened those parts of their teaching which denounced authority and led man to seek the ultimate reality within himself, at the expense of those which counselled submission to the established order.

It was this leaven of individualism which in due course was to turn the religious revival back upon itself and promote an interest in the world. Reason cannot be kept down for ever, and Protestant regard for the individual soul could and did enlarge into respect for the individual judgement. If the Reformation, in intent and immediate effect, strengthened—even reintroduced—a preoccupation with religion and theology, it is still perfectly correct to see in its breaking of the old mould also the necessary preparation for the secularisation of Europe. Whether one welcomes this or not is quite immaterial; what must be recognised is the fact that without Protestantism, without the overthrow, in so many countries, of the agency (however feeble) of intellectual control, the great strides soon to be made in secular thinking are unthinkable. Even though the Reformation rested upon assumptions and attitudes which are essentially alien to those of modern Europe, the scientific revolution and the removal of religion from political control owe a great deal to a movement which intended none of these things. Similarly the idea of toleration in matters of faith, itself a necessary aspect of the secularised state, grew from the Reformation. Assuredly, its immediate effect was to sharpen bitterness and bigotry, to strengthen the hand of partisanship and persecution, to bring joy to the rigid and intolerant. The schism forced all sides into warlike attitudes and quickly destroyed such readiness to allow differences of opinion to exist as had at times appeared in the medieval Church. But the very fact of schism soon worked the other way. Ideological wars exhaust themselves quite rapidly: men will fight more fiercely for a faith than for material advantage, but they will fight much longer for their bread than for an idea. Bread is less disillusioning. Toleration was to be the product of indifference as much as principle, and indifference flowed from the growing realisation that the points at issue were not worth battling over or were not to be decided by battles.

The Reformation was not really a movement for liberty of conscience or thought. Where it triumphed most completely, as in

Geneva or Massachusetts, it clamped a fiercer control on men's minds than had usually been employed in the old order, and it elicited from Rome an even more formidable creation of repressive machinery. Like the Catholic Church, the reformers thought that they had the one truth, and they worked with princes who regarded religious dissent as necessarily equal to sedition. But because the Reformation recalled the individual message of early Christianity, because it created two camps in each of which refugees from the other could find sanctuary, and because in the end the failure of either camp to destroy the other made religious war and persecution absurd, it is fair to say that toleration, diversity of opinion, and respect for free consciences could not develop until the monolithic power of the Church had been broken.

However, when Luther wrote these consequences lay in the unsuspected future, and it is at least arguable that the immediate, and possibly the intended, effect of the Reformation was to stifle free thought and speculation. Did Protestantism kill humanism? Obviously it did not kill the mechanics of humanist study which underlay all thinking and especially education on both sides of the divide. But it may be that it killed its spirit, and those who think that the humanist spirit was "modern"—secular, sceptical, scientific, essentially rational—would hold that it did.[3] As so often, it really depends on what one looks at. Erasmus' denunciation of obscurantists, monkery and mere formalism in religion and philosophy may make him look like a forerunner of Voltaire, and he certainly earned suspicion from the particularly dull defenders of orthodoxy, the Sorbonne and its like. But those who think him modern, or prefer him to Luther,[4] ought really to look at his popular works upon which so much of his vast influence rested: at such things as the sententious and unreadable *Adagia*, a collection of common sayings with commentaries of topical interest, or the flat and tedious piety of his ubiquitous *Enchiridion Christiani Militis* (*Manual of a Christian Soldier*). The adjectives are used deliberately: they describe what is likely to be the modern reaction to these works, so different from his immensely readable letters and or even a satire (only parts of which wear well) like the *Praise of Folly*.

His own contemporaries expressed their very different reaction by buying these books to such good purpose that Erasmus was the first, and for long the only, author who could live by his pen. Nothing so well illustrates the folly of reading back the twentieth century into the sixteenth as indiscriminate admiration for humanism: unless it is indiscriminate admiration for one of the other forms of Christianity then current. To mourn the supersession of humanism, with its credulity in the face of astrology and magic and its soft religion, as the death of reason at the hand of the wicked Luther testifies to confusion. To read Luther on Galatians or the liberty of a Christian man, after sleeping through the platitudes of Erasmus' *Manual*, is to gain understanding why the former raised men above their circumstances while the latter amused their leisure hours; nor does one have to be a Christian to see this. Certainly there were better—more sinewy—things about the humanists, and especially about Erasmus, than their plodding religion or their laboured indignation at abuses the roots of which they did not care to explore; the point is that at the time they gained adherents by what must now appear their intellectually less satisfactory side. True and critical reason of the kind that appeals across the centuries is found in Erasmus, but not in his fence-sitting views on reform. The sixteenth century is not the twentieth: its religion or its scepticism are not those of our day; its humanists would be as shocked by, as they would shock, those who too readily consider themselves their heirs.

The question which matters is whether the Lutheran Reformation was really necessary; or whether the Church could have been renewed and restored by the widespread movement of Christian humanism which looked to Erasmus, and which (as we have seen) assuredly helped to prepare the ground for the more drastic attacks of Protestantism. In their onslaught on abuses the two had much in common, and Erasmus at least, brought up in the personal religion of the Netherlands *devotio moderna*, represented one of the trends towards a less institutional form of Christianity which Luther inherited. Nevertheless, it is to mistake both the nature of the religious problem and of Christian humanism to talk as though Luther needlessly went too far and reprehensibly injected a violent irrationalism into what should have been a sensible and moderate reform. These very adjectives tell their own story. The defenders of the established order could afford to ignore sensible, moderate men. Christian humanism was a movement of the intellectuals—by no means all intellectuals—and never made the slightest impact on the great mass of Christians of all degrees. It aimed at purification without destruction, a noble aim but one which showed few signs of being realised. Here and there a reforming bishop like Giberti, a thoughtful statesman like Gattinara, or an earnest saint like Contarini might try to put its programme into practice; but the truth is that by 1520 the old order had been in no way touched or its corrupt hold weakened, and that such minor successes as Christian humanism scored thereafter owed more to fear of Luther than to respect for Erasmus. Furthermore, Luther did not just go well beyond Erasmus in passion and violence; he started from a different and more revolutionary position. The ethical preoccupations of the humanists, which led some to canonise Socrates and to equate Christianity with the teaching of the Stoics, hardly entered into his thinking. In his prophetic teaching, reform played at best an incidental part. The essence of the Reformation, and that which gave it its overwhelming appeal, was, to say it again, not its attack on abuses but its positive, and of necessity revolutionary, re-interpretation of the Christian religion.

II   Art, Literature and Learning

Religious revolution, religious revival—these facts are, up to a point, also reflected in the arts of the age, though Italy, and the Renaissance, here played a larger part than Germany and the Reformation. The bulk of the paintings produced were admittedly portraits; even painters have to live, and portraits were what patrons demanded and paid for. Those who will (and can) may see in this flood of realistic representation, certainly larger than in any preceding century, a sign of that worship of the individual which, it is said, was a mark of Protestantism. But in fact men of all religions and possibly none had their portraits painted, because it was the thing to do, because new wealth or spreading tastes encouraged an Italian fashion to find imitators all over Europe. The portrait painter was the society photographer of the sixteenth century, and his popularity illustrates the way in which the idea of "society"—of a social élite eager to record itself and to acquaint allied spirits elsewhere with its existence—dominated the Renaissance. As in all painting, one may roughly distinguish a northern or German-Flemish style and a southern or Italian among the portraits: the former best represented by the detached but extremely subtle realism of Hans Holbein the younger (?1497–1543), whose best work is found in his drawings, and the latter coming to a climax of psychological insight and devastating comment in the work of the Venetian Titian (Tiziano Vecello, c. 1490–1576). Of course, the north at this time learned a great deal from Italy, that true centre of art; but a comparison between Holbein's Windsor drawings of the English court and Titian's compassionate studies of Charles V or his relentless painting of Paul III will show the difference both of the artists and the traditions.

Portraits were painted because they were wanted. So were other pictures, but in these the artist's own dominant beliefs are more likely to appear. Even Titian, so manifestly a this-worldly artist rejoicing in the colour and classical form that were the hallmark of the *quattrocento* Renaissance, in later life abandoned the quasi-pagan framework which even his religious painting had inhabited in the 1520's and, free to please himself, began to surrender to a mysticism essentially alien to his positive and life-worshipping art. His younger contemporary Tintoretto (Jacopo Robusti, 1518–94) set the tone for that move away from the classical tradition into the baroque which is called mannerism; both his subjects and his spirit reflected the renewed hold of the Christian religion in the Italy of the Counter-Reformation. Among German artists the tendency is similar but less striking because, except for what Italy had to teach, there were no traditions of worldly painting to set against the achievements of men like Leonardo or Raphael—men who even into their treatment of sacred subjects infused a spirit of human joy or sorrow which has little to do with the supernatural. The northern painters inherited instead the troubled and demon-ridden world of the fifteenth-century malaise (as in the work of Hieronymus Bosch); even so sane a man as the great Albrecht Dürer (1471–1528) demonstrated that inheritance, for instance, in his well-known engraving, *Knight, Death and the Devil*, not only, as one would expect, in the nightmarish figure of the Devil but more subtly in the tormented figure of the Knight. Dürer did not live long enough to render his full due to the spirit of the Reformation, with which he was in total sympathy. His rival, Lucas Cranach the younger (1472–1553), spent the best part of his life at Wittenberg and acted as the most accomplished of the many propagandists who served the Lutheran cause; whether, on the other hand, one can see much religious revival in his gothic scenes and remarkable, boneless nudes—an art which not only titillates but tries to do so—is another matter. In general, however, religion both in matter and manner manifestly replaced humanist or pagan attitudes.

The most striking case of all is that of the century's outstanding artist—painter, sculptor, poet—Michelangelo Buonarotti (1475–1564). Of course, a genius of his calibre expresses himself, not his age; and a great deal of Michelangelo's long life and enormous production records quite simply the pilgrimage of one troubled and straining soul. In his inner life, his wrestling with himself and his God, Michelangelo resembles Luther. Yet there is something more generally significant about the direction of his pilgrimage. Michelangelo's work was always entirely his own, but at the same time it stood linked with the work of his time. His *David*, the sculpture which first made him famous, is a pure expression of humanity, not a story told in stone; it is therefore also an end-product beyond which the classical humanism of the Renaissance could not be developed. The work of his manhood—the ceiling of the Sistine Chapel, charged with a strictly human beauty and symbolism yet also deeply religious, or the *Moses* of Julius II's Tomb, a markedly human prophet—is Promethean: thoroughly aware of the gods, but also vigorously struggling with them, proclaiming the greatness of man even in the face of the greatness of God. When one looks from these to such works of his later years as the *Deposition* in Florence Cathedral, or particularly his last achievement, the Milan *Pietà* which has entirely abandoned the human scale of classical and Renaissance art, one moves into a different world where the spirit of religion has taken charge. The God of the Sistine Chapel is the pre-Reformation God: man's answer to the problem of the universe. That of the *Pietà* is the incomprehensible God of Luther and Loyola: no doubt concerned with man but in his own way which faith alone, not reason, can apprehend.

In poetry, too, secular themes and attitudes, though of course they continued, clearly gave pride of place to religion. Not that this is a notable age in the history of imaginative writing. Luther was a poet: it is an important clue to his person and work. In another time and position, he might have embodied his spiritual vision in an epic instead of a new Church. As it was, he confined the specific expression of his poetic genius to his treatment of the German language in his translation of the bible, and to his hymns. Among a good deal of ordinary stuff produced in that line, Luther's hymns stand out by their passion, sincerity and skill. Calvin, too, tried his hand at poetry and translated the psalms, but his prosaic temper, while it prevented him from achieving anything of note, also enabled him to see that Pegasus was not his mount, so that he gladly substituted the version produced by a real, if minor, poet, Clément Marot. These and similar examples of religious poetry all over Protestant Europe are the most characteristic writing of the day, but non-religious versification also abounded. Here Italy once again, though herself in decline, set the pace. The marvellous impetus of the Renaissance was showing signs of exhaustion; Italian literature was entering its silver age, with one tedious sonnet cycle after another applying conventional sentiments to conventional Celias and Cynthias under the direct inspiration of Petrarch's Laura. Of course there were exceptions, such as Michelangelo's sonnets, mirroring the same fierce search and despair as imbued his plastic art. But the characteristic note of Italian writing at this time is one of urbanely cynical prose, as in the comedies of Machiavelli or the resplendent gutterpress journalism of the lively Pietro Aretino (1492–1556) who made a living out of pornography and literary blackmail, and did it very well, too.

However, while the new poesy was ossifying in its homeland, it was beginning to influence other countries. The efforts which Sir Thomas Wyatt and Henry, earl of Surrey, made to acclimatise the Italian achievement in English, were greatly surpassed in France, by the work of the six writers of the so-called Pléiade. One of them, Joachim du Bellay, in 1549 published the manifesto of the school in which he called for new forms and a new vocabulary in French poetry; the most successful practitioner, Pierre de Ronsard (1524–85), wrote not only secular sonnets but also religious odes and hymns in which he lifted the literature of his country to new heights. Germany remained unaffected by these influences; resisting all things

"Welsh" (Italian) with nationalist fervour, her poets continued to write in the homely, and often clumsy, style of the past, occasionally (as in the plays of the Nuremberg shoemaker and mastersinger Hans Sachs) producing vigorous and attractive work of a sort. In general, no doubt, the Italian influence was beneficial, loosening the language and disciplining its application, a revolutionary stage in the development of flexible vernaculars which led to the peaks of Shakespeare's England and Racine's France; but some of these poets, especially Wyatt and possibly even Ronsard, wrote best when least conscious of their task as innovators.

In prose, too, the vernaculars freed themselves of the stiffness and insufficiencies of the past, again in pursuit of the example of Italian, the only European tongue to have reached full flower. One need only compare the Latin writings of Sir Thomas More with his English prose to see how superior in subtlety, though often inferior in vigour and originality, the learned language still was. When French and English had learned from Latin and Italian how to enlarge their vocabularies, ease their syntax, and variegate their moods, modern prose would emerge,[5] and much of the work of this period testifies to the birth-pangs accompanying the process. This is especially true of the one genius writing at this time, François Rabelais (c. 1495–1553). It helps to explain the exuberance of language, the heaping of synonyms and search for more, the manifestly experimental character of much of his work (*Pantagruel*, 1553; *Gargantua*, 1534; *The Third Book*, 1546; *The Fourth Book*, 1548; *The Fifth Book*, 1562). Until the recent revival of experimental writing, it is probable that these features appealed more to his contemporaries than to later readers. For them, Rabelais lives (in so far as he does: here is a writer more famous than read) because of his extravagance of invention and the roaring humour which gives life to often tedious matter. An unconventionally devout man who had been both a Franciscan and a Benedictine before he threw off the habit in disgust, he combined in his extraordinarily well-stocked mind most of the knowledge, ideas and attitudes of his age, so that he has been claimed by all the axe-grinders who have beset him, being seen now as a humanist, now as a Lutheran, and again as an orthodox Churchman of the Chesterton-Belloc brand of bibulous humour. His humanism is manifest; indeed he had learned much from his friend Erasmus without whom, it has been said, he would only have been a teller of funny stories.[6] With and through him he came to charge his marvellous fancy with a deeper purpose, presenting, for instance, in his abbey of Thélème the serious ideal of a free humanist society. But Rabelais was only occasionally as didactic as all that, nor are those the parts that make him live, any more than his notorious bawdry now stands as the obstacle to reading him which once it was. It is the satire (of the

Church) and the humour, the people and the adventures, which make Rabelais a great writer, splendid in his fusion of gothic extravagance and Renaissance discipline, of medieval romance and modern reason. Gargantua, the giant of the fairy tale; Panurge, the *novus homo* of the sixteenth century; Pantagruel, the great clumsy world seeking knowledge and peace: over all pours the huge laughter, rarely malicious, at humanity in its ineffable folly which is the hallmark of Rabelais.

If there was little prose fiction in this period, there was plenty of serious writing both in Latin and in the vernaculars. The bulk of it touched religion and theology: the really typical books of the age are such works as Luther's treatises, Calvin's *Institutes*, Loyola's *Spiritual Exercises*. The quantity of such writing, which in quality ranged from the valleys to the heights, need not perhaps be stressed again; it has often enough been hinted at in these pages. From the first the printing press—maker of reputations (Luther, Erasmus), of revolutions, of new trades and professions (printer, publisher, bookseller, even proof-reader: Erasmus, for a while, earned his living as one)—had put out more religious matter than secular, and the Reformation saw to it that this imbalance should increase. Of all the works published, translations of the bible were the most important, not only in the history of the Reformation but also in the history of languages. Luther's German translation is the most famous; begun (1521) in the Wartburg and completed in 1534, it ran into 377 editions before his death, and it virtually created a literary German language in the wealth of diverse dialects. But elsewhere, too, vernacular scriptures made their appearance, acquainting the people with Holy Writ and setting the linguistic standards of their respective nations. What William Tyndale and Miles Coverdale did for England and English in the 1530s, Lefèvre and Olivétan began for France in the 1520s. Scandinavia in particular benefited from this activity because here there was no recent tradition of vernacular literature at all; Christian Pedersen's translation (1529) and Laurentius Petri's Vasa Bible (1541) virtually opened the history of modern Danish and Swedish. In due course the bible appeared in Hungarian (c. 1540), Polish (1542), Finnish (1546), Icelandic (1584), and so on. What mainly inspired the evangelicals working in this cause was, naturally, their desire to bring the gospel to the people, as well as Luther's example; but without Erasmus' fundamental edition of the New Testament (1516) and the work of learned Hebraists on the Old, there could have been no such outburst. Enemies in all things else, Luther and Erasmus in effect collaborated in laying the foundations of that bible study and devotion which was to prove one of the main strengths of Protestantism.

However, if the mass of publication was theological and devotional, the more interesting part was often secular. The Reformation did not put an end to scholarly and popular works in other fields. Humanist scholarship excelled in philology, in the study of the ancient languages, the editing of documents, and the establishment of accurate texts. To the educated public Erasmus might be the author of the *Adagia* or the *Colloquia*, collections of proverbs and of educational dialogues neatly turned to criticise evils in Church and state. But to his fellow scholars he was the foremost Latinist of the day, the editor of the Fathers and the writer of letters in which problems of scholarship and book production jostle with friendly exchanges and complaints about bad health and worse quarters. Guillaume Budé (1467–1540) promoted education by the foundation of his college in Paris where, in imitation of the *Collège Trilingue* of Louvain (1517), Latin, Greek and Hebrew were all taught;[7] but it is doubtful if even this contributed more to learning than his fundamental work in the study of ancient Greek. Unfortunately the years with which we are concerned were disfigured by the kind of embittered controversy to which scholars are prone, the struggle over Ciceronianism. Erasmus attacked the slavish imitation of Cicero's style and vocabulary popular in Italy, on the grounds that it endangered a living Latinity, and in this he was entirely right. The curious determination to use no Latin not known to the first century B.C. prevented the further flexible development of a language which had been able to adapt itself to some fifteen hundred years of learning, philosophy and letters since then. But the cause of pedantry found its defenders, especially the Italian Julius Caesar Scaliger (1484–1558), who crowned a military career by turning scholar in France, and the French Etienne Dolet (1509–46), burned by Francis I's government as a heretic, though Calvin also denounced him. This odd pair, among others, secured the ultimate triumph of Ciceronianism, which resulted in the decay of Latin as the language was put in artificial bonds. Scaliger should not be confused with his greater son, the leading scholar of the second half of the century, who took pedantry to the point of genius.

The presses poured out books on law, for lawyers, and on history, for the general reader. Only in conservative Germany was the older tradition of chronicle history maintained without change, until even here humanist influences modified this recital of undifferentiated fact. In 1559 the first volume of a new kind of Church history, arranged century by century, was published at Magdeburg by a team of writers under the leadership of Flacius Illyricus (the Centuriators of Magdeburg). Elsewhere, the new historiography had struck sooner, as visiting Italians introduced the nations to a method in which matter was treated rationally and selectively, criticism applied to legend, and sense made of events. Paulus Amelius (d. 1529) brought the new history to France; Polydore Virgil (c. 1470–1555)

brought it to England; Peter Martyr of Anghiera (d. 1526) to Spain.
In each country these foreign observers soon bred native imitators,
like Edward Hall (d. 1548) who transformed his chronicle by turning
its last part into a properly composed history of the first two Tudors.
The finest products of the school came from Florence. Machiavelli's
History of his native city (published posthumously in 1532) is animated by his concern with contemporary events; it is more of a piece
with the openly political speculations of his *Prince* (1516) or his
Discourses on the First Decade of Titus Livius (1531) than pure
history, though very good and very personal also in this respect.[8]
On the other hand, Francesco Guicciardini (d. 1540) had given up all
hope of playing an active part in affairs before he turned to the
writing of history. His great *History of Italy* (published 1561–7)
and his *History of Florence*, which remained in manuscript until the
nineteenth century, are the reflections of a disillusioned and pessimis-
tic man of extraordinary insight, and a work of despair. The intellectual leadership of Europe was passing from Italy, mainly to France,
but also to Germany and England and other parts of Europe, in
driblets. Guicciardini, who saw little hope for mankind and doubted
the existence of any guiding principle in life, drew the line under
Italy's great age.

Rational and reflective history is one of the two outstanding intellectual achievements of modern Europe; natural science is the other.
While the age witnessed the spread of the first true beginnings of the
former, it proved curiously patchy in the latter. It is now recognised
that the later middle ages contributed a good deal to the growth of
scientific knowledge, while the main humanist attitudes operated
against a further exploitation of the beginnings made. The authority
of Aristotle, in physics, and Pliny, in the biological sciences, was if
anything greater in the fifteenth and sixteenth centuries than before.
The revival of Greek studies might add to the number of authorities
consulted, but it did not encourage any idea of criticising received
knowledge by personal observation. Moreover, those who did look at
nature were too often the victims of peculiarly handicapping illu-
sions. Far more men studied astrology than astronomy: astrology
deserves to be called the specific science of the humanists. And the
almost equally passionate preoccupation with alchemy left singularly
little in the way of accurate new knowledge; contrary to the prob-
abilities, alchemy did not found the science of chemistry. Why this
should have been so is not really clear. Humanism with its book-
learning is no doubt part of the answer, but even a man like the
extraordinary Paracelsus (c. 1493–1541), who knew nothing of
humanism or the Greeks, filled the gap not with direct observation
but with a mingle-mangle of mystical thoughts about life-forces.
Paracelsus' great idea was that chemical medicaments should replace

the herbal ones recommended by the school of Galen, and by encouraging experiments on minerals he contributed, through his disciples, a little to the history of chemical science. But more sound learning was accumulated by practical men pursuing immediate needs—the mechanics of Germany, the distillers of strong waters (admittedly at this time usually medicinal), above all the navigators from the Portuguese chart-makers and star-students onwards—than by all the "philosophers", legitimate, Paracelsian or blatantly magical.

Yet at the same time there were signs, a few of them tremendous, of a more promising future. Devoted men were collecting and publishing details of plants and animals, with some attempt to excise the fabulous and with the greater accuracy in illustration made possible by the developing arts of the engraver and the printer. Thus material was being accumulated for a truly systematic study of botany and zoology. Anatomy was profiting from more accurate dissection and medicine from experience as well as from the revived knowledge of Galen. In 1543, Andrea Vesalius published one of the really great books of the century, his anatomical treatise De humani corporis fabrica (The Structure of the Human Body), based on the arrangement of Galen's anatomical work but relying on independent research and illustrated with very beautiful and very accurate plates. That observation could overcome even received tradition was proved by the French physician Ambrose Paré whose experience as an army surgeon led him to doubt the value of cauterising gunshot wounds in boiling oil. The saner treatment which he advocated in his Method of treating wounds caused by firearms (1545) was to save many lives; in other books he studied amputation (he invented the ligature), fractures of the skull, and plague. His account of his many journeys shows him to have been just the kind of keen and relentless observer, transmuting mere curiosity into true study, of whom scientists are made. Still in the field of medicine, Servetus, using his propensity to original thinking rather more fruitfully than he did in his theology, hit upon the so-called lesser or pulmonary circulation of the blood (1553); though he had studied anatomy and practised as a physician, it is now thought that he probably arrived at his revolutionary notion by pure reasoning, without any scientific investigation. This is a method which has yielded as much error as truth, and in the sixteenth century reasoned error certainly predominated. On this occasion at least, Servetus was lucky.

But, of course, the chief scientific event of the age was the work of Copernicus on the solar system. No more reluctant or even unconscious revolutionary can be imagined. Like Luther, Nicholas Copernicus (1473–1543) turned the world upside down while looking in tradition for a better answer than that habitually given in his day.

The son of a Polish merchant, he studied at the universities of Cracow and Bologna, returning to Poland a competent mathematical astronomer of the kind familiar at the time. Like others, he became dissatisfied with the model of the universe constructed out of the geometrical astronomy of Ptolemy (second century A.D.) and the physics and cosmology of Aristotle. This had been fully rediscovered in the fifteenth century and was given authoritative exposition in Regiomontanus' *Epitome of Ptolemaic Astronomy* in 1496. According to this system, the earth is at the centre of the universe, and the heavens revolve around it at necessarily great speeds since they have to complete a revolution in twenty-four hours. The universe is finite and consists of a series of concentric crystalline spheres to which the moon, the sun, the planets, and the fixed stars are attached. The motion of the stars was explained by Ptolemy as the product of a complexity of cyclical revolutions (epicycles and deferents), and on the basis of his calculations it was possible to construct accurate tables of sidereal motion for the use of astrologers, navigators and calendar makers. But the mathematical explanation was immensely difficult, and no one ever attempted to visualise the Ptolemaic universe in physical terms. Like others, Copernicus tried to find a better answer in the best humanist manner, by going beyond Ptolemy to earlier Greeks whose ideas the great Alexandrian had superseded. How and when he arrived at his heliocentric solution (which he believed to have been that of Pythagoras) we do not know; but by 1512 he was circulating a short manuscript account of it among his friends. Publication was delayed not by fear of persecution—the Church, eager to reform the calendar, was encouraging all astronomical speculation in general and Copernicus himself in particular—but by dread of ridicule, since his notion seemed to contradict common sense. Only the enthusiasm of two Protestant visitors induced this soundly orthodox Catholic to permit his ideas to be put before the world; in 1540 there appeared an account of them in the *Narratio Prima* of George Rheticus, and in 1543 Copernicus' own *De Revolutionibus Orbium Coelestium* saw the light of day.

Copernicus suggested that the sun stands still at the centre of the universe, and that the earth, being one of the planets, moves around it. He supported this view by a variety of non-scientific arguments (as that it was more reasonable for the great life-giver, the sun, to occupy the place of honour), but also demonstrated that he could solve the problems of heavenly motion in a mathematically more satisfactory way than did Ptolemy. For the rest he preserved Ptolemy's and Aristotle's spheres and cycles, only rearranging them; no one before Kepler would accept that the stars could move along any except the most perfect curve, the true circle, so that what is really an elliptical orbit had to be depicted as a series of simultaneous rotations along two or more circles. Copernicus' really revolutionary point, and the one which needed most proof, was that he had set the earth in motion: all observation seemed to contradict this. Here he used his famous argument that an observer on a moving object will suffer the illusion that the stationary objects past which he moves are themselves in motion: motion is relative. But of course this argument could be used against him; it proved only that the earth was either moving or static, and common sense suggested that it stood still. Moreover, his adherence to the rest of the traditional cosmic physics raised difficulties not found in the Ptolemaic system; in particular, he could no longer account for gravity by Aristotle's argument that all heavy bodies fall naturally towards the centre of the universe, the earth, and was instead forced to postulate a mysterious force which he could not explain. Neither has anyone else explained it since.

In fact, Copernicus did no more than stand the Ptolemaic system on its head; his tables and Ptolemy's produced in practice the same results for those who wished to calculate the position of the stars and were indifferently used by astronomers for the rest of the century. He had only begun a revolution the implications of which he himself did not grasp. In due course it was to become apparent that a heliocentric universe overthrew some quite fundamental beliefs: the fixed stars were removed inconceivably far off and the universe might be infinite, or there might even be universes beyond our own, all speculations which for theological reasons had been condemned as heretical in the fifteenth century and were to bring Giordano Bruno to death by burning in 1600. A further scientific revolution became imminent when it was realised that Copernicus had destroyed the ancient postulate that the physics of the microcosm (earth) and the macrocosm (the heavens) are two distinct things; with the recognition that the universe is governed by one set of laws, the way was open for the search which ended with Newton. As the implications of the Copernican theory sank in, the quarrels began, but this did not happen for half a century after Copernicus' death; the triumph of the heliocentric universe had to await the revolutionary mechanics of Galileo in 1632. Not that Copernicus' achievement was ignored; there was much interest among astronomers, and the collecting of observational data which went on apace in the second half of the century increasingly suggested that he was right. But Copernicus himself had not been able to establish that his answer was true: he could only suggest that he might have constructed a better model than that of Ptolemy. Nevertheless, his achievement was very great. To argue for a moving earth required both imagination and courage. Even if, like Vesalius and the other pioneers of the age, he could do no more than start scientific study along certain promising lines, the pioneers deserved plenty of credit.

It would be as idle of this period as of any other to seek to comprehend its varied intellectual activity in any single generalisation. Tradition and innovation naturally jostled each other, as they always do, and the interests of men remained as varied and fruitful as they usually are. Yet certain features of the scene stand out more prominently than others. The revived predominance of religion expressed itself not only in the renewed vigour of theological speculation and controversy but spilled over into secular interests. Compared with the Italian Renaissance, so often truly secular or at most Platonic, this age tried to justify even its historical, scientific and linguistic studies by reference to the Christian religion. The other notable feature is the growth of vernacular literature—the development of national self-consciousness among the writers. Most scholarly work continued to be put out in Latin, because that language was better equipped for the purpose and because it ensured a much larger audience. But even here the growing demand for translations showed a new trend. In poetry, on the other hand, the nationalist demand was quite deliberate: Wyatt and Ronsard wrote as they did to prove that English and French were every bit as good as Italian. The nations of Europe were only too fully aware of their nationhood, as they could hardly fail to be in a world of growingly stronger and better organised national states.

III   The Nation State

The importance of politics in the progress of the Reformation has already been sufficiently described. One would naturally like to know whether the Reformation in its turn assisted the political development of the age. Superficially, there can be no doubt that it did. When Luther put his trust in princes, when Bucer and Calvin exploited the favour of town magistrates, when Cromwell and Cranmer ascribed ecclesiastical supremacy on earth to Henry VIII, they all necessarily enhanced the standing and power of secular rulers and advanced the consolidation of political units. But if one asks whether the revolution in religion and the Church was accompanied by a similar revolution in the political structures of Europe; the answer is much more doubtful. It is necessary to enquire into the real nature of secular government at this time.

The first thing that jumps to the eye is the apparent increase in the physical power and coherence of states, and traditionally the period is considered as one in which "the consolidation of the national state" took place. This was notable in the West. France and England went a long way towards eliminating internal diversities and subjecting all the realm to the rule of the king; Charles V not only provided unified government for his Spanish kingdoms but even attempted to turn the Netherlands into something like a federated state; in the German principalities, Lutheran and Catholic, the prince imposed his authority on all other interests and individuals. The farthest east witnessed a similar development in the rise of Russia. The "gathering of the lands" which was the main achievement of Ivan III (1462–1505) produced the vast Muscovite state free of Tatar suzerainty; Moscow absorbed Tver (1478), Novgorod (1478–94), and parts of the Ukraine (1503); and the work was continued by Vasily III (1505–33) who added Pskov (1510), Ryazan (1521) and Smolensk (1522). The creation of a major power was accompanied by the consolidation of the prince's internal autocracy; the grand duke became the tsar, and the traditional liberties of nobles and Church were progressively whittled away. Though the accession of a minor in 1533 (Ivan IV, the Terrible, d. 1584) resulted predictably in fourteen years of violent faction strife among boyar (noble) families struggling to control the government, the rule of Ivan was to prove that the new Russia was indeed an autocracy of unusual ferocity. The central kingdoms of Europe provided something of an exception to this general building up of monarchies, but the reason for this did not lie in princely unwillingness to copy the leading examples of the day. External circumstances—the Ottoman invasions and the pressure of Russia on Poland-Lithuania—caused the collapse of the Jagiellon attempt at state-building which in the fifteenth and early sixteenth centuries had promised to outgrow the power of any other European dynasty. Even so, the Habsburg heirs to the Jagiellon programme persisted and against all difficulties produced in their Bohemian and Hungarian territories some progress towards centralised government at the expense of noble privilege. Monarchy was in the ascendant; absolutism, to all appearance, just round the corner.

However, before one accepts this traditional picture too readily, two important reservations need to be made. In the first place, there was nothing new about these developments. The consolidation of monarchy is an old story; indeed, it is only a pretentious way of saying that, given the chance, rulers will extend their power to the limit. There was no "new monarchy" round about 1500: only, for the moment, more favourable conditions for the old policies of kings. The monarchies of Francis I and Henry VIII differed in very few essentials from those of Philip IV and Edward I; the whole doctrine of "free monarchy"—near-absolutism—can be found in the writings of fourteenth-century French jurists. The monarchies of about 1500 seemed new only because they had to resume this task of kingship after a simultaneous collapse of strong central authority all over western Europe. In any case, the increase of monarchic organisation and strength which is manifest in the sixteenth century, had begun everywhere long before the Reformation. Before ever Protestant doctrine justified princely control of the Church, the princes of Europe had been expanding their hold over their clergy, either in opposition to or with the agreement of popes. Luther's schism was not the first; its peculiarity lay in its being a permanent schism based on religious differences. In 1512 Louis XII of France threatened to take the French Church into schism, and as late as 1548 Rome dreaded a similar move from, of all people, Charles V; the Augsburg Interim appeared to be the first step in such a disaster. The schism of Henry VIII was at first presented as free of doctrinal quarrels with tradition, and that king was always advising Francis I to follow suit. It is clear that these rulers did not need Protestantism to teach them about sovereignty. National Churches existed, in a measure, before the Reformation and continued to exist after it even in countries which remained Roman Catholic. In this political sense the Reformation exploited and up to a point consolidated a situation into which it was born; its contribution was secondary, and it in no way created a new political system—though, of course, it created a new political situation—in Europe. If there ever was a transformation in the character of Europe's monarchies deserving the title of revolution, it would not appear to have taken place in the sixteenth century.

Secondly, it is important to note that the political trends of the sixteenth century were not only developments out of the past but also had advanced nothing like so far as seems sometimes to be thought. The nation state had arrived; its constitution was another matter. In fact, it continued very largely to be governed by the law and custom of the past. Nowhere outside the pages of Machiavelli's *Prince* was there any suggestion that the ruler's mere will should govern his realm, though Machiavelli may be said to have given voice to the arbitrary practices of Italian tyrants. Charles V's authority varied noticeably within his dominions, from the near-despotic power of a king of Naples to the near-constitutional monarchy of Aragon, just as custom dictated. Even in France, where the circumstances of the late-medieval struggle with England had so enhanced the king's prerogatives, the established privileges of such corporations as the *Parlements*, the liberties of chartered boroughs and individuals and the vigorous existence of provincial estates limited the monarch's independence sufficiently to make any talk of absolutism look rather odd. In several German principalities this was the time when territorial estates asserted themselves—in opposition or in co-operation—to a degree hitherto unknown; in none was princely rule free of recognised limits. And in England, the one country where, thanks to the creation of the royal supremacy in the Church, the tendencies of the past were at this time summed up in something like a constitutional revolution, that revolution deliberately elevated the law and custom of centuries into the principle of national sovereignty embodied in the mixed rule of king-in-parliament.

Polish publicists, looking at the strong and self-willed monarchs of the west, might think that the liberties of a nation had survived among them alone, but in truth strength was not to be identified with uncontrolled power. Indeed, that strength stemmed much more from an identity of interests between ruler and ruled, an identity which for the moment rendered the public display of constitutional safe-guards rarely necessary. The age admired and praised kings, but it worshipped the law (though it conventionally despised all lawyers as bloodsuckers). The law stood forth as the one secure thing in an uncertain world, the known framework of society and the sole protection against an anarchy from which only the strong could profit. Kings of the early sixteenth century continued to ground much of their right to rule on their task as protectors of the law; an instinctive recognition that practice must be governed by custom is to be observed in even the apparently most arbitrary actions of the state. It is ironical that a genuinely revolutionary attack on traditional political concepts should have come from that victim of the innovators, Sir Thomas More, whose *Utopia* (1516) constitutes a major indictment of the Europe of his day; as it is also ironical that More's moral commonwealth should have achieved something like reality in Calvin's puritan paradise.[9]

No one would wish to deny that the physical power of monarchs increased, with growing resources and growing armies. Moreover, the law not only protected the rights of subjects but also the lawful claims of princes; lawyers were among the leading agents of reforming monarchies. This was perhaps particularly so in those countries where a professional law, derived from the law of ancient Rome and called the civil law, replaced the always uncodified, sometimes unwritten customary law which had grown up in the countries over-run by Germanic invaders after the fifth century. France had long been the home of such Roman law principles and practices, and Charles V managed to govern his scattered realms only because he had a reservoir of administrators consisting of legists trained in Franche Comté. During the sixteenth century, the Spanish kingdoms and a good many German lands "received" the Roman law, as codes of civil and criminal law were promulgated by the ruler to replace the crudities of the customary law. It is commonly held that the Roman law naturally favoured autocracy and was therefore welcomed by princes; historians do not seem to tire of quoting the dictum "quod principi placuit, legis habet vigorem" ("what the prince has approved has the force of law") as though it identified legislation with the monarch's will, whereas it only signifies that the law of a country requires endorsement by its head.[10] In any case, the sixteenth century rightly did not regard the civil law as necessarily any more despotic than any other, as one may discover by reading the praise which Thomas Starkey (*The Dialogue between Reginald Pole and Thomas Lupset*, written c. 1535) bestowed on it in the course of a general defence of constitutionalism. It is true that the civil law had advantages for a king: it assumed the existence of a law-giver (but so in effect did developed customary law like the common law of England), and it provided a general code overriding the differences between the customs of, say, Picardy and Provence, or Aragon and Andalusia. This last was its chief attraction for kings labouring to make coherent wholes out of geographically contiguous territories which had come to them piecemeal. But no king could have used the civil law more brilliantly to help himself than Henry VII of England used the common law to restore his finances or Thomas Cromwell used it to subjugate the Church, in both cases without ever infringing its principles or details. All law was the king's, and all law also assigned specified rights to others. The point about the rule of law was not that it made puppets of kings but that it prevented strong kingship from deteriorating into despotism.

Practical obstacles, too, limited the efficacy of the sixteenth-century state. Distance and bad roads did more to save men from the burden of government than constitutional safeguards or the debates of parliaments. Most sixteenth-century governments could make themselves felt against major rebellion: neither the *Comuneros* of 1520 nor the English pilgrims of grace of 1536 really stood much chance. The resources of kings, of which national loyalty was not the least, outstripped those of all other men, even if these could command sectional or local loyalties of their own. Administrative reform did much in this period to improve the hold which the centre could exercise over the provinces. The French crown developed not only effective central agencies of financial and judicial administration, further improving on the work of Louis XI and Louis XII, but set up in the masters of requests a corps of agents who could be used to supersede the local administrators as occasion required. Charles V's empire, held together ultimately by his own person only, obtained in the hierarchy of professional councils and professional secretaries a skeleton of quite efficient imperial administration. The administrative revolution which accompanied the English Reformation provided the centralised state with the means to govern. In Spain, bureaucratic development had got so sophisticated that all action could be choked by the rival authorities of law courts and councils, only the king being able to restart it by edict: but to him these courts were useful instruments against local independence.

Nevertheless, even in these relatively well-organised states much had to be left to the dubious labours of local officials and local gentry; revenue was always difficult to collect, and new laws were very hard to enforce if they were disliked. Additions to the machinery did not always help, especially in France where during these years the sale of offices, accompanied by the creation of new offices to sell, was regularised into a system of freehold, leaving the crown helpless in the face of its own creatures. But England and France were well and effectively administered by comparison with the countries further east where the will of the centre often hardy penetrated beyond the ruler's entourage. The more one thinks of the physical obstacles to good government and effective policy, the more astonishing the actual, and often very respectable, achievements of these governments become. To a degree now hard to grasp they all depended on the voluntary co-operation of individuals, especially among the nobility and gentry, who served their king sometimes for profit, sometimes from sentiment, but always because it was their place in society to govern the members of the realm for him.

The Europe of the Reformation era therefore consisted of a number of national states, in varying degrees developed as effective political units but none of them monarchic despotisms in which the will of the ruler was law, and none of them consistently able to translate the "national will", however definite, into action. In this the age differed little from the more immediate past, and not all that much from the more distant past; it differed more sharply from the truly absolutist constitutions which in the seventeenth century the example of France was to make so popular among all sorts of princes. Yet when all is said, it would be foolish to ignore the growing signs of organised strength, the growing unity of national consciousness, the growing reality underlying the pomp of dynastic monarchy. In the long history of European kingship, which extends from Charlemagne to the first World War, the age of the Reformation marked a stage when the consolidating activity of the past was assured beyond reversal, and when it became clear that the future lay not with disparate and subordinate territories but with nation states governed by powerful, if by no means unlimited, rulers. But there was no revolution in political structure or organisation to account for the fact of the Reformation; only a situation in which the Reformation could find succour from the political ambitions and manœuvres of the powerful.

IV   Society

However, political organisation is only the outward expression of a state of society, and it is very widely held that the Reformation did, in fact, reflect, or even constitute, so major a social transformation that here will be found the explanation of both its occurrence and its success. In this business, a number of ready generalisations—once meaningful but now no more than parrot-cries—have established themselves in the historian's vocabulary, and it is unfortunately necessary to attack them if the matter is to be seen in the proper light. This means that one must enter into controversy, and controversy, moreover, with some of the great and revered.

In the first place, many regard it as proven that the period of the Reformation, extending to about the middle of the seventeenth century, witnessed a social transformation which is described either as the bourgeois revolution or the rise of the middle class. A new class, sprung in the main from merchant ranks and relying on commercial rather than landed wealth, is supposed to have replaced the so-called feudal nobility as the ascendant class in the state. The allegedly new monarchies of western Europe are said to have risen on the backs of this class, satisfying its demands by their economic and ecclesiastical policies, though in England (where the bourgeois revolution seems clearest to the exponents of the doctrine) a clash ultimately took place between the king and his bourgeois support. The Reformation is then commonly seen as the manifestation, in religion and Church government, of the economic interests of a new class with new attitudes. In its pristine form, as codified by Marx, the doctrine laid the stress heavily on the bourgeois character of this class—town-bred, mercantile, sober and industrious, its values diametrically opposed to the economically wasteful ideals of a decadent nobility. The manifest insufficiency of this theory in the face of the facts has led others to modify it by dropping the term bourgeois in exchange for middle class; since the middle class, sad victim of the schematising historian, is notoriously elastic, the good fortunes and particular policies of just about any given individual can, with care, be fitted to the doctrine.[11] The stronghold of this sub-Marxist generalisation is the textbook, especially the American textbook: in particular, idealist interpreters of history, giving due weight (as they think) to the workings of the human spirit, are fond of swallowing a large lump of this materialist dough in order to prevent the strong waters of religion and ideas from going to their heads. In denying the truth of this social analysis one is saying nothing that the real students of the period do not know; but the habit of caution is strong (and no doubt wise), and far too often one finds pieces of the exploded theory embedded in even sensible work.

In sober truth, any description of the sixteenth century, or the Reformation, which lays the stress on the "rise" of bourgeois or middle class is quite simply wrong. Sixteenth-century society was hierarchic, believing in ordered ranks from kings downwards. The various orders of society often felt a common sympathy and interest which at times cut across even the strong nationalism of the age. Kings, in particular, linked by such close ties of inter-marriage, formed almost a trade-union of their own which prevented them from allowing exasperation with each other to resolve itself into the hiring of assassins or the total destruction of defeated foes. The most pervasive ideals of the time touched on the exalted position of the landed nobleman, loyal to his prince, exacting loyalty in turn from tenants and followers, learned in his trades of war, courtierdom and estate management, upright and sincere and sometimes simple, but increasingly also educated in the humanist mode. It was for him that educational theorists like Erasmus and Vives wrote their treatises; for him Castiglione outlined the duties of a courtier; for him the poets and publishers turned out rehashed romances of chivalry. He invaded schools and universities hitherto reserved for the professional training of the clergy and the lower orders aspiring to better things. *Il gentiluomo*, the gentleman, was the paragon and model: mixture of old knight and new scholar, as full of virtues as of good manners, a self-consciously aristocratic image. Merchants who made enough money (and many, of course, did) hoped to move into that rank of society; they had no loyalty to their "class" or awareness that it was "rising". Though the move was easiest in the relatively mobile society of England, it was possible in France and Germany too, and even to a small degree in Spain, usually through service to the crown.[12] New men there were in the simple sense that the ruling class constantly recruited itself afresh; and because the landowners themselves were often fully occupied with their own affairs, government service depended in the main on younger sons or on aspirants from the ranks below the nobility. But the upshot was the same: ennoblement. This movement into the aristocracy had been going on for centuries, and it continued, though from the seventeenth century most European nobilities tried more successfully to draw a line around their caste. If town air freed the serf, court air freed the "rising bourgeois"; and the newcomer was only concerned to imitate the earlier arrivals. To call this snobbery is possible, but in a society so firmly convinced that the natural order, both in heaven and on earth, depended on rank, ambition to rise higher was both natural and pious.

It is hard to see how the notion of a rising bourgeoisie or middle class could ever have been applied to the sixteenth century, since the facts suggest the precise opposite. If there had been anything specifically bourgeois in that age, one would surely expect to see towns increase their power, money-bags outweigh land rents, burghers doing well for their order rather than leave it when they did well. But, wherever one looks in the Europe of the Reformation, the great old centres of urban life are in decline. The cities of the Hanse surrender the dominion of the Baltic to Denmark, Sweden and Poland. The Swabian League, borne up by the wealth and vigour of its affiliated towns, disappears. The ancient city of Ghent is battered by Charles V's cannon; the great city of Augsburg is bankrupted by Charles V's loans. Strassburg, manipulator of political strings and free haven of persecuted minorities, dwindles into insignificance after the defeat of the Schmalkaldic League. Even in Italy, home of cities and of an urban civilisation, nobility and princes now dominate the scene. London, Paris, Rome are all politically less effective than they have been. Antwerp is the economic centre of the Habsburg empire: if ever there was a town which should be able to assert its bourgeois strength against the power of the upper classes, here it is. Yet within two decades after 1550, its greatness is destroyed by the politics and policies of princes. Where, indeed, is that rising and politically domi-nant bourgeoisie in deference to whom kings enforce the bourgeois Reformation? No one wants to argue that towns and merchants disappeared, or even that in general trade and mercantile wealth did not increase; as we shall see, they did. But there were no social or political consequences of the kind postulated.[13] Instead, monar-chies strengthen their hand, in alliance with a nobility a great part of which they have created; the courts of princes rise to a new eminence as centres of social life; the bourgeois seek influence through attain-ment of a higher status. The age of towns, if one may so generalise, belongs to the fourteenth and fifteenth centuries, when for various reasons economic circumstances favoured them and depressed the landed classes; in the sixteenth, the social ascendancy of the nobility eliminated rivals, and, thanks to the political consolidation of states, destroyed the independence, and therefore the political and social influence, of mercantile oligarchies.

For the nobility rested their increasing status on an improvement in their economy. The growing population of the sixteenth century put a premium on food production, and land acquired a greater value, and therefore even greater attraction, than it had had since the collapse of the agrarian boom of the thirteenth century. The gentry of England, the *noblesse* of France, for a time even the landowners of Spain with their profitable interest in sheep, all benefited from this; and it is an easily demonstrated error to suppose, with some of the older histor-ians, that only new men, brought up to commercial practices, knew how to catch the favouring wind. Everywhere it was the aristocracy, not the urban middle class, who made the most out of the changed circumstances. Further east, the case is even plainer. In so far as it expanded, German industry shifted from the towns to the estates of landowners.[14] The great granary of Europe, east of the Elbe, was exploited by landowners who often succeeded in adding territorial rulership to commercial success.[15] *Gutswirtschaft*—the economy of great estates farming for the market—developed, by the seventeenth century, into *Gutsherrschaft*, a social organisation of the estate giving to the great noble political power within it and semi-independence towards others. The features of this system, which grew up on the plains of Poland, Livonia, Prussia and Bohemia, are not so different from the *encomiendas* of New Spain,[16] and in both cases the phenomenon is a product of colonisation. The victims of increasing aristocratic strength were not only the towns but even more markedly the peasants, for whom the sixteenth century opened an age of hardship. Whether, as in the east, they dropped into serfdom, or as in England turned either tenant farmer or landless labourer, or as in Germany and France simply suffered exploitation from rent-collecting landlords, the bulk of the people lost the gains which scarcity of labour had given them in the preceding century and a half.

Improving market conditions for agricultural produce were not the only thing to help the nobles towards their novel preponderance. In the east, the Turkish invasions, and soon also the pressure of Russia, created frontier situations in which defence depended upon the power of local men: typically, marcher lordships, not seen here since the collapse of the Mongol invasions, revived to add to the free power of the nobility. And in the strong western monarchies it was soon discovered that one of the highroads to wealth and influence lay through royal patronage, through the offices, grants, favours and privileges which only the king could supply in sufficient quantity. Since the nobility had the readiest access to this fountain of honour, they were the virtually exclusive beneficiaries. In return, kings were expected to be reasonably generous; careful management was regarded as a mean trait in rulers who could ill afford to squander their resources. A lavish court not only demonstrated the monarch's greatness and thus strengthened his position in the eyes of the world; it also offered the necessary sustenance to the aristocracy and gentry. Burgundy provides a striking example of how court-centred nobles came to monopolise political influence. Here, in the Netherlands, one of the medieval centres of urban wealth and greatness, the nobility, exploiting the rise first of the French dukes and then of the Habsburgs, established a firm hold over the politics and even the economy of the region. It was they, not the towns with their traditions of self-government, who a little later were to lead the struggle for independence from Spain. Everywhere, patronage organised the hierarchic social system. The old relations of master and man, of lord and servant,[17] always dependent as much on the sentiments of duty and respect as on mutual interest, came to be crystallised in an extensive network of gifts and services ranging through the ranks of society. Loyalty in consequence attached to the man who could supply patronage through his own standing with the ultimate source of it all, the monarch; if he lost power, no one blamed his servants for seeking another and more useful master. Only kings stood secure above the resulting *mêlée*.

Thus the Reformation cannot be linked with a social revolution headed by the "middle class"; if there was any social revolution at all—and the term is quite inappropriate—it consisted in the increasing monopoly of power held by the aristocracy, under the king. In any case, it has already been shown often enough that the Reformation appealed to all sorts of men. Of course, social stresses and discontents could at times assist it, but Protestantism was not the religion of social rebels seeking to destroy the men in possession. It was the religion of men spiritually dissatisfied. Especially it appealed to the young, the eager and the intelligent. Not social class but temperament and the needs of the soul attracted men to Luther, Zwingli and Calvin. The one aspect of the Reformation which might have joined hands with class grievances—with those of classes well below the bourgeoisie—was Anabaptism, drawing strength from a good many pre-Reformation facts and attitudes; and Anabaptism was kept down.

However, there is another doctrine which links the Reformation with social problems and may by many be considered subtler than the purely economic class analysis. For the past sixty years, it has been nearly unquestioned orthodoxy that there exists some kind of fundamental connection between the Reformation and what is called the rise of capitalism or the capitalist spirit. Within the orthodoxy the quarrelling has been bitter; theories have been evolved and then stood on their heads; but until recently, though some may have refused to believe the whole doctrine, no one who concerned himself with it was prepared to call its bluff. Fortunately for those who (like the present writer) have never been able to see any real sense in it, it is now possible to point to a work which removes every prop from under the notion.[18] Yet it may be doubted whether the death of the theory will become sufficiently known to prevent it having a ghostlike and sepulchral power to haunt, unless, even at the risk of a longish excursus, one proclaims the good news on such occasions as this. The whole history of the sixteenth century and beyond cannot be seen clearly unless certain general ideas, which have almost sunk into the group-consciousness of our culture, are shown for the errors they are.

It all started with the German sociologist Max Weber's famous *The Protestant Ethic and the Spirit of Capitalism* (1904; Eng. trans. 1930). This argued that the particular state of mind which produced the "modern world" was a manifestation of the same mind as underlay the Protestant revolution. The brilliant essay introduced historians to the concept of the "calling" in Lutheran and Calvinist usage (since demonstrated to have been known to late medieval writers): the treatment of worldly avocations as God-created and fulfillable in a spirit of worship. This concept, it was alleged, enabled the Protestant to see in his ordinary daily work an activity pleasing to God and therefore to be pursued as actively and profitably as possible. On the other hand, medieval and Roman Catholic Christianity were held to have condemned the world, with consequent hostility to economic activity and especially to that essential capitalist ingredient, the taking of interest on money lent. Protestantism—or rather, more particularly Calvinism and the later free sects such as the Quakers and Methodists—were therefore asserted to have been the necessary precondition of the growth of modern industrial capitalism; the ethos of Protestantism promoted—nor could anything else have promoted—the spirit of the entrepreneur; and for that reason capitalism is found flourishing in reformed countries, while the Reformation is found spreading among the commercial and industrial middle classes.

Weber's thesis, characterised by vagueness, was partly at least evolved in opposition to the Marxist view that economic and material conditions alone effect changes in economic ideas and practice. He was certainly right to stress the importance of the mind and the spirit in conditioning the economic environment itself, and the eagerness with which anti-Marxists picked him up was in part quite justified. It may be that even to-day his rejection of Marxism still occasionally attracts support for him.[19] Yet there are quite striking weaknesses in his essay. He started, astonishingly, from the notion that "the capitalist spirit" was contrary to human nature: left to themselves, all men would want only enough to maintain them in the condition in which they found themselves. This mystical concept is disproved not only by what we know of men in history, but also by all the despairing, and identical, protests against greed and self-regard which we can read from the Old Testament prophets onwards. Weber defined capitalism as "identical with the pursuit of profit, and forever *renewed* profit, by means of continuous, rational, capitalistic enterprise". In so far as this phrase is clear, and not merely tautological, it again seems to apply to all reasonably advanced economies, varying in effect but available at all times in the spirit. He illustrated his arguments, which embraced 300 years, by reference to Richard Baxter, the seventeenth-century puritan turned anti-Calvinist (whom he misrepresented), and to Benjamin Franklin who wrote his tradesman's gospel after rejecting the Calvinism in which he was brought up. Dr. Samuelsson has further shown how Weber used his mythology of "ideal types" in a transparently circular argument to substantiate the alleged facts from which he had first derived it.[20] Even the one piece of sociological analysis from which he started—Offenbach's study of the educational and

vocational habits of Protestants and Catholics in the German kingdom of Baden in the late nineteenth century—was misinterpreted by
both its author and by Weber. Properly regarded, the figures show
only that "urban dwellers tended to hold their capital in forms other
than land, that schools tended to be located in towns, and that
landless citizens tended to become engineers rather than veterinary
surgeons".[21] Like so much else in sociology, impressive theories,
looked at closely, dissolve into pointless glimpses of the obvious.

However, in 1926 the economic determinists captured the Weber
thesis for themselves, with the assistance of that non-Marxist, Christian, socialist, R. H. Tawney, and his book *Religion and the Rise of
Capitalism*. Recognising that capitalism was nothing new in the
sixteenth century nor so exclusively Protestant thereafter as Weber's
view would seem to suggest, Tawney turned the thesis round and
argued that Calvinism, in the seventeenth century, adapted itself to
the "bourgeois" and capitalist ethos of the commercial classes and
offered the encouragement of religion to the practices of the entrepreneur. The religious Reformation became once again an element in
the alleged bourgeois revolution. Tawney reversed Weber in another
and more important respect. To Weber, capitalism was one of the
glories of Protestantism: looking at the vast material expansion of
the previous three centuries and the vigour of European enterprise
and progress, he came to praise, not to condemn. Tawney, from the
point of view of a social reformer, attacked not only capitalism for its
failure to provide social justice, but also Protestantism for perverting
the Christian message of poverty and charity into a gospel in which
success sanctified the work and profit equalled godliness. His book
has had an extraordinary influence. Especially in England and America, it has greatly assisted in the decline of Protestant self-confidence
and the consequent revival of Roman Catholicism, in the reaction
against capitalism as an economic system, and even perhaps in the
West's increasing inclination to relinquish world leadership. Of
course, in the transmission Tawney's subtle thesis, expressed with
much charm and wit and apparently based on solid empirical fact,
got somewhat coarsened, but it was not misunderstood. There are
still those who, while agreeing that much of the argument will not do,
continue to hold to some really essential connection between the
spread of capitalism and of Protestantism.[22]

Yet what are the facts—or rather, in so large a subject, some of the
central facts? No one now doubts that the early reformers preached a
very old-fashioned attack on ordinary commercial practices, in opposition to the late-medieval Church's defence of them. Luther explicitly
attacked the Fuggers, and Calvin, though less uncompromising, certainly disapproved of profit-making as such. Neither offered any
method of enlarging the needle's eye for the use of the rich. Capital-

ism was fully grown in Italy and south Germany long before Luther, and the leading capitalists of the Reformation era remained faithful to Rome. Calvin very reluctantly agreed in 1545 that interest at five per cent. might be taken, in certain, carefully guarded circumstances. This has been read even by Tawney as giving the green light to free enterprise and the exploitation of others, even though Calvin and later Calvinists violently attacked all forms of "greed", and even though that sound conservative, John Eck, had twenty years earlier defended "usury" at five per cent. The characteristic note of all Protestant preaching throughout the period of expansion was moralistic, with the stress on charity rather than self-advancement, on the sinfulness of such profitable practices as the cornering of commodities or the manipulation of prices, and on the worthlessness of mere worldly success. It was only in the nineteenth century (and especially in America), when the Protestant momentum had run down, that the leaders of religion finally abandoned Calvinism and accommodated their views to the moral system of an advanced capitalism. In Reformation and post-Reformation Protestantism there is no approval of money-making as pleasing to God; the essence of the doctrine of the "calling" is certainly that men need not leave the world in order to serve God, but assuredly not that they should follow their daily task in the sole pursuit of profit. Nor is it true that reformed countries specialised in economic progress. Until war destroyed prosperity, seventeenth-century France was in the van of Europe (and not by any means kept there merely by Protestant Huguenots); commercialism was entrenched in the Netherlands long before Calvinism got there; Anglican England and Catholic Belgium became industrialised long before more notably Protestant countries. There is much else to be said against these theories, both on their content of fact and their interpretation of ideas; but those who cannot stomach this wholesale rejection of them must be referred for the full argument to the works already cited.

Of course, it would be absurd to suppose that a fine historian like Tawney had nothing in the way of fact on which to rest his views. The sermons and pamphlets of the seventeenth century form so vast a mass, and stern Protestantism had so much sympathy for the enterprising and independent mind, that plenty of quotations can be found in defence of frugality, diligence, careful living, doing one's duty in one's station in life. But it is only in the light of the preconceived theory that these expressions assume the character of a body of doctrine favourable to the capitalistic spirit and thus become a reasonable explanation for the attraction which Protestantism, and Calvinism in particular, is supposed to have had for the middle classes. In their context they are directed against mere idleness and luxury, and are firmly linked with denunciations of those particular phenomena—the right to exploit economic chances and advantages without regard for social consequences—which distinguish the "spirit of capitalism" from the normal human inclination to better oneself.[23]

A curious problem is raised by a passage in the Westminster Shorter Catechism of 1646 which could have assisted the Tawney view but does not seem to have been noticed by that party. The eighth commandment, "Thou shalt not steal", is there glossed as enjoining "the lawful procuring the wealth and outward estate of ourselves and others" and as forbidding "whatsoever does or may unjustly hinder our own and our neighbours' wealth and outward estate". Even if one remembers that wealth here means well-being, this still remains something of a millionaire's charter and has been so treated by some who were raised in the Presbyterian faith. The phrases used in this catechism grew from earlier catechisms which added thunders against "the greedy desire of riches" and against "unjust and indirect dealing"; the Larger Catechism of 1646 violently and at length denounces economic enterprise directed at self-profit; and all expositions of the catechism down to the nineteenth century echo these reservations and safeguards against the acquisitive spirit. Nevertheless, the bald omission of such safeguards in this very influential document may unwittingly have done something to assist the weakening hold of religion over secular enterprise. It was not Calvinism that freed man from the restraints of the traditional moral concepts in economics, but emancipation from religion and theology in general which enabled men, pursuing the logic of palpable economic fact, either to ignore the thunders of their clergy or ultimately to persuade some clergy to come to terms. The late-medieval schoolmen had suffered the same fate.

To sum up: there is no good reason for linking Protestantism and capitalism in the significant relationship for so long accepted as certain. Weber started with an axiom which was simply not true: that a special kind of capitalist spirit distinguished post-Reformation Europe and was most marked in Protestant countries. Neither the view that the outburst of material improvement and commercial enterprise, which characterised the centuries after 1600, in some way emanated from the new cast of mind which had also produced Protestantism (Weber), nor the view that capitalism exploited the peculiarities of the Protestant form of Christianity to free itself from all restraint (Tawney), is borne out or required by the facts. Looked at with an open mind, the whole idea of a meaningful correlation—even geographical coincidence—of these historical phenomena simply disappears. Answers have been devised for non-existent questions. The attraction of the universalising generalisation has, as so often, proved too much for the sceptical spirit which alone saves the historian from falling into the pitfalls dug by his own, very necessary, imagination. In the face of the long and ramifying controversy, sadness is the only proper feeling: sadness at so much misguided effort, and sadness at the willingness of historians to worship the graven images set up by the sociologist.

V   The Expansion of Europe

But to deny these generalisations about the bourgeois and the spirit of capitalism is not to deny that notable things were happening, and require explanation, in the economic life and structure of Europe, or that these things in great part had their beginnings in the sixteenth century. Several points strike the eye at once: an increase in population, hard to measure but none the less certain for that; a rise in prices with a relative lag in wages and rents; increased trade, involving also a greater diversity both of markets and commodities; and some consequent increase in industrial production. In other words, this was an age of expansion, an age favourable to enterprise. Nor are the causes of this far to seek, being closely if not quite exclusively linked with perhaps the most significant event of the period, the great discoveries and their exploitation.

Cortéz and Pizarro added empires to Spain. In 1519–21, Ferdinand Magellan, a Portuguese navigator in Spanish employ, led three ships on a circumnavigation of the earth which his lieutenant completed after he had been murdered in the Malayan archipelago: thus he symbolically opened the whole globe to European enterprise. In the six years before his death in 1515 Afonso de Albuquerque established and organised a Portuguese commercial empire on the mainland of India; though driven from the Red Sea, the Portuguese soon expanded eastwards, to gain control, after much fighting, of most of the trade in the Indian Ocean. Portuguese were also settling along the coast of Brazil, maintaining themselves there in spite of conflicts with the Spaniards. The seamen of France and England were beginning to wake up to the chances offered by this enlargement of the known world, even though merchants and capitalists, let alone governments, hung back as yet, having more urgent matters in hand. Spain and Portugal knew what they had got; their jealously, if unsuccessfully, guarded monopoly of trade with their conquests proves that. The new regions supplied luxury goods like spices and silks from the east, dye-woods from the west; but in particular the west supplied bullion. The Americas from the first exported considerable quantities of gold and silver, and after the opening of the mines of Potosí in Peru in 1545 the stream of silver remained steady and large for the best part of a century. In return, Europe exported African slaves, cloth, weapons, metal manufactures and household goods to the colonists in America; cloth and bullion to the east.

Compared with trade in Europe, this transpontine trade was not extensive, and in the east it was by no means all new trade, much of it amounting only to a re-routing from the Mediterranean. (It should, however, be remarked that until the early seventeenth century the Mediterranean remained one of the world's great trading areas.) The effects of Europe's expansion were in great part indirect: through the inflation which the influx of specie and the increase in commerce produced at home. In Spain, prices rather more than doubled in the half-century 1500–50, with the serious increase starting after 1520; Antwerp rates followed suit very rapidly, and thereafter the rest of Europe was affected. Such a relatively steep inflation had disturbing effects, the more so because it followed upon a prolonged period of price stagnation, the result in part of economic depression and in part of the shortage of money in circulation. Even before America came to the rescue of silver-starved Europe, the mines of Bohemia and the Tyrol had been exploited more energetically and trade had helped itself with efficient instruments for the creation of credit, especially the bill of exchange, an Italian invention which enabled large transactions to be carried on without the physical transfer of cash. But credit instruments are, in the last resort, only as good as the capital which backs them, and in a period of population increase Europe was very short of liquid capital as represented by precious metals. Thus American silver assisted the release of an internal trade potential already stimulated by the revival of markets after the fifteenth-century wars and depressions.

The buoyant market and the inflation had their predictable consequences: profits for anyone who had anything to sell, hardship for anyone living on a fixed or insufficiently elastic income, hardship to the pure wage-earner (a rare figure in the sixteenth century) but possibilities of improvement for even the small man with skills or products to sell. Governments, faced with rising costs and laggard revenue, encountered the difficulties which they tried to solve by the intensive borrowing that resulted in the disastrous crashes of 1557. Landowners either lived on rents of declining value or did their best to exploit their lands directly by farming for the market; many did very well that way, and others, in due course, managed to screw more out of prospering tenants who were quite often protected against rent-increases by the customary law. Commerce alone found the economic climate totally favourable and saw trouble only in the interference of man—in war, embargo, taxation. As has been pointed out already, however, this does not mean that commercial success came only to the "bourgeois": the upper classes used the same obvious techniques to exploit their possessions and the grants of princes. It was, in other words, an age naturally constructed for entrepreneurial success, and equally naturally entrepreneurs responded. Not that everybody prospered: of course not. Some who prospered most, like the Fuggers with their commercial empire resting on mining rights in New Spain and old Austria, also overreached themselves, committed their fortunes too heavily to the support of princes, and went into premature decline. In general this was an age when wealth accumulated: reserves of wealth, whether in bullion, or lands of rising value, or fixed capital of various sorts (buildings, industrial equipment, shipping) all increased very markedly. Considering her favourable position, Spain participated less than she ought to have done in this general laying up of treasure; she was content to act the spendthrift with her silver, an attitude encouraged by traditional contempt for commercial activities (associated with Jewish or Moorish heretics) and by the constant drain of heavy taxation which was the price she paid for supporting the foremost dynasty in Europe. But even here, the first half of the century saw some increase in real wealth; in France, England, the Netherlands that increase was marked, and in the older centres of prosperity, such as Germany and Italy, political decline and troublesome war did not prevent some further improvement at this time.

It is this accumulation of capital, assisted by the quite novel abundance of bullion, which deserves to be called the most important economic feature of the age. For there can be no capitalism without capital. If European capitalism after 1550 differed from similar earlier phenomena it was not in its spirit or ambitions, but in the means at its disposal. It was not the Protestant ethos which it exploited, but vastly enlarged reserves and vastly greater liquidity. The continued expansion, never seriously arrested, which, together with industrial technology, has led to the unique enlargement of wealth characteristic of the modern world, stemmed from those beginnings. Its outcome was unique, but its early days were not. The economies of the nineteenth and twentieth centuries assuredly show special characteristics. But these characteristics owe nothing to some peculiar capitalist mentality or to the Reformation. Instead, they derive from a very special set of circumstances which prevented the growth of the sixteenth and seventeenth centuries from suffering the relapse which had attended all such growths in the past. As recently as the thirteenth century an agrarian and trading boom (resulting from increased populations and expanded trade routes: from an enlargement of the market) had come to nothing because the natural cyclical misfortunes of mankind had supervened. Over-expanding populations lead to diminishing returns from over-used land and therefore to famine, which quickly reduces the population (and therefore the market) and produces a major slump, especially if that reduction is further accelerated by such epidemics as the bubonic plague of the fourteenth century. Modern capitalism has (so far) succeeded in breaking through this natural cycle by means of medical and technical advance. Arrest disease, improve transport, lower costs and speed up production by industrial progress, and the market will continue to expand; the large cycle of growth and collapse will cease to operate, however many small cycles of boom and slump may occur within a generally expanding economic universe.

This is what happened to Europe after the far from unprecedented sixteenth-century boom had run its course, and the reason for it happening must in the main be sought in two facts: the natural expansion of the market achieved by the opening up of the globe, and the technological triumphs which followed in the wake of the scientific revolution of the seventeenth century. Neither of these events is to be directly linked with the Reformation, though both can be seen to begin their operation in the era of the Protestant revolution. Perhaps, despite its small positive contribution to science, technology or exploration, one should still respect the old view that the Renaissance, reviving interest in the Greeks, stimulating concern with new studies, and encouraging man to trust to his own powers, played its part in the great movements which enabled humanity to achieve a new grip on its environment. Still, the Reformation should not be ignored even in this context. Because of it, the Europe that expanded was not united in religion and therefore more varied, more adaptable and potentially more successful than the Europe of a monolithic papal Church could ever have been. Dissatisfaction with the religious policy of European powers also assisted, by increasing the important flow of colonising emigrants. And as for science and technology, though these were most certainly not monopolised by Protestants, it may still be asserted that the Reformation helped in the freeing of the intellect. It had not intended to do so, nor did it at first seem likely to do so. Narrow passions, bigotry and persecution were far more manifest in its immediate wake. There is sound sense in the complaints of those who see reason and free enquiry threatened by the revival of religion and the *furor theologicus* that replaced more rational and humane attitudes; even though it is absurd for anyone to suppose that religion could have been revived by reason and free enquiry. Yet when the passions had produced war and exhaustion, when most men had agreed to differ on the details of the faith, it was seen that by breaking the authority of the Church, by liberating the individual responsibility of men, and by preserving so much of the intellectual achievement of humanism, the Protestant Reformation had helped to give a new range and a new strength to the human mind and spirit.

Of all the events of the time, the expansion of Europe remains, in retrospect, the most fateful. In the first half of the sixteenth century, this small appendage of the main landmass of the world entered upon its career as the inspiration and the ruler of that world. It can hardly have looked so at the time. The ancient empire and civilisation of China seemed vastly more powerful and looked upon European visitors with a courteous superiority to which they often responded with an impressed respect that was later to be sadly lacking. The subcontinent of India, not markedly smaller than Europe itself, and the home of a civilisation subtler than any yet produced in the west, was about to fall under the energetic sway of the Mogul emperors with their aggressive policies; nothing seemed less probable than that within two hundred years India would be torn by European conflicts. The highly organised Asiatic empire of the Ottoman Turks was pressing into the very vitals of the Christian Europe which in due course was almost contemptuously to hold it off with one hand, while engaged in gathering in the globe with the other. In spite of all that has been said against too catastrophic a view of the sixteenth century, the Europe of Luther and Charles V was a region of great changes. One may take what view one pleases of movements which we summarise under the titles of Renaissance and Reformation; one cannot overlook them or the greater flexibility which they produced. Without falling into the error of supposing that "the middle ages" were entirely static, one must still recognise the cracking of traditional moulds and traditional convictions which marked the sixteenth century. Above all, in this age Europe was tilting away from the landmass to the oceans—to that open side where success awaited the enterprising few to the benefit of the many. Through Turkey, and to a lesser degree through Russia, Asia was once more at her old game of pushing back the eastern frontier; such heartlands of medieval Europe as Hungary or Poland became border lands. The Reformation, with its political consequences, helped to depose Germany from the place of first importance which it had intermittently held since the ninth century. Political events, reinforcing the logic of the Mediterranean's gradual decline, ended the long era of Italy's greatness in wealth and culture. In the *conquistadores* of Spain, the mariners of Portugal, the traders of Lisbon and Seville and Antwerp, the Atlantic seaboard announced its readiness to initiate the four centuries of European hegemony on earth.

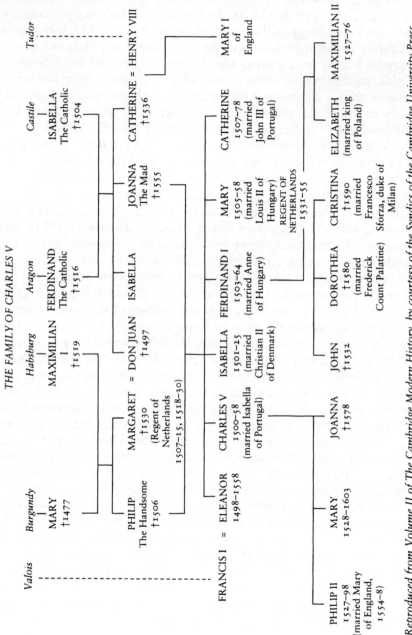

THE FAMILY OF CHARLES V

Valois   Burgundy   Habsburg   Aragon   Castile   Tudor

MARY †1477

MAXIMILIAN I †1519

FERDINAND The Catholic †1516

ISABELLA The Catholic †1504

PHILIP The Handsome †1506

MARGARET †1530 (Regent of Netherlands 1507–15, 1518–30)

= DON JUAN †1497

ISABELLA

JOANNA The Mad †1555

CATHERINE = HENRY VIII †1536

MARY I of England

FRANCIS I = ELEANOR 1498–1558

CHARLES V 1500–58 (married Isabella of Portugal)

ISABELLA 1501–25 (married Christian II of Denmark)

FERDINAND I 1503–64 (married Anne of Hungary)

MARY 1505–58 (married Louis II of Hungary) REGENT OF NETHERLANDS 1531–55

CATHERINE 1507–78 (married John III of Portugal)

PHILIP II 1527–98 (married Mary of England, 1554–8)

MARY 1528–1603

JOANNA †1578

JOHN †1532

DOROTHEA †1580 (married Frederick Count Palatine)

CHRISTINA †1590 (married Francesco Sforza, duke of Milan)

ELIZABETH (married king of Poland)

MAXIMILIAN II 1527–76

Reproduced from Volume II of The Cambridge Modern History, by courtesy of the Syndics of the Cambridge University Press

Afterword to the Second Edition
by Andrew Pettegree

Geoffrey Elton was a unique figure in the British academic community, and this is a history of the Reformation era unlike any other. Its enduring influence is a tribute to qualities which were essential to the man, and which characterised all of his writing: clarity of thought, an incisive ability to organise his materials, brilliant phrase-making. Rereading this book for the purposes of this essay brought home to me how much I, like most of my generation, have been influenced by Elton's Reformation. Here, rather to my surprise, I rediscovered formulations and phrases which, almost subliminally, seem to have formed my understanding of the period.

This is all the more remarkable since Elton was not in the modern sense a historian of continental Europe. Elton made his reputation, and enjoys his enduring fame, as an interpreter of English constitutional history, the abiding love of his mature career. Apart from his responsibility for the Reformation volume of the *New Cambridge Modern History*, *Reformation Europe* was his only major foray into continental history. If this makes Elton seem a rather surprising choice to undertake a volume in the highly ambitious and hugely successful Fontana History of Europe Series, then this was perhaps not as remarkable then as it would be now. All the great figures of Elton's generation of Early Modern historians, Elton himself, A. G. Dickens, Hugh Trevor-Roper, moved more casually across national boundaries in their published scholarship than would now be thought usual, all making major contributions in the fields of both British and European history. Reading Elton's work again makes it seem all the more regrettable that modern traditions of specialisation have made these boundaries seem almost impenetrable. For Elton brings to the study of this wider canvas a sense of informed detachment which is one of this book's many strengths. Writing away from his main field of research, the author seems almost visibly to relax; in particular there is none of the irascible disputatiousness with which he pursued critics of his *Tudor Revolution in Government*. The result is a brilliant, fast-flowing narrative which combines clarity with insight: a true classic.

It is a classic also in the sense that it is the product of an age which is manifestly not our own. Reading it now, it evokes something of the lost age before historical scholarship felt the full impact of the social upheavals of the 1960s. There is no trace here of the new social history which emerged during this period, and seemed likely for a time to permanently re-order the way history would be written. The French *Annales* school (like all things French) was deeply foreign to Elton's way of thinking. Yet in a curious way Elton's text seems less dated now than it might fifteen years ago, as with the passage of time many aspects of history writing have turned full circle. In particular, Elton's concentration on key personalities and their intellectual thought-world as a means of understanding an era now seems less anachronistic than it would in the 1970s. For this is manifestly not, as Elton concedes in his preface, a history of European society in the early sixteenth century. Rather it captures in a remarkable and often dramatic way some of the key conflicts which shaped and defined the age.

This was appropriate enough, because in his own life Geoffrey Elton was no stranger to the dramatic events which shaped our own, equally turbulent century. Gottfried Ehrenberg (as Elton then was) was born in Tübingen, Germany, in 1921, the second son of the distinguished classical scholar, Victor Ehrenberg. The Ehrenbergs were a prosperous family of professional people and academics; in addition to his father, his uncle Richard was also an academic of distinction. Richard Ehrenberg was clearly a leading influence on the young Gottfried (Elton would later dedicate to him the German edition of his *Reformation Europe*), and it is from his uncle that Elton seems first to have found his love of the sixteenth century. Ehrenberg was in his day a leading authority on the period and his two major works, a study of capitalism in the age of the Fugger and an analysis of Anglo-German relations during the age of Queen Elizabeth, still repay study today. Indeed, taken together the careers of uncle and nephew offer a poignant commentary on the history of Germany in the early twentieth century. Ehrenberg's *Hamburg und England im Zeitalter der Königen Elizabeth*, first published in 1896, is an unmistakable product of the Dreadnought era. In Ehrenberg's presentation England is bound, as an integrated nation state, to get the better of the weak and divided German cities. Expressed in an impeccable historical context one can still sense clearly the pressures that drove England and Germany into competition and emnity by 1914.

But the Ehrenbergs, though patriotic, were also Jewish, and in 1939 Victor Ehrenberg decided to abandon Prague, where he had a post in the German university, and remove his family to England. They left a month before Hitler occupied the city; Gottfried's aunt, who elected not to leave, was shot the following year. In England a family connection secured the two boys entry to Rydal School, where Gottfried first resumed his interrupted school work and then obtained a degree, an external London B. A., through a correspondence course. The change of name, to Geoffrey Elton, was suggested by the British Army when he was called up in 1943. Demobilisation, a London doctorate (working under Sir John Neale), and a post at Glasgow university followed in short order. In 1950 he was appointed to a lectureship at Cambridge, where he remained for the rest of his life. The publication of his first book, *The Tudor Revolution in Government* in 1953, announced both the arrival of a major talent, and of the field, English constitutional history, that he would now make his own. Successive textbooks and studies, notably *England under the Tudors* (1955) and *Reform and Reformation* (1977), and his influential Ford Lectures, *Policy and Police* (1972), ensured that Elton's presentation of the Tudor period as a time of radical constitutional innovation, and his celebration of the work of its primary instigator, Thomas Cromwell, soon passed into the mainstream. From a remarkably early stage Elton's were the views against which others were measured; not least by the successive shoals of graduate students, seventy in all, which were a permanent feature of his mature Cambridge career.

It is obviously of relevance to ask how these life experiences may have affected Elton's historical perceptions. Certainly they left him with a deep love and passionate commitment to the history of his adopted home. Elton later said of his coming to England that it was like arriving in a country into which he felt he should have been born. He truly loved England with the zeal of a convert, and was a doughty defender of what he believed to be the best British values. More subtly, but no less profoundly, one may also see in the experiences of Elton's youth the origins of his deep and abiding conviction of the power of strong personalities to shape their age. Certainly, Elton's family history would have left him in no doubt that individual historical figures do matter, and a strong sense of the ability of leading actors to shape Events characterises all of his historical work. In his writings on England this led him to frame the history of constitutional change largely as the achievement of a bureaucrat of genius, Thomas Cromwell, who Elton in effect rediscovered. But the same instinctive search for powerful personalities also pervades his view of sixteenth-century Europe.

With several books behind him and a growing reputation as a pugnacious and original scholar, Elton was a well-established figure when he was invited by his Cambridge colleague, J. H. Plumb, to contribute to the planned new Fontana History of Europe. Judging from the correspondence which Elton preserved in his papers, he hesitated before taking on what he recognised would be a considerable commitment. But the challenge from Plumb—a lifelong rival—proved too insidious, and in December 1960 Elton signed the contract. He began to write in March 1962 and delivered the required 90,000 words, on time, nine months later. At times he was writing at the rate of 3,000 words a day; for a survey work of this breadth and scope a remarkable rate of progress by any account.

Published first by Collins in hardback in 1963 *Reformation Europe* was an immediate success. In reviews it was recognised as a marvellous achievement even by those with whom Elton had crossed swords in the past. When reviewers had entered reservations Elton, being Elton, frequently wrote a private letter to offer his counter-observations. The Elton papers, now the property of the Royal Historical Society, included exchanges with Lawrence Stone, Christopher Hill and Joel Hurstfield, among others. It is clear from this correspondence (to which I have had access for the purpose of this essay), that even in its day this was regarded as a conservative book. The thread that runs through these first exchanges was Elton's defence against the charge that he had ignored or underplayed the social and economic element in favour of a strong political and religious narrative. And indeed, the gap between the history Elton would write and Stone or Christopher Hill was even then well nigh unbridgeable; though the exchanges between them, public and private, remained always courteous. Indeed on one occasion, writing to Christopher Hill, Elton is moved to suggest mutual congratulations that they continue to disagree in a proper spirit—a rare quality, he believed, in an academic world populated increasingly by prima donnas.

Forty-five years and many hundreds of thousands of sales later, we may take a longer perspective on Elton's Europe. Yet some of the observations of perceptive commentators on its first publication ring equally true now. As we have seen, Elton made no apology, then or later, for eschewing the vogue for total history. This was not a choice made through neglect or ignorance of the major continental schools that even as Elton wrote were transforming the landscape of historical writing. Fernard Braudel's *La Méditerranée et le monde méditerranéen à l' époque de Philippe II* (1949), which one could almost call the flagship enterprise of the *Annales* school, was well known if not yet translated into English. Elton understood what was intended with such a panoramic survey, which introduced its narrative of the events of the reign with a long (900-page), discursive survey of the landscape, environment, economy and culture of the lands. But all his instincts revolted against it. Reflecting only a few years later on the various approaches to writing history in his highly successful and still very readable text, *The Practice of History* (1967), Elton turned directly to Braudel:

> The long ascendency of Ranke, primarily concerned with international relations and diplomacy, has been replaced by such influences as that of the French *Annales* school, which wishes to understand a whole society in every detail, in all its interrelationships and activities.... [Braudel's *Mediterranean World*] offers some splendid understanding of the circumstances which contributed to the shaping of policy and action; the only things missing are policy and action. There is a clear and admirable sense of life, but how these lives passed through history is much less clear. To me, at least, the *Annales* method—certainly until it lost itself in rhetoric and self-adulation—represented a valuable, perhaps necessary, stage in the development of historical writing, one which attacked genuine deficiencies and did a great deal to remedy them, but it must not be regarded as in some way the sole consumma- tion of the historian's duties. (*The Practice of History*, pp. 167–8)

One may legitimately question whether this was altogether fair to Braudel; there is in fact a perfectly serviceable account of "policy and action" in *The Mediterranean World*, albeit buried deep in the book. But that is not the point. Elton was instinctively drawn to history writing which took its main theme in political narrative and analysis. It was not that he regarded this as in any sense a soft or easy option. Fresh from the effort of writing *Reformation Europe*, Elton con- fessed in *The Practice of History* that he found the writing of narrat- ive in many respects more taxing than the analytical history at which he excelled (though that might have had more to do with the relat- ively unfamiliar subject matter, than the method, *per se*).

Elton's main objection to *Annales* was an unshakeable conviction that a book must have a main theme; a theme, in his own words, "sufficiently dominant to carry others along with it". And:

> In practice, it has to be admitted, this means that the main theme even today will be nearly always "political": it must consist of the actions of governments and governed in the public life of the time. (*The Practice of History*, p. 172).

Reformation Europe was certainly true to these precepts. Elton presents the age as a drama formed principally through the conflicts of its leading actors. No history of the sixteenth century would now begin, as Elton does, with Martin Luther, nor even with the Reforma- tion; though thankfully, the contrary fashion for writing the history of the age almost without mentioning Luther seems also to have passed. In this respect the pendulum swing of historical writing has been quite kind to Elton. The return of the fashion for narrative writing, in particular the vogue for biography, makes Elton's presentation of the dramas of the Reformation seem quite topical. Certainly, in the hands of the master it demonstrates very ably just how much this approach to history writing has to offer.

In particular Elton's interest in personality allows him to create a powerful sense of the engagement between the leading actors of the age and their circumstances. We see that Martin Luther and Charles V both had choices when they confronted each other at the Diet of Worms. These were choices constrained and formed by their very different education and upbringing, but in both cases character determined the fateful decision: on the side of the reformer to maintain his defiance, on the side of the Emperor to let Luther go. Along the way there are some splendid individual judgements on other players who strut across the stage. Elton was a big personality and it is no surprise that he is drawn to the large characters. Courage gets high marks, as does style (Elton had plenty of both). Well-meaning but indecisive statesmen are more harshly treated, and Popes, from Clement VII ("weak, hesitant and always a little late") to Paul IV ("mad") rarely escape unscathed. Some of these judgements are a little invidious, since Elton would, on occasions, allow his opinions to run ahead of his knowledge. His views on sixteenth-century church music (p. 32) betray a tin ear rather than a profound acquaintance with the subject. But on the politics of the central drama of the age he remains a sure-footed guide.

If politics and religion are undoubtedly the main organising themes of the book, then what is missing? No two generations write history in the same way, and ours has both different preoccupations, and different opportunities from the era in which Elton wrote. There is no doubt that for him Germany and England were the most interesting parts of Europe and the Reformation its central drama. The terms of reference of the series excluded England from explicit narrative attention, which suited Elton well enough; he has said what he had to on England elsewhere. But the concentration on the central Reformation conflicts means that some other parts of western Europe, which would now play a large role in any consideration of the moving forces of the sixteenth century, get comparatively short shrift. Apart from a useful narrative of the Valois–Habsburg wars, France, one of the most interesting emerging cultures of the period, does not command much attention. This is a pity, for in Francis I, France possessed one of the most arresting figures of the age, whose significance went far beyond his role as an arch-foe for Charles V. Historians would now recognise that the Renaissance monarchy, which achieved a strikingly advanced state of development in France during this period, was one of the most significant manifestations of the emerging nation state. It is also now widely recognised that the intellectual presuppositions underlying these developments had a great deal of common currency on both sides of the Channel. Elton would not have missed the significance of this work for his own studies of the Tudor monarchy. There is also not much on the Netherlands; already a powerhouse of north European culture if not yet the international flash-point it would become in the second half of the century. Because in the first half of the sixteenth century it did not command much "political" attention, being securely under the control of its ruler, Charles V, it receives little attention in Elton's narrative. But in fact the culture and civilisation of Erasmus's homeland was already beginning to make a profound mark on the European intellectual world, not to mention its economy.

Most interestingly, Elton's own background seems to have left him with no particular desire to write about Eastern Europe. One cannot help but feel that this is an opportunity missed. At the time that Elton wrote *Reformation Europe* Eastern Europe was a secure and apparently permanent part of the Soviet bloc, to all intents and purposes closed to western scholars of the pre-modern era. This sense of foreignness and impenetrability resulted in its virtual exclusion from many textbook surveys of Europe. But Elton of all people was in a position to know that modern circumstances were in no way a reflection of sixteenth-century reality. In the pre-war Europe of Elton's childhood cities like Prague and Budapest were as much part of the German central European cultural network as Munich and Vienna. Wittenberg, where Elton begins his narrative, is less than one hundred miles west of Prague, where he spent his formative years. Both were far distant from the Rhineland towns which for forty years became the accidental centre of the post-war German state.

In the last ten years all of this has turned full circle once again. There are generations of students now at university who will have no active memory of a time when Europe, for all practical purposes, ended thirty miles east of Vienna, or Berlin was a divided city. These governing realities of the post-war, Cold War era are themselves now consigned to history. A new history of Reformation Europe written today would undoubtedly reflect these changed circumstances, and the happy rediscovery of those sixteenth-century intellectual and cultural connections that made of central Europe a cultural unity that largely ignored the weak and rather fluid political boundaries of the period. Indeed, thanks to the reopening of Eastern European archives made possible by the collapse of Soviet power these changes are already occurring. New studies of the impact of Protestantism on strange and unfamiliar lands—Bohemia, Moravia, and Transylvania, for instance—have already yielded some striking results. Indeed it is not too much of an exaggeration to say that we now know that

Luther's message found its strongest resonance outside Germany in lands to the East, such as Bohemia, Hungary and Poland. Yet these are countries which scarcely feature in many general histories of the Reformation, except as the home of Luther's mediaeval precursor, Jan Hus, and as a refuge for radical refugees who fell foul of the magisterial reformers.

This aspect of Elton's text was not much remarked upon in its day. Contemporary critics concentrated their fire on what they saw as the relative neglect of social and economic issues. Elton, for all that he acknowledged conscious primacy of the political narrative, did not altogether accept this charge. He believed rather that by embedding passages of analysis in the description of events he would create a true picture of the age. Ultimately the reader must decide to what extent this difficult assignment is achieved. But even in his own terms Elton is deploying such analysis to explain the motives of the central actors, rather than explore the lives of those upon whom the actions of the great impacted. In general terms ordinary people appear in Elton's narrative only when they do extraordinary things: the German peasantry in the Peasants' War, the hapless inhabitants of the Anabaptist kingdoms of Münster.

This would now be recognised as a great deficiency. One of the great achievements of history writing in the generation since Elton published *Reformation Europe* is the recognition that it is possible to write the history of the silent: the non-influential, unchanging inhabitants of Early Modern Europe. It would be impossible to write such a history now without some sort of survey of the conditions of everyday life. Elton gives us very little of this—nothing on food, clothing, health or disease, transportation or livestock—the basic building-blocks which in fact wholly formed the living experience of most humans in the period. Elton was certainly not oblivious to the value of this work. Much of the most influential and pioneering work in this field, was after all, done in Cambridge, amongst others by members of the Cambridge Population Group. It is inconceivable that work of this kind would not be powerfully represented in any revision that Elton might himself have undertaken of this text.

The interest in the living experience of the broad mass of the population also has, of course, a most profound impact on the way in which we study the history of religion. This was a central concern of Elton's *Reformation Europe*, and produced some of his most penetrating, as well as his most provocative judgements. The account of Luther is clear-minded and profound. On Zwingli, Elton felt on less certain ground, and sought the guidance of George Potter, the Zwingli specialist then at Sheffield university. The result is a fair-minded and sympathetic account of the Swiss reformer, and of his differences with Luther. For the Radical Reformation, Elton could

not discover the same sympathy. Elton regarded the radicals as misguided and shallow; their disregard for temporal authority was
uncongenial to him; the fissiparous tendencies of their self-tutored
systems of belief excited his contempt. Elton's somewhat brutal dis-
missal of the Radical Reformation excited comment at the time, and
he was forced to defend himself against the charge of unfairness. It
was a point on which he remained sensitive, if unrepentant. The very
short preface to the second edition of the Reformation volume of the
New Cambridge Modern History (1990) devoted a large chunk of its
space to arguing that his views on the radicals had been borne out.

It would be less easy to sustain this argument with respect to
Elton's presentation of Genevan Calvinism. Here there is a striking
contrast between the clarity and balance Elton brings to an analysis
of Calvin's ideas, and his presentation of Geneva after Calvin had
established his domination of the city:

> The more democratic institutions in the city's civil government disap-
> peared, and the surviving top council came in effect to be an agent of
> the now all-powerful consistory. Laws of mounting severity were
> passed—against blasphemy and adultery, for attendance at church
> and compulsory schooling, concerning cleanliness and public health.
> Many of them were sensible and necessary, others bigoted and stultify-
> ing; all were the same to Calvin.... Calvin's Geneva should not be
> disbelieved or despised: it should be treated seriously, as an awful
> warning. (See above, pp. 162–3)

How could Elton come to believe such a terrible parody? In fair-
ness to him, the full transcripts of the deliberations of the Genevan
consistory, which reveal an altogether more sympathetic institution,
are only now being made available to scholars through publication;
the originals, preserved in Geneva are almost unreadable to any other
than trained experts. And Elton's remarks were not that far distant
from the contemporary fashion for seeing Calvinism as an effective
proto-modern insurgency movement; for historians of the Cold War
era, the vision of Geneva as "Moscow on the Leman" spreading its
tentacles through Catholic France, was very plausible. But the passion Elton invests in this passage could only be explained by his deep
antipathy to the puritan ethic; indeed, anything that smacked of
religious totalitarianism was deeply uncongenial to him. Catholic
zealotry fares little better, and none are so savagely treated as Thomas Müntzer, the educated man who lent his learning to the "revolutionary fantasies" of the mutinous peasants and led them to their
destruction.

Given the strength of feeling that Elton expressed on these issues,
one can only think that he would have been greatly cheered by the
new trends in research into the religious culture of Early Modern

Europe since he wrote his text. These have revealed that ordinary folk were in fact far less malleable in their religious beliefs than would be suggested by a total concentration on the official Reformation. This represents by far the most significant sea-change in research since Elton wrote, and has truly transformed both our understanding of early modern belief systems and the conclusions we draw about the success of the evangelical enterprise. Elton's approach to Luther's ideas—essentially through an analysis of the reformer's intellectual formation and theology—was entirely conventional for its day. Scholars of that generation, if they concerned themselves with the wider consequence of the reformers' initiatives, would investigate solely how these precepts were *applied*. Now all that has changed. It is now recognised that the beliefs of the mass of the population bore little resemblance to the tidy, well-ordered systems of the trained theologians. Nor did they readily abandon their beliefs on the urgings of those in power.

Our changing sense of the questions that should be asked of popular belief can be traced, for England at least, to two milestone books. Keith Thomas's *Religion and the Decline of Magic* (1971) opened our eyes to a world of magical, semi-pagan and customary belief which pervaded the lives and beliefs of the masses in Early Modern Europe. To the reformers the medieval church was a vast and creaking institution in need of urgent restitution. But to the vast majority of ordinary believers, it was more, to paraphrase Thomas, a vast reservoir of magical power, capable of deployment for a variety of secular purposes. The priestly caste was respected as the agency of these powers, but by no means an exclusive agency. The relationship between this world and the next was both close and complex, mediated and explained through a web of rituals and folk festivals that were often Christian only in the loosest sense. Our sense of the dignity and interest of these rituals also owes a great deal to Peter Burke's seminal study, *Popular Culture in Early Modern Europe* (1978), a book which can be said to have pointed the way to what has become one of the most fruitful areas of research of the last thirty years.

Geoffrey Elton was certainly aware of the value and importance of the work inspired by these books. In his own time he greatly encouraged, and learned from the work of his Cambridge colleague, Robert Scribner, the author of a ground-breaking and still influential study of the popular visual culture of the German Reformation, *For the Sake of Simple Folk* (1975). Scribner taught us that the reformers were fully aware of the need to accommodate their message to those of meaner understanding: indeed, after the first flush of enthusiasm in the 1520s the rise of the sectaries seems to have convinced some of the reformers that they succeeded too well. Elton would probably have been less sympathetic to a strand of research which has argued that because the reformers did not manage to create the informed Christian people that they had envisaged the Reformation in some sense "failed". This debate, initiated by a seminal article and book by the German scholar Gerald Strauss (see Further Reading), now seems in its turn somewhat anachronistic. Historians of both Protestantism and Catholicism now recognise the task of transforming society was a work of many generations, if not centuries. In terms of a study of such a limited time-scale as Elton's *Reformation Europe* all that could realistically be asked was that the Reformation should have achieved a degree of political success; though even this hung in the balance until the very end of the period.

The debates inspired by this generation of research into popular belief are themselves far from wholly resolved. In particular, in very recent years historians have begun to question the sharp dichotomy between elite and popular culture implied by the rediscovery of an autonomous popular voice. It is now recognised that while elite culture was and remained exclusive to the literate minority, this did not exclude the elite from interest and participation in popular culture. There is plenty of evidence that members of the highest reaches of society valued and participated in practices and ceremonies that we think of as distinctly "popular" in the sense of being anti-intellectual or irrational. It is also important that a sympathetic investigation of its ritual practice and traditions does not lead to a romanticising of this society. There is a distinct trend in some recent influential studies to present too stark a contrast between the smoothly functioning world of medieval social ritual and the destructive pressures of the Reformation. To articulate the manner in which the rituals of belief functioned to promote social cohesion and harmony in the mediaeval world is not to say that all mediaeval communities were cohesive and harmonious. Descriptions of the rich tapestry of mediaeval belief and practice can lead almost unintentionally to the creation of an imagined and scarcely plausible archetype where all these ritual practices lubricated the smooth and well-oiled machinery of parish life. One can scarcely believe it actually existed in any one place or time.

Put another way, late mediaeval religion now has for historians of the sixteenth century all the fascination of a lost world. The destruction of this world through the intervention of the Reformation seems almost an act of wanton vandalism. This would indeed be a world turned upside down to writers of Elton's generation; readers of *Reformation Europe* would be in no doubt of the author's view of the essential nobility of the movement. And there are certainly dangers in the contrary view. Reading and admiring recent work on religious life before the Reformation, we can too easily forget that there are real evidential difficulties here. It is more difficult even than for the Early Modern period to identify how widely disseminated were the beliefs and practices that have been the subject of so much recent scholarly attention. This is a note of caution entered in respect of some fine, fresh and invigorating work. It suggests, above all, that this is a debate that still has some way to run.

In the last chapter of *Reformation Europe* Elton turns away from narrative and considers the spirit of the age. The placing of this chapter at the end of the book suggests a certain diffidence and indeed Elton confessed some misgivings about having embarked on such a wide-ranging survey of the art, literature and social organisation of the age. Sensibly, he opted to concentrate once again on areas of strength; this chapter has much more to say on the intellectual underpinnings of early modern society than the broader conditions of existence. Thus there are useful reflective passages on theology, book culture and literature, and brief surveys on new developments in the world of science and political thought. The succeeding sections on broader social and economic trends have not worn so well. This is partly because Elton frames this discussion in terms of debates which were no doubt lively at the time, but are now barely remembered. Religion and the rise of capitalism, the Reformation and modernity, the great inflation, all these were no doubt important issues for historians of that time; now they seem more like museum pieces.

This is perhaps slightly unfair, because in at least one case—the debate on the "rise of the middle class"—it was Elton who largely killed it off, not least in this book. His conclusion is worth citing:

> The Reformation cannot be linked with a social revolution headed by the "middle class"; if there was any social revolution at all—and the term is quite inappropriate—it consisted in the increasing monopoly of power held by the aristocracy, under the king. (See above, p. 222)

In its day this would have been bold; now it represents a case which has largely carried the day. The extent to which Early Modern society continued to be dominated by aristocratic values, and the nobility remained the dominant class has survived any notion of the "crisis of the aristocracy", a crisis which now seems to have been largely illusory. Indeed the consensus of scholarship would now seem to suggest that there was no real crisis of the nobility until the French Revolution; though that, admittedly, was rather acute.

Strangely, given the nature of his own specialist work on England, Elton is also curiously downbeat about the emergence of the new nation state. Given the subjects that lay at the core of his specialist scholarship, it is perhaps strange that he admits no fundamental shift in the nature of monarchical government since the High Middle Ages.

The assertion that "the monarchies of Francis I and Henry VIII differed in very few essentials from those of Philip IV and Edward I" is curious indeed from the pen of the author of the *Tudor Revolution in Government*. It is hardly likely that Elton intended to distance himself from this earlier work; more likely the subject was not of great relevance to his central preoccupation in this book with the Empire, and particularly the towering figure of Charles V. Of all the parts of western Europe the Empire remained, in terms of its central administrative institutions, the most relatively under-developed. This by and large forced Charles to rely on traditional methods of government: his own presence, and when that was not possible, family proxies. Elton gives predictably short shrift to Charles's brief flirtation with concepts of universal monarchy as the heir of Charlemagne.

Also of relevance in this connection is the fact that Elton was much more comfortable dealing with written, documentary evidence than with the cultural expressions of regality. Historians have gained much since Elton's day from the collapse of boundaries between disciplines, and the consequent broadening of the subject. There are now very few limits to the frameworks of analysis that are seen as legitimate for the pursuit of historical enquiry. Nowhere has this been more significant than in our recognition of the extent to which society functioned through systems of ritual engagement and customary practice that were every bit as binding as written law. For the rulers of the new age it was necessary both to observe these conventions and to enhance their own place within them. Thus while all were moved to make war, the customary sport of kings, they also lavished their subjects' wealth on tangible monuments to their own power and dignity: palaces and portraits, medals and sculpture. All were employed in a pageantry of ever greater elaboration and intricacy.

To do justice to this it is necessary to comprehend the potency of art, as much as its beauty. It is also important to recognise that the arts were far from being the exclusive preserve of the governing classes. One of the most familiar physiognomies of the age was that of Martin Luther, a man of relatively humble social origins. Yet from the time that he first became a public figure, Luther was sketched and painted in images that became as familiar, perhaps even more so, than those of most of Europe's rulers. This reflected in part his fame, but was also a conscious effort to make of the reformer an icon of the new movement (ironic enough, in a movement which had rejected the cult of saints). So Luther became, quite literally, one of the first to have his image deliberately manufactured for a mass audience; in portraits turned out in industrial production by the workshop of Lucas Cranach, in woodcuts, engravings and wood carving. As

Luther's movement took root, these images themselves became objects of veneration; a trend which serves as a final reminder of the enduring mediaevalism of this new age.

Perhaps it is fitting that this brief appreciation of Elton's text has concluded where he would have wanted us to begin, with Charles V and Martin Luther. They were men with many similarities: energy and courage, breadth of vision and determination, somewhat gross physical appetites. It was Europe's tragedy that they should have to be antagonists; in the event the unity of western Christendom would be irreparably damaged by the clash of their conflicting sense of Christian duty. It was an irony which another of the age's greatest men—Erasmus—might well have appreciated, had the peace and tranquillity of his own hard-won prosperity not been fatally damaged by the corrosive impact of the Reformation conflicts.

Notes

Chapter 1 Luther

1 Papal decrees are called Bulls after the lead seal (*bulla*) attached to them, and are named after their initial words.
2 The spiritual princes of Cologne, Mainz and Trier; the secular rulers of Bohemia, Saxony (Ernestine Saxony; Albertine was ruled by a duke), Brandenburg and the Palatinate.

Chapter 2 Charles V

1 It was not until 1707–16 that the kingdoms of Castile and Aragon were formally united.
2 For a summary of the situation cf. H. Hantsch, "Le problème de la lutte contre l'invasion Turque dans l'idée politique générale de Charles-Quint," in *Charles-Quint et son Temps* (1959), pp. 52 ff.
3 Below, p. 221.
4 Below, p. 171.
5 Below, p. 182f.
6 Charles was not properly crowned until 1530, by Pope Clement VII at Bologna; he was the last Holy Roman Emperor to seek papal coronation.
7 The full translation was not published until 1534. Earlier vernacular versions existed, both in German and in other languages, but they were generally poor and remained without influence.

Chapter 3 Years of Triumph

1 Above, p. 8.
2 Above, pp. 9 f.
3 Below, pp. 58 f.
4 F. Lars, "Der Bauernkrieg und das angebliche Ende der lutherischen Reformation," *Luther-Jahrbuch* 1959.
5 See also below, pp. 60 ff.

6   Below, pp. 122 ff.
7   Below p. 49.
8   *Leutpriester*, usually and rather inanely translated literally as "people's priest".
9   Below, pp. 58 ff.
10 Below.
11 B. Moeller, *Reichstadt und Reformation* (Schriften des Ver. eins für Reformationsgeschichte, 1962).
12 In the sixteenth century the word was phonetically, if inaccurately, translated as "lance-knights"; it really meant originally something like militia-man—a foot-soldier recruited from his region.
13 Below, pp. 190 f.

Chapter 4 The Radicals

1   E. G. Rupp, "Word and Spirit in the first years of the Reformation," *Archiv für Reformationsgeschichte*, vol. 49, pp. 13 ff.
2   Above, p. 30.
3   Below, p. 101.

Chapter 5 Outside Germany

1   In this chapter it will be necessary to go beyond the year 1530 because much of the spread of Lutheranism belonged to the decade after that date.
2   Below, p. 162.
3   Below, pp. 122 ff.
4   Below, p. 156.
5   Below, p. 163.
6   The "Trilingual College" of the University, founded in 1517, in which lectures were given in Latin, Greek and Hebrew, was designed on Erasmian lines and promoted his approach to theology and the classics.
7   Below, p. 213.
8   Below, p. 177.
9   Above, p. 37.

Chapter 6 The Formation of Parties

1   H. Kellenberg, "Zur Problematik der Ostpolitik Karls V." in *Karl V.: der Kaiser und seine Zeit* (1960), pp. 118 ff.
2   S. A. Fischer-Galati, "Ottoman Imperialism and the Religious Peace of Nuremberg," *Archiv für Reformationsgeschichte*, 1956, pp. 160 ff.
3   For the Swabian League, see above, p. 8.

4   As a pupil of mine once put it: "The medieval popes were always
     elected in their old age; therefore they never had a chance to start a
     dynasty." Paul III had done his best in his youth.
5   For Paul III as a reformer see below, pp. 129 ff.
6   For the two Saxonies cf. below, p. 174.
7   Above, p. 20.
8   On Contarini cf. below, pp. 125 f.
9   Gropper's career has been described by W. Lipgens, *Kardinal Jobernes
     Gropper* (1951); the book has been criticised on the grounds that it
     overestimates Gropper's Erasmianism (H. Jedin in *Historisches Jahr-
     buch* 1955, pp. 687ff.) and underestimates the contribution of politics
     in Gropper's preservation of the old religion at Cologne (L. Hatzfeld in
     Archiv für Kulturgeschichte, 1954, pp. 208 ff.).
10   The essence of the doctrine may be expressed in Contarini's definition:
     "Two kinds of justification, one inherent in us…the other given to us
     in Christ." I.e., while justification comes essentially by faith and from
     grace, faith, is perfected by good works deriving from the justness
     created in baptism. This definition laid the stress on the Lutheran
     (and Pauline) doctrine but contemplated a greater degree of free will
     and human perfectibility than Luther would accept.
11   These points are taken up below, pp. 169 ff.

Chapter 7 The Revival of Rome

1   Above, p. 81.
2   Above, p. 118.
3   Above, p. 75.
4   Above, p. 73.
5   P. Hughes, *A Popular History of the Reformation* (1956), p. 233; L. V.
     Pastor, *Geschichte der Päpste*, v (1909), p. 252.
6   *Ibid.*, v. 29.
7   Arguments of this order tend to blame Luther for isolating a particular
     traditional doctrine, whereas he should have treated it in cautious
     conjunction with other, sometimes contradictory, traditional doctrines.
     Without finding Luther's theology, with its high irrational content,
     particularly attractive, one may still prefer his clear spiritual vision to
     that sort of academic timidity. For an example of this kind of attack—
     by an Anglican of high views—cf. J. P. Whitney, *History of the Refor-
     mation* (rep. 1958), pp. 171 ff.
8   For the actual history of the Council of Trent cf. below, pp. 178 f.,
     182 f.
9   Above, p. 119.
10   Above, pp. 69 f.
11   Too much, it seems to me, is often made of the "military" antecedents
     of Loyola and the Jesuit order. True, they called for the service of a
     soldier, but the image is surely also suggested by the ancient concept of

the Church militant on earth. As for the title of general, this (carrying at the time no military meaning that I am aware of) was common in the orders of the friars; in any case, the Jesuits at first elected a "praepositus" or head. In the second half of the century the Society passed briefly through a phase of revolt against the rigid authoritarianism of the founder (G. Lewy in *Church History*, 1960, pp. 141 ff.).

12 Below, pp. 190 ff.

Chapter 8 Calvin

1 Luther all his life had to fight against the temptation to doubt God's grace: R. H. Bainton, "Luther's Struggle for Faith," *Festschrift für Gerhard Ritter* (Tübingen 1950), pp. 232 ff.

2 Above, p. 80.

3 W. Niesel, *The Theology of Calvin* (1938; Eng. trans. 1956); F. Wendel, *Calvin: The Origins and Development of his Religious Thought* (1950; Eng. trans. 1963).

4 As T. F. Torrance puts it, if Luther's was the theology of faith and Bucer's that of charity, Calvin's is that of hope (*Journal of Ecclesiastical History*, 1955, p. 59).

5 Above, pp. 71 f.

6 These theories are discussed below, pp. 217 ff.

Chapter 9 War and Peace

1 Above, pp. 117 ff.

2 This is true not only of the German *Landsknechte*, the Swiss and the Italians who formed so large a part of all the armies, but also of the Spanish *tercios* and the French legions which came nearer to being genuine national standing armies.

3 Above, p. 136.

4 M. Salomies, *Die Pläne Kaiser Karls V. Für eine Reichsreform mit Hilfe eines allgemeinen Bundes* (1953).

5 E.g., its statement on the Lord's Supper avoids the question of transubstantiation but implies that doctrine by saying that "whereas in the sacrament of the eucharist there are the true body and blood of Christ, Christ must be duly worshipped in that sacrament". All that was here conceded was communion in both kinds.

6 H. Jedin, "Die Deutschen am Trienter Konzil 1551/2," *Historische Zeitschrift*, 188 (1959), pp. 1 ff. Not even the German bishops had ever been very eager to attend the Council: they were mostly aristocratic scions only accidentally also princes of the Church and "thought with discomfort of the theological debates taking place there" (Jedin in *Historisches Jahrbuch*, 1955, p. 690).

7 K. E. Born, "Moritz von Sachsen und die Fürstenverschworung gegen Karl V.," Historischa Zeitschrift, 191 (1960), pp. 18 f.

8 The famous phrase, "cuius regio eius religio", which summarises the result, does not occur in the recess of the Diet.

9 The policy of the Carafa family is exhaustively analysed in L. Riess, Die Politiik Pauls IV. und seiner Nepoten (1909).

10 J. Delumeau, "Les progrès de la centralisation dans l'État pontifical au XVIe siècle," Revue Historique, 226 (1961), pp. 399 ff.

11 F. Braudel, "Les emprunts de Charles-Quint sur la place d'Anvers," Charles-Quint et son Temps (1959), pp. 191 ff.

Chapter 10 The Age

1 As was shown above (p. 153), Calvin's stricter theology, in many ways a development of Luther's, in effect introduced impurity into God's love for men by ascribing the purpose of predestined election to God's desire to prove His mercy!

2 "Innerweltliche Askese", which does not mean the asceticism of man's inner world (the private asceticism of the soul), as some translators would seem to suppose, but the "asceticism" of living the religious life in the ordinary world.

3 E.g. H. R. Trevor-Roper, Historical Essays, pp. 35 ff.

4 Does one have to prefer one or the other?

5 The same is no doubt true of Spanish: sed totaliter ignoro.

6 A. Renaudet, Humanisme et Renaissance (Geneva, 1958), p. 177. Renaudet also remarks that without Erasmus Calvin would have written the Institutes "en scolastique". This seems to me meaningless: if Calvin had written in the manner of a schoolman he would assuredly not have produced the Institutes.

7 Cf. above, p. 81 n. 6.

8 Machiavelli receives fuller treatment in the first volume of this (Fontana) series.

9 J. H. Hexter, More's "Utopia": The Biography of an Idea (1952), pp. 91 ff.

10 The common interpretation would seem to require a placet in place of the placuit.

11 Cf. the witty and accurate demolition job done by J. H. Hexter, "The Myth of the Middle Class in Tudor England," in Reappraisals in History (1961).

12 E.g. E. Perroy, "Social Mobility among the French Noblesse in the later Middle Ages," Past and Present, 21 (1962), pp. 25 ff.

13 In Germany, in particular, towns like Hamburg, Danzig and Frankfurt rose to fill, to some extent, the gap left by the decline of others; but they did so by abandoning political ambitions and independent influence.

14 R. Ludloff, "Industrial Development in 16th-17th century Germany," Past and Present, 12 (1957), pp. 58 ff.; F. Lütge, in Jahrbücher für Nationalökonomie und Statistik, (1958), pp. 84 ff.

15 F. Lütge, *Deutsche Sozial-und Wirtschaftsgeschichte* (1952), pp. 155 ff.; M. Malowist, "The Economic and Social Development of the Baltic Countries from the 15th to the 17th centuries," *Economic History Review*, 2nd Series, xii (1959–60), pp. 177 ff.

16 Above, p. 25.

17 Servant, in this sense, means anyone who attached himself to a social superior, to work for him in a variety of ways and in return to receive protection, profit and promotion. The term does not define any absolute social standing: nobles were servants to kings, gentlemen to peers, and so on.

18 K. Samuelsson, *Religion and Economic Action* (translated from the Swedish by E. G. French, ed. D. C. Coleman, 1961). For other recent contributions to the controversy see also C. H. and K. George, *The Protestant Mind of the English Reformation* (1961), pp. 144 ff.; W. S. Hudson, "The Weber Thesis re-examined," *Church History*, 1961, pp. 88 ff.; A. Biéler, *La Pensée Economique et Sociale de Calvin* (1959), pp. 477 ff.; H. Lüthy, "Nochmals 'Calvinismus und Kapitalismus'," *Schweizerische Zeitschrift für Geschichte*, 1961, pp. 129 ff.; R. de Roover, *L'Évolution de la Lettre de Change* (1953), esp. pp. 145 ff. The earlier discussion, summarised in these works, is conveniently available in a collection of extracts, *Protestantism and Capitalism: The Weber Thesis and its Critics*, ed. R. W. Green (1959).

19 Cf. the comments by L. Strauss on Hudson's sceptical paper quoted above, p. 222, in *Church History*, 1961, pp. 100 ff.

20 Hudson (see p. 222, n.) maintains that Weber only professed to offer a hypothesis for testing. But this will not do: when he was attacked, he firmly entrenched himself in his imaginary fortress.

21 Samuelsson, *op. cit.*, p. 145

22 Cf. C. Hill, "Protestantism and the Rise of Capitalism," *Essays...in Honour of R. H. Tawney* (1961), pp. 15 ff. Even Mr. Hill's subtlety and charm cannot, it seems to me, disguise the fact that he is defending a faith in despite of the facts.

23 Dr. Samuelsson (*op. cit.*, p. 80) points out that the doctrine of thrift, regarded as central in the Tawney thesis, was proclaimed with much greater vigour in the Catholic France of Colbert than in Oliver Cromwell's England; and also that thrift is not the major element in capitalism which Weber and Tawney made it. No one ever got to be really rich by saving pence and living frugally; he needed other methods and used them—methods which not even the doctrine has found Calvinists defending.

Further Reading
by Andrew Pettegree

The following recommendations replace those of Elton's original edition. I have tried to include work which I know that he admired, but I have not extended the bibliography into areas which he did not regard as meriting consideration in his text. In the main, therefore, these notes on further reading follow the structure of Elton's own outline bibliography, though given the extent of new publications in this area over the last thirty-five years there is virtually no overlap in terms of content. Where works listed below were first published in a language other than English I have given the date and place of publication of the English translation.

General texts

In 1990 Elton supervised publication of a revised version of his volume in the *New Cambridge Modern History*, though critics would argue that to have been useful a much more radical revision should have been undertaken. Nevertheless new articles by Robert Scribner and Volker Press (on Germany), James Stayer (Anabaptists), and Mia Rodriguez-Salgado (the Valois–Habsburg wars) are valuable. A more ambitious venture is Tom Brady, Heiko Oberman and James Tracy (eds.), *Handbook of European History, 1400–1600* (2 vols., Leiden, 1994). In the economic and social sphere new work has transformed both methodology and our knowledge of the way lives were led. Fernard Braudel's three volumes published collectively as *Civilization and Capitalism, Fifteenth–Eighteenth Century* (London, 1981) cover, respectively, *The Structures of Everyday Life*, *The Perspective of the World* and *The Wheels of Commerce*. The work of Elton's uncle, Richard Ehrenberg, *Capital and Finance in the Age of the Renaissance: A Study of the Fuggers and their Connections* (London, 1928) has proved an enduring classic. See also Catharine Lis and Hugo Soly, *Poverty and Capitalism in Pre-Industrial Europe* (Hassocks, 1979), now supplemented by Robert Jütte, *Poverty and Deviance in Early Modern Europe* (Cambridge, 1994). On sickness and disease, see especially Charles Webster (ed.),

Health, Medicine and Mortality in the Sixteenth Century (Cambridge, 1979). Otherwise, the best work is often to be found in the study of specific localities. Bob Scribner, *Germany: A New Social and Economic History, vol. I: 1450–1630* (London, 1996); Emmanuel Le Roy Ladurie, *The French Peasantry, 1450–1660* (Aldershot, 1987).

The Reformation

Elton enormously admired Heiko Oberman's *Luther: Man between God and the Devil* (New Haven, 1982). One can see why; this is a bold and brilliant reinterpetation which places the intellectual personality of the reformer back in the centre of the picture. A. G. Dickens, *The German Nation and Martin Luther* (London, 1974) is still stimulating and readable, though now a little dated. On the Reformation controversies Scott Hendrix, *Luther and the Papacy* (Philadelphia, 1981), Mark Edwards, *Luther and the False Brethren* (Stanford, 1975), David Bagchi, *Luther's Earliest Opponents: Catholic Controversialists, 1518–1525* (Minneapolis, 1991). For the Peasants' War and its implications, Peter Blickle, *The Revolution of 1525* (Baltimore, 1977). Relevant documents are collected in Tom Scott and Bob Scribner, *The German Peasants' War: A History in Documents* (London, 1991). Peter Blickle, *Communal Reformation: The Quest for Salvation in Sixteenth-Century Germany* (London, 1992) is an interesting attempt to provide a new conceptual framework which has not yet achieved general acceptance. An effective response to Blickle is Tom Scott, *Freiburg and the Breisgau: Town–Country Relations in the Age of Reformation and Peasants' War* (Oxford, 1986). Medium and message have dominated the debate over the impact of the Reformation since Elton's day, a debate largely shaped by Robert Scribner, *For the Sake of Simple Folk: Popular propaganda for the German Reformation* (Cambridge, 1981). See also now Mark Edwards, *Printing, Propaganda and Martin Luther* (Berkeley, 1994), Miriam Chrisman, *Conflicting Visions of Reform: German lay propaganda pamphlets, 1519–1530* (London, 1996), Peter Matheson, *The Rhetoric of the Reformation* (Edinburgh, 1998). For the urban Reformation, Steven Ozment, *The Reformation in the Cities* (New Haven, 1975), R. Po-Chia Hsia, *The German People and the Reformation* (Ithaca, 1988). For the debate over the long-term impact of the evangelical programme of reform, Gerald Strauss, 'Success and Failure in the German Reformation', *Past and Present*, 67 (1975), pp. 30–63; Strauss, *Luther's House of Learning: Indoctrination of the Young in the German Reformation* (Baltimore, 1978). The Swiss Reformation awaits a convincing new synthesis. G. R. Potter, *Zwingli* (Cambridge, 1976) is still sound; see also Robert C. Walton, *Zwingli's Theocracy* (Toronto, 1967). On Calvin and Geneva there are two works of ground-breaking originality: William J. Bouwsma, *John Calvin: A Sixteenth Century Portrait* (New York, 1988), and William G. Naphy, *Calvin and the Consolidation of the Genevan Reformation* (Manchester, 1994). Also valuable is T. H. L. Parker, *Calvin's Preaching* (Edinburgh, 1992).

The spread of the Reformation outside the German-speaking lands is much more fully studied than in Elton's day. See Andrew Pettegree, *The Early Reformation* (Cambridge, 1992) and *The Reformation World* (London, 1999); Jean-François Gilmont, *The Reformation and the Book* (Aldershot, 1998); Ole Peter Grell, *The Scandinavian Reformation* (Cambridge, 1995); Alastair Duke, *Reformation and Revolt in the Low Countries* (London, 1990), Francis Higman, *Piety and the People: Religious Printing in French, 1511–1551* (Aldershot, 1996). Karin Maag (ed.) *The Reformation in Eastern and Central Europe* (Aldershot, 1997) contains some truly ground-breaking work. For new interpretations of the English Reformation, J. J. Scarisbrick, *The Reformation and the English People* (Oxford, 1984) and Eamon Duffy, *The Stripping of the Altars: Traditional Religion in England, 1400–1580* (New Haven, 1992). Susan Brigden, *London and the Reformation* (Oxford, 1989) is a definitive study of England's only real city.

On the Radicals, G. H. Williams, *The Radical Reformation* (3rd ed., Kirksville, MO., 1992) is a much revised standard. Abraham Friesen, *Thomas Muenzer, a destroyer of the Godless* (Berkeley, 1990) is thankfully a more generous assessment of its subject than Elton's. Hans-Jürgen Goertz, *The Anabaptists* (London, 1996) is an excellent treatment of the radical movement. For the Reformation movement as a whole *The Encyclopedia of the Reformation* (4 vols., New York, 1996) contains a host of well-written and authoritative articles.

Catholic reform

This has now been the subject of much scholarly attention, though with a general recognition that its real impact at parochial level was only felt at a much later period. R. Po-Chia Hsia, *The World of Catholic Renewal, 1540–1770* (Cambridge, 1998) is an excellent introductory survey. N. S. Davidson, *The Catholic Reformation* (Oxford, 1987) is shorter but still very useful. On Catholic efforts at reform before Trent see Peter Matheson, *Cardinal Contarini at Regensburg* (Oxford, 1972) and Elizabeth Gleason, *Gasparo Contarini: Venice, Rome and Reform* (Berkeley, 1993). The myth of the Inquisition has been effectively exploded since Elton's day. See especially the work of Henry Kamen, *The Spanish Inquisition* (London, 1965), Stephen Haliczer, *Inquisition and Society in the Kingdom of Valencia, 1478–1834* (Berkeley, 1990) and William Monter, *Frontiers of Heresy: The Spanish Inquisition from the Basque Lands to Sicily* (Cambridge, 1990). For patterns of belief in Catholic Europe see also Alastair Hamilton, *Heresy and Mysticism in Sixteenth-Century Spain: the Alumbrados* (Cambridge, 1992) and William A. Christian, *Local Religion in Sixteenth-Century Spain* (Princeton, 1981). On the new religious orders see John W. O'Malley, *The First Jesuits* (Cambridge, Mass., 1993). Strangely, we still lack a modern analytical study of the Council of Trent. See *The Canons and Decrees of the Council of Trent*, ed. H. J. Schroeder (Rockford, Ill., 1978), for a good edition of the text.

Political history

As an introduction, M. S. Anderson, *The Origins of the Modern European State System, 1494–1618* (London, 1998) is wise and thoughtful. The best study of Charles V is that of Manuel Fernandez Alvarez, *Charles V* (London, 1975), though the classic of Karl Brandi, *Charles V* (London, 1939) is still useful as well as highly entertaining. It is astonishing that as sympathetic a character as Maximilian I has not attracted a good English-language biography. The management of the Imperial lands is variously approached in John M. Headley, *The Emperor and his Chancellor. A Study of the Imperial Chancellery under Gattinara* (Cambridge, 1983), James D. Tracy, *Holland under Habsburg Rule, 1506–1566* (Berkeley, 1990) and Steven Haliczer, *The Communeros of Castile* (Madison, 1981). The end of the reign is examined in detail in M. J. Rodriguez-Salgado, *The Changing Face of Empire: Charles V, Philip II and Habsburg Authority, 1551–1559* (Cambridge, 1988). Thomas Brady, *Turning Swiss: Cities and Empire, 1450–1550* (Cambridge, 1985), is a fascinating exploration of what might have been for the Habsburgs in their German lands. On France, R. J. Knecht, *The Rise and Fall of Renaissance France* (London, 1996); his *Renaissance Warrior and Patron: The Reign of Francis I* (Cambridge, 1994) is the second, revised edition of his classic study of Francis I (1982). On Francis's less regarded successor, Frederic Baumgartner, *Henry II* (Durham, NC, 1988) and on the Habsburg–Valois conflicts David Potter, *War and Government in the French provinces. Picardy, 1470–1560* (Cambridge, 1993). War-making and its impact on society had produced some highly creative and innovative scholarship since Elton's day. See J. R. Hale, *War and Society in Renaissance Europe, 1480–1620* (London, 1985), and for a longer perspective, Geoffrey Parker, *The Military Revolution* (Cambridge, 1988). For England, Elton's own *Reform and Reformation, England 1509–1558* (London, 1977), should be read in conjunction with John Guy, *Tudor England* (Oxford, 1988) and Penry Williams, *The Tudor Regime* (Oxford, 1979). John Guy (ed.), *The Tudor Monarchy* (London, 1997) is an excellent introduction to the latest research.

Overseas discovery

The best introduction is probably now G. V. Scammell, *The First Imperial Age: European Overseas Expansion, c. 1400–1715* (London, 1989). J. H. Parry, *The Age of Reconnaissance* (Berkeley, 1963), is still useful, and very readable. There is much very fine work in J. H. Elliott, *Spain and its World, 1500–1700* (New Haven, 1989). See also Ross Hassig, *Mexico and the Spanish Conquest* (London, 1994). For an insight into the mind of the *conquistadores*, Herman Cortés, *Letters from Mexico*, ed. Anthony Pagden (New Haven, 1986). For the organisation of New World societies, P. K. Liss, *Mexico under Spain, 1521–1556: Society and the Origins of Nationality* (Chicago, 1975).

Intellectual movements

Erasmus continues to fascinate; Léon-E. Halkin, *Erasmus: A Critical Biography* (Oxford, 1993) is sound and up-to-date, though not critical in more than the technical sense. R. Coogan, *Erasmus, Lee and the Vulgate* (Geneva, 1992) throws interesting light on the darker side of Erasmus's character. Peter G. Bietenholz, *Contemporaries of Erasmus* (3 vols., Toronto, 1985–7) is an invaluable handbook of those who knew, admired or opposed the great Dutchman. The ongoing new translation of the *Correspondence of Erasmus*, ed. Peter G. Bietenholz (Toronto, 1974–) is also a fantastic resource. Charles G. Nauert, *Humanism and the Culture of Renaissance Europe* (Cambridge, 1995) is a useful general survey. See also Roy Porter and Mikuslás Teich (eds.), *The Renaissance in National Context* (Cambridge, 1992). The wider intellectual trends of the era are surveyed in a masterful fashion by J. H. Burns (ed.), *The Cambridge History of Political Thought, 1450–1700* (Cambridge, 1991). On the transforming technical innovation, Lucien Febvre and Henri-Jean Martin, *The Coming of the Book: The Impact of Printing, 1450–1800* (London, 1984) is outstanding. The thought-world of the unlettered is brilliantly evoked by Keith Thomas, *Religion and the Decline of Magic* (London, 1971); that of the self-taught in Carlo Ginsburg, *The Cheese and the Worm* (London, 1980). Peter Burke, *Popular Culture in Early Modern Europe* (New York, 1978) is a masterly survey.

Index

synods 167
Syria 101

Taborites 93
Tartaglia, Niccolò 47
Tatars: of the Crimea 89; Kazan 89
Tauler, John 11
Taussen, Hans (1494–1561) 83
Tawney, R. H. 150, 226, 252; *Religion
and the Rise of Capitalism* 224–6
taxation 47–8, 228, 229
Tetrapolitan Confession 101–2
Tetzel, John 4
Teutonic Knights 37
Theatines 128, 140, 143
theocentrism 151
theology 196–7; medieval sources for
radical 55; revival of 14–15
Thiene, Gaetano di (1480–1547) 125,
128; *see later* Cajetan, Saint
Thomas, Keith, *Religion and the Decline
of Magic* 242
Thomism 134, 136
Thurgau 41
Thuringia 34, 59, 177
Tintoretto (Jacopo Robusti, 1518–94)
202–3
Titian (Tiziano Vecello, c.1490–1576)
202; portrait of Charles V 17
Toggenburg 41
toleration 38, 57–8, 66–7, 161, 187–9,
199–200
Torgau, Lutheran League of (1551) 38,
185
Torquemada, Thomas de 70
Toul 185
Toulon 171
Tournai 21
towns, German self-governing 7, 8,
10–11, 14
trade 7, 20–1, 22, 25, 68, 227, 231;
cloth 46; Levantine 100; luxury
goods 227; spice 20–1, 100
translations 212
transubstantiation 43–4, 101, 154, 250
Transylvania 74, 90, 92, 94, 186, 239
Trent, Council of: (1545) 136, 175, 179;
decree on justification (1547) 137;
move to Bologna (1547) 179, 180;
Protestant representatives at 137;
reconvened (1551–2) 145, 182–3
Trevor-Roper, Hugh 233
Trier, archbishop of 33, 247
Trolle, Gustavus, archbishop of
Uppsala 86–7
Truchsess, George 34
Tudor Revolution in Government
(Elton) 234, 235

Tunis, captured (1534) 109
Turks *see* Ottoman Empire
Tver 213
Tyndale, William 82, 124, 206
typhus epidemic (1547) 179
Tyrol 16, 34, 61, 62, 187; mines 7, 54,
228
Tyrolese Brethren 61

Ukraine 88, 89, 213
ulema 99
Ulm 38
Ulrich, duke of Württemberg 106, 177
Umbria 190
Unitas Fratrum (Bohemian Brethren) 93
universities 7, 14
Unterwalden 40
Uri 40
Ursulines 128
usury 225
Utopia (More) 215
Utraquist nobility 94; *see also* Hussites
in Bohemia
Utrecht 21
Utrecht, Adrian of 23; *see also* Adrian
VI, Pope

Valais 41
Valdés, Alonso de 72
Valdés, Juan de (1500–41) 73–4;
Dialogo de Doctrina Christiana
71–2
Valencia 22, 23
Valladolid (1527) 71
Valois 40, 49, 109, 110, 163, 190; and
Habsburgs *see* Habsburg-Valois
wars
Vasa, Gustavus 85, 86, 87; *see also*
Gustavus I, king of Sweden
Vasily III (1505–33), tsar of Russia 89,
213
Västeras, Diets of: (1527) 87; (1544) 87
Vaucelles, truce of (1556) 189, 191
Vaud 112
Venice 26, 50, 51, 68, 72, 99, 100, 112,
125–6, 128; 'orators' of 48
Venloo, Treaty of (1543) 171
Vera Cruz 24
Verden 185
Verdun 185
Vergerio, Pietro Paolo 111, 161
vernacular: literature in 212; services in
the 31, 40; translation of Calvin's
Institutes into 163; translations of
the Bible 29, 206
Verona 126
Vesalius, Andrea 211; *De humani
corporis fabrica* 209

Lightning Source UK Ltd.
Milton Keynes UK
28 November 2009

146782UK00002B/12/P